PROTECTING THE ELDERLY

CHARLES LOCKHART

PROTECTING THE ELDERLY

HOW CULTURE SHAPES SOCIAL POLICY

THE PENNSYLVANIA STATE UNIVERSITY PRESS
UNIVERSITY PARK, PENNSYLVANIA

Library of Congress Cataloging-in-Publication Data

Lockhart, Charles, 1944–
    Protecting the elderly : how culture shapes social policy /
    Charles Lockhart.

        p.   cm.
    Includes bibliographical references and index.
    ISBN 0-271-02130-6 (alk. paper)
    1. Aged—Services for—Government policy—Cross-cultural studies.
    2. Culture—Political aspects.   I. Title.

HV1451 .L65 2001
362.6—dc21   2001021056

To the memory of Aaron Wildavsky

CONTENTS

PREFACE

Only a few contemporary students of comparative politics employ culture as a prominent explanatory variable. By the 1970s comparativists were increasingly intrigued with the capacity of cross-societal institutional differences to explain variation among a broad range of dependent variables; and culture—a central concern among major comparativists in the 1950s and 1960s—was already becoming marginalized as a contributor to a field of comparative politics based on empirical generalization. Culture's position on the sidelines of comparative politics has been made even more tenuous by the growing practice of applying the deductive approach of rational choice theory to comparative political research, an activity that began in earnest in the 1980s and has since developed extensively.

Thus this is hardly an auspicious juncture at which to introduce an approach to comparative politics that starts with and develops a particular theory of culture, the "grid-group" theory of Mary Douglas and Aaron Wildavsky. What possesses me to engage in such an enterprise? One factor is my conviction that political life involves activity that is purposeful in deeper, more significant ways than institutional analyses frequently suggest. I do not dispute that cross-societal institutional differences contribute to variation in a range of important dependent variables. Indeed, I think it likely that analysts who focus on matters such as actors' institutional roles and duties as well as on institutional missions and standard operating procedures do a good job of explaining why many political actors behave as they do much of the time. But they do not explain the origins of many cross-societal institutional differences. These differences arise in part from peculiarities of historical circumstance, and in part as the result of disparate human purposes. Political actors sometimes effect conscious decisions, based on criteria exogenous to whatever current institutional roles they may hold, and construct institutions with varying particular characteristics. And where does their guidance for this come from if not from culture? While the structure of broader institutions may contribute to the character of the narrower institutions they contain, the structure of the broadest societal institutions cannot explain their own design. At this level the explanation has to be exogenous to institutions; and the distinctive institutional design preferences, what I call institutional formation imperatives, of the adherents of rival cultures is one promising source. I stress the limited character of this criticism of institutional explanations. Institutions clearly have considerable explanatory capacity, but no theory—institutional theories included—explains everything, and explaining why certain institutions (e.g., public social programs) take particular forms is not one of the strengths of contemporary institutional analysis.

Disparities among human purposes provide a second reason why I advocate a more thorough inclusion of culture in the comparative study of political life. As a consequence of their limited attention to preference formation, rational choice theorists run a risk of being either wrong or vacuous. If they employ their conventional assumptions, the egoistic and hedonistic purposes of "economic man," then they will misinterpret and misrepresent some situations in which humans clearly act from other motives, such as affection and duty. If, however, they admit a broader range of motivations and conceptions of self-interest, then the explanation for whatever persons do becomes their varying self-interests. But as a theory of preference implementation, rational choice generally provides no means of ascertaining in advance the particular ways in which specific persons will conceive of their interests. So it affords no way of predicting how various persons might behave across a range of situations. Persons' persistent efforts to realize certain interests efficiently do not explain why they conceive of their interests in one fashion rather than another. The explanation of disparate interests is exogenous to an instrumental or preference implementation conception of rationality. Yet the distinctive beliefs and values of the adherents of rival cultures can explain why various persons conceive of their interests differently. Thus employing culture to clarify the process of preference formation may facilitate our identifying in advance persons with rival, culturally constrained, and distinctive conceptions of the self and its legitimate interests.

So relying on complementary contributions from instrumental rationality, disparate and culturally constrained preferences, and rival institutional formation imperatives seems to me to offer promise of a more adequate theory with which to predict and explain both similarities of societal trajectory and cross-societal differences of interest to students of comparative politics. Mixtures of these three elements might vary from one application to another. The mixture that I offer here is heavy on culture, in order to draw attention to this contributing element whose promise currently appears to be underappreciated among comparativists. My central argument is that grid-group theory's three, ubiquitous, socially interactive cultures entail rival, culturally constrained rationalities whose adherents strive—in varying degrees under different circumstances—to construct distinctive institutional designs. Further, societies vary in terms of the influence of these rival institutional preferences among their political elites, and the design characteristics of their institutions reflect these differences. I demonstrate these propositions in the character of societal decision outcomes involving public social programs serving the elderly.

Portions of the description of the theory which follows in Chapter 1 as well as a number of the examples that I use to illustrate various points throughout the manuscript have developed over a number of years. Thus brief passages similar to some in this manuscript have appeared in several places: the *Western Political Quarterly, Utilitas, Sociological Perspectives,* the *Journal of Theoretical Politics,* the *Journal of Contemporary Thought,* and the *Review of Politics.* I thank Westview Press and Sage Publications for permission to reprint somewhat more extensive passages of similar material.

I have benefited from the assistance of many wonderful friends and colleagues, both across my professional life generally and on this project. In particular, I am grateful to Paul Diesing for setting an inspiring example during my days as a graduate student. Subsequently, Gary Freeman, Peter A. Hall, Richard M. Coughlin, Gunnar Grendstad, Richard F. Galvin, Gary Bonham, and Dennis Coyle have all provided professional, intellectual, and—especially valuable—moral support for a number of years.

Jeffrey Legro made it possible for me to expand my understanding of the interface of culture and rationality. David P. Conradt and Irwin L. Collier, Jr., eased my search for data on German pension policy. Marianne Bobich and Hugh Macdonald, both reference librarians at TCU, were also helpful in this regard. T. J. Pempel, Daniel I. Okimoto, and Chalmers Johnson provided guidance to my efforts to improve my capacity for dealing with Japanese policymaking. John Creighton Campbell was extremely generous in clarifying numerous aspects of Japanese pension policy for me. Naturally, I remain responsible for any mistakes in the analysis that follows.

Further, Richard J. Ellis read and commented on early versions of several chapters. Andrew J. Nathan helped to sharpen my argument by relentlessly posing trenchant questions. Richard W. Wilson was kind enough to read the manuscript on multiple occasions, and his numerous comments have contributed immensely to refining both my argument and its presentation.

I particularly want to acknowledge the exceptional guidance and support that I have been fortunate to enjoy from three persons. The first is Aaron Wildavsky. In 1989 it was my good fortune to participate in a National Endowment for the Humanities Summer Seminar on political culture that Aaron directed. Early in my professional life Robert Jervis, Alexander L. George, and Adda Bozeman had sparked my interest in thinking systematically about rival interpretations of social life, particularly from the standpoint of their propensity for generating misperception among international adversaries. The system of rival intrasocietal patterns of social cognition and interpretation which Aaron introduced in this seminar, arising most immediately from his work with Mary Douglas on grid-group theory, enticed me immediately. This seminar and ensuing contact with Aaron certainly enlivened my intellectual life, and I hope that this influence has augmented my capacity for contributing constructively to the development of an empirical science of comparative politics as well.

The second is Sanford Thatcher. Sandy saw promise in this book where others had not, and he labored doggedly through several rounds of review to bring that promise to fruition. I am extremely grateful for his insight, persistence, and support.

The third is Jean Giles-Sims, my wife and a family sociologist with a penchant for microtheory and quantitative data. She has lived much longer and in much better humor with this project than I have had any right to expect. I am extremely thankful for her continuing support and counsel.

PART ONE

ONE

INTRODUCTION

Among advanced industrial societies, employing public pensions and related programs to protect the elderly became an increasingly central activity over the course of the twentieth century. Since Bismarck's development of modern social programs in the 1880s, aging has become widely recognized as one of the vicissitudes of life for which ameliorating societal measures are appropriate. The distinguishing feature of modern social policy, made famous by Bismarck's pioneering efforts, is contributory social insurance. In contrast to earlier public measures aimed at mitigating poverty, this device facilitates the efforts of responsible households to surmount episodic social hazards. Persons contribute to social insurance funds during their adult working lives and draw on program benefits when confronted by hazards covered by this insurance. Pensions for the elderly are the most widespread and popular type of social insurance (Coughlin 1980). Such programs are also commonly the largest single line items in the public budgets of advanced industrial societies.

While nearly all industrial societies had initiated social insurance programs of some sort for the elderly prior to the Second World War, the three decades following the war witnessed extraordinary growth in the breadth and depth of these programs and public social policy generally. By the late 1970s it was becoming clear that some of this growth would be reined in (Heclo 1981). Throughout the 1980s Ronald Reagan in Washington, Margaret Thatcher in London, and other national leaders across advanced industrial societies managed to reverse some of the earlier growth in social programs (Pierson 1994; OECD 1994b, 80). Their retrenchment efforts grew out of broad societal changes that mobilized adherents of an individualistic cultural perspective. First, advanced industrial societies began to recognize their growing vulnerability to various aspects of globalization: e.g., increasingly competitive global markets and the related heightened mobility of capital. Under these circumstances governments found it increasingly difficult to insulate healthy socioeconomic conditions within their domestic domains from disruptive external forces. Less settled economic circumstances heightened complaints about the high taxes extensive social programs absorbed and, more important, prompted thoughts that perhaps these new circumstances required a more self-reliant orientation throughout society. Second, across the 1970s recognition of the limits of social programs grew. Mismatches between various public assistance efforts (e.g., programs aimed at brief episodes of single-parenting) and changing lifestyles (e.g., the increasing prevalence of long-term single-parent households) provided the most frequent examples of these limits (Esping-Andersen 1996, 6–7), but social insurance limitations were recognized as well. Public medical-insurance programs could not, for instance, assure health to persons who smoked, drank too much, indulged in poor diets, and followed sedentary lifestyles. Accordingly, Howard Jarvis, who had been considered an extremist crank prior to his success in limiting California's property tax rates, became a consultant to individualistic public officials across advanced industrial societies.

Pensions for the elderly, while generally retaining considerable support, were hampered by additional problems specific to them. First, in some societies (e.g., the United States) the unsettling consequences or at least recognition of the consequences of "program maturity" developed. For instance, prior to the 1970s the United States social security program had, by bringing new groups under its coverage, progressively expanded its revenues, and many of the persons who had been paying into the program across its life had not yet begun to receive benefits. In comparison to current and future "mature" circumstances, the social security program was still in an early stage with a high worker/beneficiary ratio and no problems in meeting its benefit obligations. Such problems became visible in the late 1970s. Second, while the specifics varied from one society to another, the populations of all advanced industrial societies were progressively aging. Long-term projections for worker/beneficiary ratios showed continued declines that prompted worries that the characteristically generous program benefits of the 1970s might not be sustainable. Moreover, in some societies (such as the Federal Republic of Germany) a trend of earlier retirement exacerbated the social policy problems posed by an aging population (Gruber and Wise 1999).

In the face of these challenges public pensions for the elderly were cut back during the 1980s. In the 1990s there were calls for further cuts. Thus the issue of how to protect the elderly remains current indeed. Yet societies responded differently to these problems, and my central task in this study is to explain why. For instance, Germany and the former Soviet Union relied more heavily on revenue increases than on benefit reductions, thus largely sustaining existing levels of protection. In contrast, the United States and Japan relied more heavily on benefit reductions. I argue that cultural conceptions of what is appropriate provide the key variable in explaining how societies responded to 1980s pressures on public protection for the elderly (cf. Blyth 1997). Rival, culturally constrained rationalities, based on distinctive value clusters, produce different institutional preferences, which are rational or efficient in light of their distinctive moral bases. Further, variations in the relative influence of rival cultures among relevant, organized societal elites affect the shaping of social policy decisions.

JUSTIFYING A PARTICULAR THEORETICAL APPROACH

As Lichbach and Zuckerman (1997) argue, variations of the political culture approach form one of three general types of theory commonly employed by political scientists engaged in comparative analysis. The two others are rational choice theory and institutional analysis.[1] Among contem-

---

1. The "first wave" of post–Second World War comparative work emphasized cultural contributions to explanations of political life (see, for example, Almond 1956, Almond and Coleman 1960, Almond and Powell 1966, Almond and Verba 1963, Apter 1965, Eckstein 1961, Epstein 1967, LaPalombara 1964, Pye and Verba 1965, and Weiner 1967). High-profile work

porary political scientists, political culture theory is likely the least commonly applied of the three. I employ a particular version of political culture theory, Douglas-Wildavsky grid-group theory, in this examination of why societies responded differently to the difficulties of public programs protecting the elderly in the 1980s. Grid-group theory is an especially powerful tool for linking instrumental rationality to culturally constrained value clusters (motivational bases), whose adherents, in turn, strive to construct distinctive institutional designs. Thus the theory highlights constructive complementary contributions among the three prominent approaches analyzed by Lichbach and Zuckerman.

INTRODUCING GRID-GROUP THEORY

Grid-group theory is an approach to cultural explanation that was conceived in sociology (Durkheim 1951), refined in cultural anthropology (Evans-Pritchard 1940; Douglas 1978, 1982a, 1982b, 1986, and 1992) and has recently been advanced and applied in political science (Coyle and Ellis 1994; Ellis 1993; Thompson, Ellis, and Wildavsky 1990). It explains how persons derive a limited range of answers to basic social questions such as how the world works, what humans are really like, to whom I am accountable and how I hold others accountable to me (Wildavsky 1994). Grid-group theorists argue that a person's answers to these questions produce orientations toward two basic social dimensions: the legitimacy of external prescription (grid)[2] and the strength of affiliation with others (group). The

emphasizing culture has continued (such as Almond and Verba 1980; Eckstein 1988; Inglehart 1977, 1988, and 1997; Lipset 1990, 1991, and 1996; Putnam with Leonardi and Nanetti 1988 and 1993; Verba et al. 1987; and Verba, Nie, and Kim 1978), and some scholars have skillfully composed explanations combining cultural and institutional factors (such as Aberbach, Putnam, and Rockman 1981; Beer 1965; and Heclo 1974 and 1977). But across the 1970s an essentially new field of comparative politics that emphasized institutional explanations developed (see, for example, Berger 1981; Hall 1986; Huntington 1968; Johnson 1982; Katzenstein 1977, 1984, and 1985; Pierson 1994; Rae 1967; Rae and Taylor 1970; Steinmo, Thelen, and Longstreth 1992; and Wilensky 1975 and 1976). Even more recently, rational choice theorists have become actively involved in the study of comparative politics (such as, Bates 1991 and 1997, Golden 1990, Levi 1988, Lichbach 1995, North 1990, and Rogowski 1989).

2. By "legitimacy of external prescription" I refer to the varying ease with which persons accept that other persons' judgments are valid for and binding on them. For a career enlisted person in a military service, for instance, this legitimacy is apt to be high, since he or she will have chosen a life that routinely involves accepting the orders of officers by and large without question.

theory thus helps to fill a notorious void in the social sciences (Becker 1976, 133). It explains how distinctive social relations preferences are formed as a consequence of various grid and group positions (Schwarz and Thompson 1990, 49). The range of actual social practice is constrained, since only four general ways—each admitting variations—of responding to these issues are socially viable.[3] Preferences for various forms of social relations prompt supporting justifications or cultural biases and vice versa. Together, the preferences and justifications create distinctive ways of life or cultures (Lockhart 1999, 864–67). (See Figure 1.)

For instance, where low tolerance for external prescription is reinforced by weak feelings of group membership, we find an individualistic way of life organized by self-regulation among voluntary, shifting, contract-based

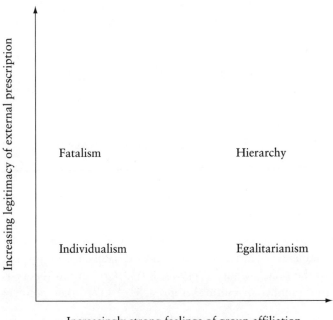

FIG. 1

<hr>

3. While this claim is controversial, it is obviously less limiting than the widely accepted notion that only variations on two ways of life—hierarchy and individualism—are socially viable; see Lindblom 1977. Additionally, Fiske (1993), Maruyama (1980), Lichbach (1995), and Peters (1996) have independently derived similar typologies. There is also a fair amount of empirical analysis supporting this claim; see Evans-Pritchard 1940, Dumont 1980, Strathern 1971, and Uchendu 1965. Finally, grid-group theory admits a fifth, non-socially interactive way of life—the hermit's—which I do not find relevant to this study; see Thompson 1982.

networks of persons. Promoting such a way of life among persons perceived as self-interested, with roughly equal broad competencies such as rationality, is one purpose of Smith's *Wealth of Nations*. Increasingly strong feelings of group affiliation together with weak prescription entail a way of life that grid-group theorists call egalitarian. From this perspective broadly equal humans, unmarred by natural flaws destructive of social harmony, ideally prefer to organize into small groups that reach collective decisions through discussions designed to produce consensus. This process is reminiscent of Rousseau's descriptions of the social ideal in *The Social Contract*. High feelings of group affiliation in conjunction with perceptions legitimizing strong external prescription create the realm of hierarchy. In this view unequal humans with various social shortcomings that require improvement through institutional guidance are arrayed in vertical collectives. The ideal polis portrayed by Plato in *The Republic* illustrates this way of life. And finally, weak feelings of group affiliation intersect with perceptions of external direction to create a way of life grid-group theorists call fatalism. The unhappy combination of recognizing constraint by others but not feeling part of any broader social collective predisposes fatalists to social avoidance rather than varying forms of social interaction. One manifestation of avoidance is that fatalists rarely construct works of political theory; their views have, however, been well portrayed by others (Banfield 1958; Turnbull 1972).[4]

DISTINCTIVE FEATURES OF GRID-GROUP THEORY

Culture's centrality to social explanation depends largely on how it is defined. As Eckstein laments: "The term *culture*, unfortunately, has no precise, settled meaning in the social sciences" (1988, 801).[5] Grid-group theory is only one of a large number of cultural approaches.[6] Like other political

4. There are a few exceptions to fatalists' general reticence. See Ecclesiastes 9:11 and Schopenhauer's *The World as Will and Representation*.

5. This unsettled meaning at least provides a heuristic openness (Kaplan 1964) that conceptual innovations such as grid-group theory can utilize.

6. In addition to the various political cultural approaches mentioned in note 1, cultural approaches are widely employed in sociology, cultural anthropology, social psychology, and—less constructively (Limerick 1997)—in areas of the humanities. Even economists occasionally draw on culture (North 1990). Prominent examples include, in sociology, McAdam (1994), Parsons and Shils (1951), and Swidler (1995); in anthropology, Benedict (1934), Geertz (1972), and Shweder (1991); and social psychology, Feldman and Zaller (1992), Pye (1962), and Whiting (1983). The culture-based literatures in all three of these areas are voluminous.

culturalists, grid-group theorists conceive of culture, in part, as the beliefs and values (i.e., the cultural biases) with which various social groupings justify their rival ways of life. But they also recognize cultures in the distinctive institutional preferences that arise from rival beliefs and values, phenomena that others may view as cultural artifacts rather than as culture per se. Lane (1992), Eckstein (1996 and 1997), and particularly Ross (1997) have recently produced fine surveys of cultural approaches to comparative politics and related areas.[7] It would seem superfluous to repeat their constructive efforts here. Rather, I want to focus on discussing three distinctive characteristics that give the theory unique advantages for the work I undertake in this study.

First, like other cultural approaches, grid-group theory sustains a dual interest both in selective patterns of attention and interpretation and in shared identity. Yet the theory provides a particularly productive schema for distinguishing a small number of rival patterns of selective social attention and interpretation (Douglas 1982b). Thus it offers advantages over alternative theories in terms of contrasting various political actors' differing ontological foundations, especially the varying conceptions of human environments and human nature reflected in their distinctive institutional preferences. Also, by focusing on such fundamental, identity-constituting concerns the theory facilitates our understanding of how persons become the adherents of rival cultures.

Second, in contrast to a convention by which cultures (sometimes allowing for multiple subcultures) are thought of as roughly coincident with societies (i.e., French, German, or Chinese culture), grid-group theorists argue that all four of their theory's global ways of life are present in varying proportions in all societies.[8] Like the interaction of different amino acids in biological systems, each way of life provides services for the others that they cannot create for themselves. Societies thus are typically "multicultural" in this sense. Societies face widely varying historical contingencies that prompt distinctive collective responses. Indeed, the varying proportions of rival cultures in different societies likely arises from these variations in historical experience. Although the peculiarities of the historical contingencies that

7. Ross (1997, 46, 50, and 62) is particularly clear about distinguishing grid-group theory from other theories of culture because it focuses on interaction between distinctive motivating values and associated social structures.

8. Empirical confirmation of this tenet in instances of large-scale societies remains in its early stages. See Grendstad 1999, Ellis and Thompson 1997, and Coughlin and Lockhart 1998.

societies confront influence the specific character of their policy responses, grid-group theory's cultures have—as their association with rival social theorists in the previous section suggests—distinctive predispositions for specific institutional design. The characteristic institutional preferences of rival ways of life suggest that the sharp distinctions Lowi (1984) and other institutionalists draw between culture and structure are misguided. Instead, the two realms are locked in a symbiotic relationship; culture is an important source for the formation and sustenance of social institutions and vice versa.

Third, unlike many other conceptions that do not associate culture with dynamism, grid-group theory easily incorporates cultural contributions to political change. Since it associates rival cultures with distinctive value clusters and institutional preferences, and because it perceives societies as composed of these multiple, rival groupings, the theory portrays culture as integral to political change. Individualists, for instance, seek to implant their institutions and the distinctive values they embody more thoroughly throughout society, and adherents of other cultures seek to do the same for their institutions and their values. The inevitable result of this intercultural, but intrasocietal, conflict is political change as conditions raised by successive historical contingencies favor one culture or coalition of cultures and then another. As the opportunities for one culture wax, those of another wane, so different cultures sequentially build varying types of institutions. If one culture is highly dominant—hierarchy in the Soviet Union, for example—the pace of change may slacken for a time. But as we have recently witnessed, the possibilities for innovation will eventually improve as environmental changes present conditions affording better opportunities to other cultures.

TRANSLATING DISTINCTIVE FEATURES INTO UNIQUE ADVANTAGES

Instrumental Rationality

I begin with an instrumental conception of rationality: rationality as the efficient pursuit of consistent ends. Rational choice theorists often employ models of rationality that actual persons can likely only at best approximate in certain domains of social life. Monroe (1991a, 1991b, 1995) provides excellent analyses of both the most significant of these discrepancies and the efforts of some theorists (e.g., Simon 1983) to construct more realistic conceptions of rationality. I think that these various discrepancies between theoretical conceptions of rationality and actual behavior are of limited significance as problems for social analysis. I accept that humans are loosely rational goal seekers. But I see the penchant of rational choice theorists for leaving unspecified the particular ends that various persons prefer as a more serious problem. By this view of exogenous ends, persons prefer what they have chosen, whatever that may be, and this tells us too little too late. As Macaulay (1852, 299) put it:

> One man goes without a dinner that he may add a shilling to a hundred thousand pounds: another runs in debt to give balls and masquerades. One man cuts his father's throat to get possession of his old clothes: another hazards his own life to save that of an enemy. One man volunteers on a forlorn hope: another is drummed out of a regiment for cowardice. Each of these men has, no doubt, acted from self-interest. But we gain nothing by knowing this, except the pleasure, if it be one, of multiplying useless words.

Monroe (1995) seeks a solution to this problem through the concept of identity. That is, to the degree that we define ourselves in terms of distinctive sets of constrained value priorities, the ends that we pursue admit specification in advance. Other scholars agree that various persons pursue different sets of constrained value clusters with distinctive priorities (Sen 1977; Etzioni 1988). Teske (1997) contends that both political activists among the citizenry and some political elites are apt to have well-developed identities with distinctive value priorities that guide their political activity. For such persons Monroe insightfully shifts terminology to "rational action," since their activities arise from socialized preferences rather than truly open choices or decisions.

It seems to me that this is how culture works as an ally, rather than a rival of rationality. These two perspectives—political culture and rational choice—are frequently portrayed as incompatible competitors (Eckstein 1988; Elster 1989a, 1989b, and 1989c; Inglehart 1997; Rogowski 1974), but others (Grief 1994; Young 1996) show that customs often arise as rational responses to repeated social stimuli. Distinctive rational experiential bases for cultural peculiarities frequently appear, for instance, in the literature on "organizational cultures" (Kreps 1990; Legro 1996). Yet for conventional rational choice theory, personal preferences remain beyond the scope of legitimate inquiry. Realization of given preferences can be rational, but preferences are themselves exogenous (Becker 1976, 133). But once we accept that experiences with the world vary sharply and that distinctive patterns of selective social attention and interpretation naturally arise from such differences, preferences can be rational in the sense of being deducible from particular experience-prompted patterns of cognition. But they may not be just preferences (tastes) any longer; some are value priorities whose support is virtually required by one's cultural identity. Thus both forming preferences and striving to realize them efficiently can be rational activities, but referring to these activities as stages of rational action (Monroe 1991a) rather than rational choices is more appropriate.

Culturally Constrained Value Clusters

Cultural identities would be particularly helpful if we thought of them, not in the conventional sense of "national" cultures and various subcultures, but rather as transcending societal boundaries so that adherents of a few global cultures, distinguished by their value priorities, could be found in all, or at least many, societies. Political ideology offers a crude version of culture in this sense. Social conservatives, (classical) liberals, and socialists exist in many societies, providing the bases for various multiparty systems, and each perspective retains numerous familiar basic features across societies. These "cultures" are conventionally portrayed as occupying various points on a single dimension, but this way of interrelating them leads to conflating important distinctions (Coughlin and Lockhart 1998). Accordingly, most contemporary schemata for distinguishing general, socially ubiquitous cultures employ two dimensions (see Inglehart 1997; Maddox and Lilie 1984; Rokeach 1973; Rosenberg 1988; Thompson, Ellis, and Wildavsky 1990; and Triandis 1995). Each of these schemata works from distinctions among various "core values" (Feldman and Zaller 1992; Sniderman et al. 1991). I favor Douglas-Wildavsky grid-group theory for what appear to be its—currently—unique capacities for eliciting complementary contributions from conceptions of rationality, culture, and institutions.

Grid-group theorists conceive of culture as including the beliefs and values with which various social groupings justify their rival ways of life. These cultural biases are based on beliefs about the natural and social environments that rest ultimately on experience (Douglas 1986). Distinctive conceptions of human nature follow from particular beliefs about the world. Together, these beliefs about humans and their world locate persons on the grid and group dimensions, support characteristic value clusters, and spawn preferences for distinctive institutions that are also indices of culture. So if we know a person's culture, we know as well her value priorities and practical political preferences (Lockhart 1999, 864–67, 870–73).

For instance, persons whose life experiences, both firsthand and via precept, predispose them to perceive bountiful and resilient natural (Locke, *Second Treatise*) and social (Nozick 1974) environments characteristically adopt a culture of individualism. In light of these experiences, they are prone to view humans as motivated by egoistic hedonistic concerns and as holding significant and roughly equal broad capacities such as rationality. These humans are thus properly motivated and sufficiently capable of mastering their own fates in an abundant world. This ontology accounts for the individualists' preeminent value: a particular ("negative"—Berlin 1969) conception of liberty. Accordingly, individualists prefer to rely primarily on self-regulation among persons, and a network of contractual (voluntary) relations that shifts over time as interests do is their preferred social institution. For them, government—with its inherent coercion—should be limited in its domain and activity.

In contrast, persons whose experience produces a view of human environments as fragile are likely to become adherents of egalitarianism. Not only do they see the natural environment as subject to depredation, but they think that social contexts—the inner city—are easily perverted as well. In order to complement this delicate context, the egalitarian vision of human nature stresses creatures naturally benign in their motives and broadly equal in both basic capacities and needs (Gewirth 1978). Yet humans are easy prey for social stratification, which damages central egalitarian values of relatively equal interpersonal respect and material condition. Egalitarians believe that by undoing natural human equality, stratification creates arrogance in the dominant and resentment in the subordinated, perverting in the process the natural goodness of all. Accordingly, egalitarians prefer social relations among relatively small societies that share a limited material bounty fairly equally—exemplified by the aphorism "live simply so that others may simply live" or as Schumacher (1973) put it, "Small is beautiful"— and reach collective decisions through open discussion resulting in consensus (Downey 1986; Zisk 1992).[9]

Persons whose experiences suggest a more complex, tolerant/perverse

9. Both the low-grid cultures (i.e., individualism and egalitarianism) frequently form coalitions with hierarchy in order to gain specific benefits and to better project their way of life into society at large. Thus varying forms of limited government and social democracy are adopted by individualists and egalitarians, respectively

world are likely to adopt hierarchy. For them, both natural and social environments are sufficiently robust to support some exploitation, but if humans press too hard, disaster is apt to follow. Figuratively, humans live on mesas, not needing to worry about minor variations of the table-top terrain, but having to stay clear of the encircling cliffs. This view of the human environment elicits a conception of humans that, in contrast to those of the low-grid cultures, attributes great importance to disparities of specific talents. Experts in various matters are required to discern crucial natural and social boundaries not equally evident to everyone as well as for ascertaining how humans should adjust their behavior in conformity with these limits. For hierarchists, then, many of the same obvious interpersonal differences that individualists and egalitarians believe to be inconsequential take on moral and social significance. This ontology focuses priority on the values of expertise as well as the social harmony and order that may be derived from expert knowledge. Accordingly, hierarchists prefer to organize society into vertically arrayed institutions. Experts guide these institutions, attempting to order persons' lives with sanctioned activities. In this way the lives of less capable and more seriously flawed persons are improved, and the social collective runs more harmoniously.[10]

So each of these cultural ontologies generates distinctive value clusters that foster rival conceptions of a range of practical matters, including the appropriate character of human interests and political institutions. Persons apply cultures, then, not only to interpret the world around them, but also to shape their social environments. In short, the selves—and the interests associated with them—perceived by the adherents of each of these cultures are distinctive and constrained, allowing tight relations between persons' cultures and the specific practical interests they seek to realize (Lockhart and Coughlin 1992; Wildavsky 1994; Lockhart and Wildavsky 1998). In this way culture and rationality complement each other in explaining human action. In conjunction with instrumental rationality, grid-group the-

---

10. The relatively low levels of social interaction sustained by fatalists lead me to reduce the attention accorded to them in this study. Fatalists are rarely found among the political elites of developed societies whose actions with respect to social policy form my focus here. Briefly, fatalists perceive context as random and humans, fittingly, as capricious. Accordingly, they attempt to stay out of harm's way by minimizing their interaction with unpredictable, uncontrollable forces. Thus fatalists are characterized by what Eckstein (1991) calls "frustrated or analgesic" behavior. I think Eckstein exaggerates the differences between this sort of behavior and goal-oriented activity. Staying out of harm's way is, in certain circumstances, an appropriate goal.

ory produces three socially interactive "rationalities," each dedicated to the practical realization of a distinctive set of values.

Ferejohn's (1991) characterization of "thick" rationalities offers a conception similar to that which I am proposing. By this term he denotes the efficient pursuit of distinctive sets of values. So far, so good. But Ferejohn, like some other scholars who view rational choice theory favorably, goes on to privilege the values on which conventional applications of this theory implicitly focus, acting as if these values were natural in the sense of fitting with an accepted conception of human nature (i.e., "economic man") and required no explanation. By this reasoning only other value sets are arbitrary, thus requiring explanation, perhaps even unscientific interpretation (Geertz 1973), and acquiring the adjective "thick." Yet as Almond (1991), Noll and Weingast (1991, 241), Petracca (1991), and particularly Rosenberg (1991) all contend, the egoistic and hedonistic, economic-man values frequently employed by rational choice theorists are no more natural to humans than values deriving from love and duty.

Minimally since Hume (1951, 172–76), for instance, humans have been recognized as having multiple motivational bases (interest-, affection-, and principle-driven) that result in distinctive value priorities. Contemporary scholars have reaffirmed this value-priority pluralism (see Etzioni 1988, Jencks 1990, Mansbridge 1990a and 1990b, Sen 1977, and Wolfe 1993). Gridgroup theory enables us to recognize Hume's three distinctive motivations (interest, affection, and principle) as socially embedded in individualistic, egalitarian, and hierarchical cultures, respectively, and to "dethrone" economic-man (individualistic) value priorities as no more natural than others (Lockhart and Wildavsky 1998). A mother's affection for her child is as natural as an entrepreneur's preference for an alternative offering a better benefit/cost ratio. The egoistic and hedonistic value assumptions generally employed in conjunction with rational choice theory may be commonly utilized when persons think about the economic realm, but they are not preeminent in other spheres of social life (Hochschild 1981; Walzer 1983; Monroe 1995) and do not merit privileged, "no-explanation-necessary" status in comparative political research. What might be called "pure" rational choice theory is strictly instrumental; ends are exogenous. All ends used in conjunction with rational choice theory make assumptions about various ontological and normative issues.[11] None of these assumptions merits a prima facie

11. Thus while Wildavsky (1994) retained the less appropriate "decision" terminology, he did so in the plural (a theory of rational decisions), distinguishing three issues. These are in turn: ontological (How does the world work and what are humans really like?), normative

global privilege over others. As a theory of preference implementation, rational choice cannot legitimately violate its explicit, preferences-are-exogenous stance by implicitly favoring some clusters of values over others.

Grid-group theory enriches rational choice's emphasis on preference implementation by adding a focus on preference formation. By explaining distinctive patterns of selective social attention and interpretation and their associated values preferences, grid-group theory helps us understand what persons want and why. It facilitates our understanding of how persons develop the particular clusters of ranked values that are distinctive to rival cultures. These rival cultures, in turn, provide a basis for understanding and predicting constraint among political preferences. Better understanding of these issues is surely an appropriate central objective for the social sciences. Grid-group theory thus enables culture to complement rationality, and it affords similar opportunities for institutional analysis as well.

Institutional Formation Imperatives

This brings us to the issue of how persons go about efficiently realizing the distinctive practical purposes or interests that derive from the varying value priorities of rival cultures. Certainly in those instances in which interests are persistent, this is generally accomplished by creating and maintaining particular institutions, designed to embody specific values. So a cultural schema employed as a means for distinguishing motivations arising from rival value clusters should ideally carry clear institutional implications. These implications are found most obviously in what I call institutional formation imperatives. By this I mean that the adherents of rival cultures strive to construct institutions that realize their ontologies and values. Thus individualists create markets and related institutions (competitive elections, multi-voiced mass media) that support liberty among relative equals. In contrast, hierarchists build centralized institutions such as "peak" associations for representing sectoral interests and central-state bureaucracies through which the most capable persons can organize a harmonious common life for all. Egalitarians generally prefer consensus among ordinary citizens, a means of fostering equal interpersonal respect, to both the adversarial self-

---

(What values are relatively more merit worthy, or what purposes should persons strive to realize in specific situations?), and instrumental (How are given purposes best realized?). His point in highlighting these three issues was to direct attention to rational choice theory's emphasis on the third, while frequently handling the other two through sometimes implicit assumptions about an intersubjective reality and economic-man preferences.

interest of the individualists and the reliance on centralized expertise advocated by the hierarchists. Accordingly, they support socioeconomic rights and develop participatory institutions among citizens and workers. Thus persons use cultures, not only to interpret their worlds, but also to shape them, and the bulk of this shaping occurs through the construction of distinctive institutions. Cultural tenets and institutions require one another. Without particular institutions, adherents of rival cultures have sketchy means for shaping human experience in accordance with their distinctive beliefs and values. Moreover, without appropriate cultural tenets, particular institutions have no justification in terms of beliefs and values.

Denying that institutional formation is guided by culturally constrained rationalities leaves little but happenstance as an explanation for institutional design.[12] Surely happenstance contributes; the complexity of human interaction in all but the most narrowly contrived instances and the resulting likelihood of what appear as chance occurrences having unforeseen effects are both so high that factors relevant to the explanation of social life are bound to be exogenous from the perspective of any given theory (Jervis 1997). Thus institutional development is apt to occur against a background of historical contingencies that can be recognized and whose influence can be taken into account, but the contingencies themselves may defy explanation (Heclo 1994). Yet the construction of human institutions does not simply involve reaction to events. It is a purposive activity, driven by certain beliefs about events as well as values and their associated practical interests that make sense in light of these beliefs.

THE STRUCTURE OF THIS BOOK

In the remaining chapters of Part One, I use selected evidence to explain further the three distinctive features of grid-group theory, refining and extending the theory in the process. I draw on illustrative examples involving the United States, the former Soviet Union, the Federal Republic of Germany, and Japan. I stress that my purpose here is illustration for theory development; I make no claim that my examples confirm broad generalizations (Eckstein 1977, 108–13). In Ragin's terms, I "use theory to make sense

---

12. "Happenstance" will shortly be expanded to include shifting historical contingencies and the character of existing societal institutions at particular points in time.

of evidence and . . . use evidence to sharpen and refine theory" (1992, 224–25). In Chapter 2, I revisit the ontological foundations that grid-group theory distinguishes. I show that grid and group orientations can arise in early life. Moreover, these distinctive beliefs may continue to guide persons, including prominent political elites, throughout their adult lives.

In Chapter 3, I develop the rival value clusters associated with grid-group theory's three socially interactive cultures and show that the adherents of these disparate clusters are likely to prefer distinctive institutional designs. Then I employ brief heuristic examples drawn from the Soviet Union and Japan to illustrate more specifically how variations in the relative influence of rival cultures among societies can contribute to cross-societal institutional differences.

I employ illustrative examples drawn from the United States and Germany in Chapter 4 to show how the presence in societies of rival cultural perspectives and preferences, in conjunction with successive historical contingencies, produces multiple mechanisms of political change. My dependent variable in this chapter is change in the character of public policy; while the key explanatory variable involves shifting relations among cultures. In contrast to Chapter 3, in which my purpose is to show that differences in the relative influence of rival cultures among societies can contribute to cross-societal institutional variations, my comparisons in Chapter 4 are intrasocietal but across time.

In Chapters 5 through 8 (Part Two), I draw on the culturally constrained rationalities and institutional formation imperatives that I introduced above in a more systematic effort to demonstrate that culture is an important explanatory variable. Using case studies, I examine the most prominent 1980s social policy decisions affecting the elderly in the United States, the Soviet Union, Germany, and Japan. I examine two distinct processes. One involves human purposes (i.e., Who wants what and why?). I show that the disparate, culturally constrained rationalities associated with grid-group theory's three socially interactive cultures produce the institutional design preferences that I have suggested for them. The second process is causal (i.e., Who gets what and why?). While other variables contribute as well, important characteristics of these social policy decisions clearly reflect the relative influence of rival cultures among relevant, organized, societal elites. This second (causal) process is independent of the first (purposive) one. The world often works in such a way that what persons want is of little consequence in determining what they get (Skocpol 1979). I acknowledge that various methodological issues accompany this exercise in using theory to make sense of evidence, and I turn to them shortly. In Chapter 9, I offer two sorts of conclusions. First, I evaluate grid-group theory's contributions to the explanation of these major social policy decisions, concluding with some thoughts on methodological concerns. Second, I outline the advantages and drawbacks, in terms of affording socioeconomic protection to the elderly, offered by different variations in the relative influence of rival cultures among societal political elites.

METHODOLOGICAL ISSUES

Causes and/or Human Purposes?

King, Keohane, and Verba (1994) have recently offered extensive advice on how scholars with qualitative concerns can contribute to the development of causal inference and thus cumulative social science. I appreciate their efforts and have constructed numerous aspects of this study in light of their advice. Nonetheless, although King, Keohane, and Verba seem to accept various "logics of discovery," they want to impose a single "logic of justification" (Diesing 1971), holding practitioners of various modes of discovery accountable to justification criteria imported from physics.

Laitin (1995) suggests that their intolerance on the matter of justification indicates greater concern with research design than with the development of crucial concepts. Toulmin (1961, 48–59 and 67–73) argues that scientific advances arise from the development of crucial concepts. Like Lichbach and Zuckerman (1997), I think that the three most promising concepts available to comparative politics are rationality, culture, and institutions. So I want to employ my versions of these concepts to explain why societies reacted differently to related pressures on their social programs supporting the elderly in the 1980s.

Yet social science approaches employing rationality or culture characteristically focus on human objectives and interests or motivations and purposes rather than mechanistic causes, similar to those of physics, which King, Keohane, and Verba (1994) often use in their examples. Fortunately, purposive approaches can be expressed in hypotheses (e.g., that persons whose identity rests on certain values prefer—and under various conditions strive in varying degrees to construct—particular institutional designs), and appropriate research design is as important for tracing the social effects of such human strivings as for constructing causal paths devoid of intentionality. So preferences and the various social strivings that they induce can be used in conjunction with mechanistic variables in predicting and explaining social outcomes.

This combination is even desirable. The rival, culturally constrained rationalities that I have introduced offer considerable capacity, not only for predicting and explaining human purposes in the sense of who wants what institutional design and why, but their relative influence among a society's organized political elite contributes to predicting and explaining as well major aspects of the outcomes of social policy decisions (i.e., who gets what and why). So the distinctive human purposes represented by rival cultures represent an important explanatory variable or cause of these decision outcomes. Nonetheless, these decisions clearly rest as well on other factors. These include the unpredictable character of the specific historical contingencies that societies confront and which present varying threats and opportunities for realizing the distinctive values clusters of rival cultures. Additionally, existing institutionalization patterns constrain the specific means political actors choose for protecting or enhancing their rival value priorities in a variety of ways.

Moreover, interactive effects occur among cultural influences, the character of historical contingencies, and the form of existing institutions. Accordingly, gaps arise between predominant cultural preferences and institutional results in a variety of ways. For instance, conflicts between the adherents of rival cultures over the institutional design of important policy development steps may end, not with a clear victory for one and thus resulting institutional designs easily recognized as expressions of particular cultural preferences, but in compromises of various sorts that produce institutional designs representing mixtures of cultural influences. Further, as both Jervis (1997) and Zuckerman (in Lichbach and Zuckerman 1997) have pointed out, the complexity and inherently interactive character of social systems as well as the frequency of significant but seemingly chance occurrences within them make the outcomes of societal decisions unpredictable in at least some specific respects. Yet the relative influence of rival cultures among relevant political elites is often a strong predictor of important aspects of decision outcomes.

Even if complex social policy decisions cannot be predicted in all their specifics, they can be explained ex post facto. Accordingly, in the case studies of Part Two, I adopt King, Keohane, and Verba's (1994) recommendation for employing George and Smoke (1974, 95–97) and George and

McKeown's (1985) method of "structured-focused comparison" in a manner that traces the processes by which political actors work their way through what Cook (1993, 6) calls "pressured decision points." For King, Keohane, and Verba this approach both illuminates a causal path and produces a number of observations, thus guarding against indeterminacy. I employ this procedure as well to trace the social effects of human purposes: that is, to trace the transformation of culturally constrained value clusters into efforts to construct distinctive institutional designs.

I did not collect original data for this study. Rather, I follow George and others in subjecting standardized case studies to a set of questions tailored to my specific concerns. My hopes for the originality of this study are captured by Gould: "Our greatest intellectual adventures often occur within us—not in the restless search for new facts and new objects on the earth or in the stars, but from the need to expunge old prejudices and build new conceptual structures. No hunt can have a sweeter reward, a more admirable goal, than the excitement of thoroughly revised understanding" (1995, 13).

The Interaction Between Cultures and Institutions

Culture and institutions—as these concepts are broadly understood—have an inherently symbiotic relationship; each fosters and sustains the other (Elkins and Simeon 1979). Few imagine that we can pursue the comparative study of political life without focusing on institutions, and control issues do not go away when researchers ignore the influence of culture (Steinmo 1994), in effect categorizing as "exogenous" or "given" those preferences which culture helps to form, or relegate culture by fiat to a limited residual status (Johnson 1982). While I have already acknowledged the influence of institutional and other structural (e.g., historical contingencies) factors in shaping major social policy decisions, my emphasis in this study is on the contributions culture makes to these decisions.

Accordingly, I have chosen to focus on a class of decisions that offers exceptional opportunities for recognizing cultural influences. Cultural and institutional analysis are each stronger than the other in specific arenas. So I think that grid-group theory is apt to be most fruitfully employed in a specific range of situations. In a few instances historical contingencies may appear with such speed and force that disagreement and adaptive interaction among cultures are overwhelmed and political elites are left to cope as best they can through existing institutional mechanisms. Alternatively,

many other relatively routine situations pose implications sufficiently modest that, as historical (e.g., Steinmo, Thelen, and Longstreth 1992) and related (e.g., March and Olsen 1989) institutionalists suggest, political actors
are apt to carry out the standard operating procedures of their institutions
dutifully, even if these conflict with their own culturally derived preferences.[13] Among the instances between these two extremes are those that
Cook characterizes as "pressured decision points" (1993, 6). These situations afford political elites time to create innovative responses and are serious enough to engender struggles among alternative institutional designs
based on rival value clusters. This is the most fruitful territory for grid-
group theory. Conventional rational choice applications can model individualists' preferences in these situations, but the preferences of adherents of
other cultures are likely to appear as "irrational norms" (Elster 1989a) from
this egoistic hedonistic perspective. Grid-group theory reveals these situations as struggles among rival cultures, each striving to realize efficiently or
rationally distinctive clusters of constrained and predictable values through
the construction of different political institutions.

What to Do About the Levels of Analysis and Related Issues?

As a group, political culture theories have often been criticized for the casu-
alness with which those who employ them move back and forth between
macro and micro social levels. In comparative politics, for instance, culture
at the macro level often refers to matters such as shared patterns of social
attention and interpretation and shared conceptions of (likely partial) identity. So the prevalence of particular institutions in a society might be attributed to their embodiment of the values central to a predominant shared
identity (e.g., a preference for relatively unregulated markets—and thus negative liberty—over state-prompted corporatism as a means for organizing
economic relations in a society in which individualists are preeminent). Ross
(1997, 47–48) identifies this capacity for linking individual and collective
identities as one of the intellectual contributions of culture. Yet questions
arise concerning how we can use a macro-level characteristic (the predominance of an individualistic culture in society) to explain the actions of particular individuals and how individual preferences produce macro-level
outcomes.

13. These procedures are among what I call institutional maintenance imperatives in order
to distinguish them from the institutional formation imperatives.

I approach the first of these questions by considering persons as adherents of particular cultures. To the degree persons fulfill this assignment, they will act on the basis of beliefs and values shared across the culture and pursue institutional designs consistent with those of their fellow adherents who collectively form the macro-level culture. Such a stance—like nearly everything else about the contemporary practice of political science—is controversial. However, as Ross (1997, 55–56) relates, a number of prominent political scientists—from Almond and Verba (1963) through Inglehart (1997)—have employed such a stance in their work. On matters such as the appropriate character of social policy, attentive political activists among the citizenry and political elites are much more likely to fulfill roles as adherents of particular political cultures or at least to see such issues as relevant to those roles than are ordinary citizens (Ellis and Thompson 1997; Teske 1997).

This brings us to the second question, how individual preferences produce macro-level outcomes. Once again, while what I am doing may be controversial for some, it is similar in its assumptions to high-profile work undertaken by others. For instance, Inglehart (1997) and Flanagan and Dalton (1984) have shown that changes in the collective structure of individual values contribute to changes in political institutions such as party systems. I attribute social policy outcomes, in part, to the relative frequency of various cultural perspectives among relevant political elites. Bates (1990, 37), drawing on Popkin (1979, 245–59), stresses the pitfalls that can accompany assuming that persons can and will act on their preferences. Certainly hazards do plague this enterprise (Arrow 1951, 3; Barry and Hardin 1982, 375–78), but I think that they are minimized in my work here by two factors. First, I focus on political elites who are already generally well organized into rival factions for pursuing particular, culturally specific values and interests. So means for aggregating the preferences of these influential individuals exist. Second, as Rosenberg (1991) and Monroe (1995) suggest, in the political sphere and especially among elites, some values and the practical interests associated with them are apt to become integral aspects of persons' identities. So striving for or opposing particular sorts of social program protection for the elderly is more likely among political elites adhering to rival cultures than is revolutionary action among rural peasants (Popkin 1979). In the absence of effective organization the downside risks are higher for the latter, and they are apt as well to derive little sense of identity from new and unfamiliar revolutionary activities (Teske 1997).

Which Societies to Examine?

Throughout this study I draw largely on the experiences of four societies: the United States, the Soviet Union, Germany, and Japan.[14] These societies provide wide variation on important explanatory and dependent variables. For instance, one dependent variable employed in the case studies of Part Two is whether these societies rely more on increased revenues or benefit reductions in dealing with the financial pressures posed by their public programs for the elderly, and these societies offer clear variation on this criterion.

These societies also offer wide variation on a key explanatory variable: the relative influence of distinctive cultures, particularly among political elites. The United States is the most thoroughly individualistic of large-scale societies (Huntington 1981; Lipset 1990 and 1996; Verba et al. 1987). By the 1980s the Soviet Union represented a thoroughly hierarchical society. Several studies (Baker, Dalton, and Hildebrandt 1981; Conradt 1978, 1980; Grendstad 1999; Inglehart 1997; Rohrschneider 1994) characterize the Federal Republic of the late 1980s (i.e., prior to reunification) as having influential egalitarian, individualistic, and hierarchical elite cultures (see also Padgett 1989, 125). Japan represents a more thoroughly high-group (i.e., hierarchical and egalitarian) society than Germany with less individualistic influence (Inglehart 1997, 93; Flanagan 1979, 1987). Additionally, while these four societies exhibit similarities among the pressures confronting their public social provision for the elderly, there are also differences in the relative immediacy and severity of their difficulties.

Moreover, this purposive sample includes the most prominent examples from each of the four commonly employed categories of developed societies: liberal democracies, communist states, social democracies, and non-Western "late developers." This strategy has its drawbacks. These examples may fail to be representative of their categories as a whole. In each category I have chosen the dominant case for my sample, and there is evidence (Katzenstein 1985; Freeman 1983) that small states follow practices different from those adopted by dominant powers. These four societies do, nonetheless, provide a broad range of variation on key explanatory and dependent variables.

14. Grid-group theory is as applicable to developing as to more highly developed societies, but only the latter have extensive social programs, so I focus on varieties of moderately to highly developed societies.

Why Focus on Examples from the 1980s?

In explaining particular social policy decisions in Part Two, I seek to emulate the example that Katzenstein (1977) applied to various national reactions to the early 1970s "oil shocks." By examining different national reactions to a common stimulus, Katzenstein created a series of relatively comparable case studies (see also Gourevitch 1986). The widespread economic difficulties posed by various contingencies of the 1980s, the demographic challenges revealed during this decade, and the frequent though not universal retrenchment in social programs (OECD 1994b, 80) in response to these developments represent a related opportunity for explaining different societal reactions to similarly daunting situations.

In each society I examine what I regard as the preeminent social policy issue, particularly in light of the concern for protecting the elderly, of the 1980s. In the instances of the United States, Japan, and Germany these decisions involve changes in delivering pensions to the elderly in 1983, 1985, and 1989. In the Soviet instance the future of consumer price subsidies provides the most crucial issue, with peaks of activity in 1987 and again in 1989–91. Following Cook (1993, 6), I consider these instances to be "pressured decision points." That is, these situations forced political decision makers to reveal their priorities on a central political issue. These priorities, in turn, divulge the distinctive beliefs, values, and institutional preferences of political actors adhering to rival cultures.

Culture cannot explain everything (Elkins and Simeon 1979), but grid-group theory offers promise that is not currently available from other political culture theories for using culture as a primary independent variable in explaining various middle-range political phenomena such as cross-societal social policy differences. Thus it makes sense to inquire carefully into how grid-group theory can contribute to and enrich social explanation. To get this process under way we need to know more about how preferences originate. When and how, for instance, do persons become adherents of the rival ways of life that the theory distinguishes? And how does this process of acculturation constrain the social preferences of mature political elites? These are the tasks of the next chapter.

T W O

ORIGINS OF SOCIAL PREFERENCES

Why persons want what they do is surely among the great underinvestigated—as well as controversial (Wilson 1993; Thompson, Ellis, and Wildavsky 1990)—questions of the social sciences. Versions of rational choice theory—while commonly assuming egoistic hedonistic motivation—treat the origins of preferences as exogenous, outside the legitimate realm of inquiry—how persons obtain whatever it is that they want (Becker 1976, 133). Eckstein (1988) summarizes the work of one group of scholars who do address the origins of preferences. The answers that these political culture theorists offer draw on the transmission of relevant beliefs and values through socialization—particularly early socialization. Answers of this sort are challenged by others, prominently lately by various institutionalists (e.g., Hall 1986; Johnson 1982; Katzenstein 1984 and 1985; March and Olsen 1989; and Steinmo, Thelen, and Longstreth 1992). These institutionalists argue that the character of the institutions in which adults, especially political elites, spend their lives shapes what they want as political actors.

So the issue that has bedeviled social theorists at least since Durkheim (Durkheim and Mauss 1963, 11) remains. Do basic social relations preferences derive from beliefs about how it is desirable to live (beliefs that presumably draw on conceptions of how the world works and what humans are like) or lessons about how it is necessary to behave in order to fit into particular institutional frameworks (frameworks that likely reflect reactions to contingency as well as purposive design)? This question admittedly exaggerates distinctions between the two alternatives. What persons believe to be an appropriate way to live will rest in part on what their experience suggests is feasible. And whatever the pressures placed on them, institutions will have missions deriving in part from what persons consider to be appropriate general objectives. So beliefs about appropriateness and responses to exigency intermingle in practice. They are nonetheless conceptually distinct sources of motivation and may dominate distinctive spheres of socialization.

SPHERES OF SOCIALIZATION

Individual preferences clearly represent the socially constructed results of interaction among persons across time (Wildavsky 1991, 305). At issue is the nature of the interactions. These interactions are surely lifelong (Renshon 1989), but while learning continues into adult phases of life, "first-wave" political culture theorists argue that early learning acts as a filter that "conditions later learning and is harder to undo" (Eckstein 1988, 791). The examples that I develop below offer considerable support for the importance of early learning, much of which occurs by precept rather than by direct experience. Nonetheless, previous socialization studies have frequently erred in their conception of political culture by focusing too narrowly on the development of attitudes that are political in a needlessly explicit and strict sense (e.g., party identification). In contrast, grid-group theory focuses on the development of a few fundamental beliefs (e.g., a person's views on whether humans are equal or unequal) that pick up the political aspects in all social relations even if these aspects are implicit and subtle. Beliefs about human nature and motivation as well as beliefs about the character of human environments foster preferences for constrained clusters of values, associated interests, and particular institutional means for realizing them. Individualists such as Nozick (1974), for instance, perceive plentiful natural and social environments as well as capable, roughly equal and self-interested persons and thus develop preferences for a particular conception of liberty and what they interpret as the consensual, contractual, market-based institutions that embody this conception.

By developing such fundamental beliefs and values, early learning creates basic cultural orientations that provide coherent interpretations of how the world works and are further developed in different ways during adult life as a consequence of various new experiences, occasionally including sharply disruptive events (Sigel 1989, 459; 1995, 19–20). Institutionalists generally argue that these later experiences acquire preeminence in shaping the social preferences of adult life. Surely later socialization is important. Some persons clearly experience significant changes in their cultural biases during their adult lives. I want to suggest a means of merging some claims of both first-wave political culture theorists and some institutionalists in a sphere-oriented view of socialization. I distinguish between spheres on the basis of two criteria: the depth and breadth of issues and the nature of the socializing agent.

Depth and Breadth of Issues

Some socialization focuses on broad deep questions concerning who we are and how it is appropriate to live. Wildavsky (1994) offers examples: who am I, what do I do, how does the world work, what are humans really like, to whom am I accountable, and how do I hold others accountable to me. In acquiring answers to these questions we learn something of our cultural identity in terms of our preferences for basic forms of social relations. I refer to socialization directed at such fundamental questions as basic socialization (see also Brady, Verba, and Schlozman 1995).

Fundamental questions concerning how it is appropriate to live comprise the central focus of the early stage of socialization. These are precisely the questions that the process of cultural initiation is designed to address (Whiting 1983). Socialization during childhood and adolescence is not, of course, devoted exclusively to these basic questions, but through both precept and experience, lessons relevant to such questions are characteristically woven into the fabric of early life.

Later life experiences frequently deal with narrower, often shallower, issues. But there are occasions on which adult life raises and probes basic issues of cultural identity, sometimes shifting preferences across alternative patterns of social relations. These episodes may be elicited by hazardous or otherwise exceptional personal experiences prompted by inclusion in general social conflagrations (e.g., wars or revolutions) as well as by conscious efforts to prompt personal development (e.g., further education or initiating psychotherapy). Erikson (1956) argues that distinct stages of development continue into adult life, and in recent years guiding the continued development of American adults has become a growth industry. Thus dealing with issues of basic socialization during adulthood has become more recognized than in the past. So while basic socialization occurs largely in early life, many persons also experience episodes of socialization in adulthood.

In addition to occasional lessons of basic socialization adults are also immersed in socialization that tailors their behavior to the requirements of particular institutions. This sphere of socialization prepares humans for performing specific roles, rather than shaping their cultural identities. While lessons of basic socialization may occasionally be acquired in these various domains, the acquisition of more specific lessons is the norm. As we shall see, in many instances the later lessons of adult professional socialization fit well with those of earlier basic socialization, the former specifying and refining the latter. But in the process of modifying the more general lessons of basic socialization, adult professional socialization may sometimes introduce fundamental conflict.[1]

Nature of the Socializing Agent

Various theorists of human development (Erikson 1956; Kagan 1984; Rogers 1961) agree that the effective sources of early socialization are other persons who are prominently involved in youngsters' lives. This is necessarily the case for infants and small children, who have at best limited conceptions of institutions, rules, roles, and exigencies. They accept what significant others teach—both intentionally and inadvertently—because of their close relationships with these persons. These relationships may extend beyond family members to include neighbors, teachers, ministers, etc. The necessary dominance of personal relations in socialization declines sharply as children become adolescents. Nonetheless, institutions that seek to mold adolescents generally and appropriately attempt to reinforce cognitive mes-

---

1. One important example of this sort of conflict occurs in the military. Marshall (1947, 50–59, 78–79) contends that even in the Second World War within units that fought regularly, no more than a quarter of American troops actually used their personal weapons against the enemy. Revulsion at killing (attributable to basic socialization) evidently outweighed both adult military socialization and fear of being killed. Recently, however, Marshall's claims have been challenged by others, including his own grandson. See Smoler 1989 and Marshall 1993.

sages by relating them through persons who have developed personal relations with the youngsters, and the personal relations of peer groups become prominent socialization agents. Thus during the formative period of early life, within which basic socialization lessons are concentrated, agents socializing through personally directed face-to-face activity predominate. Among adults, the messages of basic socialization, while they remain personal, are less commonly delivered face-to-face. Thus deliberative reflection that prompts new patterns of living can arise from (for example) reading a guide for coping with the dilemmas of mid-life.

Further, in the large, relatively impersonal institutions in which most contemporary national political elites work, Weber's rational-legal form of authority (Bendix 1977) is characteristically more, and personal relations accordingly less, important in socialization. Exigencies of organizational role and institutional mission in a challenging world frequently require elites to act in ways that they might prefer—on the basis of basic socialization—to avoid. Personal relations remain, importantly under these circumstances, as humane adhesives that bind such institutions together, and personal peculiarities contribute to variations in behavior (Downs 1967). But the central core of socialization about fulfilling one's duty derives from the nature of one's role (March and Olsen 1989). Lessons on role fulfillment form part of the institution's standard operating procedures. These guidelines in turn reflect conditions prevalent in the social environment with which the institution must deal.

Boundaries of Relevance

This sphere conception of socialization suggests that if what we want to explain are the day-to-day routines of organizations, or what I call institutional *maintenance* imperatives, then the nature of adult professional socialization is our best guide. But if what we want to explain is why particular institutional forms (i.e., the institutional *formation* imperatives introduced in the previous chapter) are chosen over others, then basic beliefs about the human condition and human nature, factors laden with messages about appropriate institutional design, are apt to be more helpful. Thus institutionalists (e.g., March and Olsen 1989) are frequently correct that policy preferences of adult political actors arise from the constraints of their institutional roles and organizational missions. But I am concerned to demonstrate the limitations of this view. While adult political officials may have few opportunities for acting on their basic socialization, such instances are sometimes crucial in shaping the nature of societal institutions.

Consider an instance of institutional formation. Late-eighteenth-century European colonists in North America worked their way through several governmental variations. Two possibilities—dominion status in an empire and a loose confederation of local, popularly elected legislatures limited in their legitimate powers—were predictably preferred by hierarchists and egalitarians, respectively (Lockhart 1999, 870–73). The writings of Samuel Boucher and Thomas Paine provide characteristic examples of hierarchical and egalitarian views on humans and their world (Levy 1992, 86–91 and 73–80). Boucher was as well an implacable advocate of remaining part of the British empire, whereas Paine worked for local legislatures. These men exemplify the associations of hierarchy with empire on one hand and egalitarianism with limited local government on the other (Wood 1969; Main 1964).

But these options were successively challenged and overcome by the Revolution and the replacement of the Articles of Confederation with a new Constitution. This Constitution was furthered by a coalition between individualists and hierarchists. The latter, having lost on the issue of dominion, found the Articles incapable of delivering the security and order their interests required and sought improved circumstances through a coalition with some individualists who, following egalitarian attacks on certain forms of property, shared important objectives with hierarchists (Beard 1965). As Madison's appeals for ratification of the Constitution (*Federalist 10* and *51*) reveal, its checks and balances as well as separation of powers define the form of governing institutions considered appropriate among those whose views of nature as bountiful and humans as self-interested construct the grid-group position of individualism. If Madison and others had simply accepted their roles in existing institutions and engaged in their corresponding duties, as March and Olsen (1989) argue adults tend to do, then these new institutions would likely have never developed. Instead they drew on their earlier basic socialization, thus choosing to discard empire as well as limited local legislatures and to create new structures better suited to their cultural biases. Such choices may be relatively unusual, but they are also apt to be quite important for explaining institutional form.

A Cautionary Note on Culture and Personality

We ought to consider a cautionary point about any form of acculturation through social learning—that is, the experience-driven acquisition of broad patterns of cognition as well as identities that are shared by many persons. Common experience does not necessarily produce identical perspectives or social preferences. As Greenstein (1992) suggests, culture and personality each transcend the other in different ways. Culture represents a roughly common element shared across multiple persons. But within each person culture comprises only a portion of the personality. Other portions of personality remain relatively independent of culture, and some are idiosyncratic.

Two caveats arise from the fact that culture represents only a portion of an individual personality. First, what it means to share an experience is an elusive matter that draws on aspects of the personality that are independent of culture. What an external observer perceives as an experience common to several persons may be perceived differently by these persons. So even the cultural aspects of personality are likely to be shared imperfectly across persons as they internalize somewhat different messages from common experiences. Second, even truly shared perspectives do not always produce the same practical social preferences, since these cultural aspects of personality may be related differently to other personality aspects across persons. So a few persons who share a culture with others may be preoccupied with matters centered in various noncultural aspects of personality and thus ignore culture-mobilizing cues in new experiences to which most adherents of the culture are attentive. In spite of these limitations, it is clear that many persons do share significant aspects of cultural orientations arising from similar experiences. But we need to keep in mind that this sharing is imperfect.

SPHERES OF SOCIALIZATION AND GRID-GROUP THEORY

I apply this sphere conception of socialization in conjunction with grid-group theory to show that persons can acquire long-lasting cultural identities prior to entering the institutions of adult life. Further, the consequences of basic and largely early socialization can be fairly easily categorized into grid-group theory's four types (Banfield 1958; Pye 1988; Thompson, Ellis and Wildavsky 1990, chap. 14). Grid-group theory is certainly more capable at categorizing social orientations than is the traditional left-right continuum of political ideology in this regard (Coughlin and Lockhart 1998). By this I do not mean that everyone in a given society becomes an individualist or a hierarchist or an egalitarian or a fatalist. Societies are multicultural; and particularly under the conditions of relatively tolerant pluralism that exist in many advanced industrial societies, children may well be influenced by significant others who adhere to different cultures. Socialization by the agents of multiple cultures frequently produces persons who hold bifocal cultural biases. Persons socialized in this fashion retain sympathies for multiple ways of life and are likely to practice different cultures in varying social contexts: individualism and/or hierarchy in the workplace as opposed to egalitarianism in the family, for instance (Hochschild 1981; Walzer 1983).

At certain junctures persons with bifocal cultural biases may begin applying one of their cultural faces, previously used in one particular domain of life, in another domain. Such transitions are often prompted by historical contingencies that raise issues suggesting the appropriateness of applying an approach familiar in one context to a different context recently transformed by changing circumstances. Consider, for instance, the situation of a successful attorney who is also a wife and mother. Following a series of academic and professional mentors, she applies an individualistic cultural bias toward workplace issues. But in accordance with themes introduced to her by contemporary feminists, she practices egalitarianism in her home: roughly equal spousal sharing of household responsibilities and participation of the children in family decisions etc. This attorney has, then, an IE (or EI) bifocal cultural bias (Lockhart 1999, 876–77).

Historical contingencies may alter the cross-pressures weighing on such a bias and contribute to political change in the process. The emergence of the family leave issue that sharpens tensions between the home and the workplace, for example, may prompt this attorney to broaden the application of her egalitarian cultural bias to an aspect of the workplace by endorsing new supports for working parents at the expense of the firm's economic efficiency. In so doing she does not replace her culture of individualism with a new culture of egalitarianism; rather she shifts marginally the way she applies her two preexisting cultures across domains of social life.

Issues that prompt such shifts arise from contingencies that are not easily predicted, but the intrapersonal mechanism that triggers the revised application of particular cultures can be specified. This trigger is appropriately viewed as a shift in relevant analogies that has the effect of relocating a boundary between social categories. Up to this point, the attorney of our example has associated workplace matters with an individualistic efficiency model and affairs relating to the home with an egalitarian caring model. This association remained stable as long as she continued to view her coworkers as workers, but the family leave issue led her to see some of her coworkers as parents and suggested to her the relevance of the caring model. If a number of persons apply egalitarianism to a matter on which their practice has previously been individualistic, these marginal shifts in the application of bifocal cultural biases may alter the relative influence of rival cultures on a specific range of issues and thus create conditions conducive to political change. So bifocal cultural biases complicate applications of grid-group theory, but they do not detract from a tendency for persons to view broad swaths of social life in ways that are easily coded by the theory.

As we shall see, for some political elites the professional socialization of adult life reinforces the culture(s) dominant in their basic socialization. Thus many aspects of political learning in this period are easily filtered through earlier learning and engender only incremental changes in elite cultural biases, characteristically involving more specific guidance about a relatively narrow range of situations (Eckstein 1988). Nonetheless, the tasks involved in governing are apt to prompt modification of the preferences deriving from early socialization. In a few instances institutional exigencies will be particularly forceful, and persons who in other circumstances would not kill become involved in projects entailing the massive destruction of civilian populations, such as the fire bombings and nuclear attacks of the Second World War. Thus while the lessons of adult professional socialization are often narrower and shallower than those of basic socialization, they can nonetheless be powerful within their particular social domains.

EXAMPLES

I illustrate the process of early cultural acquisition and its influence on later life as it unfolded in the lives of four contemporary political figures representing the societies that I examine in this study. I employ these examples to illustrate the following points: (1) persons can acquire their basic social relations preferences (and thus become adherents of one of grid-group theory's cultures or bifocal combinations of them) as a result of early basic socialization; (2) cultures acquired early in life can guide political elites (and presumably others too) in later life on central matters such as career choices and orientations toward a broad range of public policy issues; (3) several factors contribute to the capacity of cultural orientations acquired in early life to guide adult political preferences—(a) the fundamental identity-constituting nature of the issues (e.g., conceptions of human nature) central to the cultures that grid-group theory distinguishes, (b) self-selection into careers compatible with early socialization, and (c) a complex and ambiguous social reality that lends itself to rival interpretations. I stress that I am illustrating processes, using theory to interpret evidence (Ragin 1992, 224–25), not confirming empirical generalizations.

Ronald Reagan

Ronald Reagan was born in 1911 and spent his youth in Illinois, primarily in the small town of Dixon.[2] His father was a salesperson who experienced little economic success and was an alcoholic. His mother, a kind and creative woman, was extremely active in the Christian Church (Disciples of Christ). Reagan was closer to his mother, while his older brother, Neil, gravitated toward his father.

Thus a Christian community nurtured Reagan in his youth. He was involved in the plays and related activities that his mother engaged in through her church. He acquired a sense of optimism from his mother and social confidence from these activities. His pastor became the first among several extrafamilial father-figures for him. From high school through college Reagan worked summers as a lifeguard at a park near Dixon and acquired a remarkable record of life-saving rescues. He disapproved of the undisciplined behaviors (among them drinking) of some of the park's clientele, including those he rescued.

Much of Reagan's early learning about how to live thus involved adopting his mother's sense of communal values and responsibility for less capable persons.[3] He yearned for stability and felt comfortable with discipline and authority (Wills 1987, 34–35). He developed as well a fear of dependency arising, according to Dallek (1984, 15–17), in part from his experiences with his father's alcoholism. Reagan also learned from his father the salesperson's stock-in-trade of infusing customers with optimism.

These varying influences were all reinforced during Reagan's years at

2. According to Reagan himself: "There [in Dixon] was the life that shaped my mind and body for all the years to come after" (Reagan with Hubler 1965, 23). My account draws on Cannon 1982, Edwards 1987, Reagan with Hubler 1965, and Wills 1987. See also Reagan with Lindsey 1990.

3. For instance, following his mother's extraordinary example (for the household in which Reagan grew up was poor), Reagan donated ten percent of his income to the Hollywood and Beverly Hills Christian Church during the years he worked at Warner Brothers (Edwards 1987, 56). See also Edwards (1987, 72–73) on Reagan's early communal values.

nearby Eureka College, a Disciples' school.[4] With the help of a reference from his pastor, Reagan joined a fraternity immediately. During Reagan's first semester, Eureka was the scene of the dramatic finale of a lengthy struggle between the faculty and the president over the latter's proposal for a substantial reorganization of the college prompted by financial problems. This struggle culminated in a student strike. Several members of Reagan's fraternity were leaders of the strike, and Reagan, who on the basis of his church experiences was already a confident public speaker, was prominent among those who addressed the meeting that precipitated the strike. Reagan's recollections of this episode reveal an orientation commonly exhibited in his later life. He glosses over the long-standing and intricate nature of the conflict, reducing it to a struggle between the forces of good and evil (Wills 1987, 52).

High-grid high-group themes dominated Reagan's childhood and adolescent socialization. The community that his mother and pastor provided was disciplined. Thus Reagan acquired tutoring in correct behavior that the persons who needed rescuing at Dixon's swimming park presumably lacked. Further, this community promoted self-improvement and encouraged responsible contributions according to one's capacities. Thus Reagan developed a cultural bias with a strong hierarchist component. He actively sought inclusion in group activities, evincing a sense of responsibility toward the collective, and he was intolerant of undisciplined behavior. Somewhat more surprisingly, Reagan acquired some early sympathy for individualism as well—an HI bifocal cultural bias. This latter lens appears to have arisen in part from the experience of growing up dependent on a breadwinner who was alcoholic. Reagan reacted to this experience with the marked dislike of dependency characteristic of individualism. Additionally, while his mother's Christianity accepted stratifying persons on the basis of their individually demonstrated capacities for living according to the Gospel, she nonetheless instilled in Reagan a disdain for discrimination based merely on ethnicity—an orientation sharing common ground with individualistic views. His individualism acquired only limited development in his early years, prompting little independent thinking or unconventional action. However, it would later provide Reagan with a basis for a cultural shift as his life experiences increasingly moved him in an individualistic direction.

Unemployment plagued Reagan for a few months following his college

---

4. For similarities between the social community of Eureka College and Dixon, see Edwards 1987, 85, 95.

graduation in the Depression year of 1932. He applied himself to several modest jobs and gradually advanced to a position of responsibility at a radio station in Des Moines, Iowa, where he spent roughly five years. Here he became a local celebrity, much sought after for appearances and speeches. His popularity was initially based on his creative broadcasts of Chicago professional baseball games. Reagan worked from brief wire accounts in Des Moines and imagined the details he broadcast. In doing so he demonstrated a remarkably quick wit as well as coolness under pressure, capacities likely developed in his earlier church stage experience but which in his new celebrity status reinforced his perception of himself as a capable individual. The inspirational character of sports journalism in this era fit well with Reagan's style. He also voluntarily joined the Army Reserves in Des Moines and frequently used Camp Dodge facilities for riding and other recreation. He approved of the discipline, obedience, and dedication of the military men he encountered (Wills 1987, 111).

Reagan moved to Hollywood in 1937 and developed a successful career in the film industry, particularly at Warner Brothers as a light romantic comic lead. He was soon joined by some of his Illinois friends, and he brought his parents to California. He and his friends—still several from his midwestern days—frequently socialized with his parents. Reagan thus fit well with the political and social conservatism—"wholesome Hollywood" (Cannon 1982, 77)—of the film industry in this era. Working in make-believe may have reinforced his individualistic sense—already visible in the Eureka College strike and his stint as a sports radio celebrity in Des Moines—that persons can make crucial contributions to events. But the Reagan who moved to California with friends and family and socialized with this multigenerational collective retained his hierarchical face as well.

In Hollywood Reagan became active in the Screen Actors Guild (SAG). His membership on its board of directors brought him into regular contact with some of the major stars of this period—persons who did not need a union. Reagan's initial reactions to organized labor activities came from observing the efforts of these stars to win collective agreements that improved the lives of others with far less bargaining power. He was quite favorably impressed with the selflessness of their activities.

Reagan worked on training films in the Army Air Corps during the Second World War. On his return to commercial films in 1945, he renewed his participation on the SAG board. Labor activities in the film industry during this period were convoluted, with troubling influences—organized crime and Moscow-oriented leftists—contributing to the complexity of the mix.

Reagan's "union" activities in the latter half of the 1940s provided a primary locus for his acquiring adult professional socialization leading to revision of the relative emphasis among his earlier views. While he remained intrigued by Franklin Delano Roosevelt's (FDR) New Deal and war effort, which had vastly expanded the federal government, he began to apply his individualism more thoroughly in the public realm. For instance, he dropped his (recently acquired) membership in a prestigious golf club that discriminated against Jews—his boss, Jack Warner, among them (Edwards 1987, 203). Further, he began to oppose communists in his industry from a perspective that gradually led him into the Republican Party. According to Edwards (1987, 293–94), Reagan's conception of himself as a liberal was both shallow and narrow, based on FDR's charisma and the help that the New Deal had provided for his family during the Depression. Reagan was developing the more obviously bifocal beliefs and values that formed the moral vision that he later applied in public life: individualistic elements centering on his preference for minimal government interference in economic activities along with his hierarchist belief in the private (Christian-based) obligation to help persons less capable of coping with life's vicissitudes. These conflicting elements are characteristic of the economically conservative (individualistic) and socially conservative (hierarchical) wings of the present-day Republican Party.

So Reagan's early postwar SAG activities involved him in several of the prevailing political issues of the time and pitted him against a shifting series of adversaries that he came—at least briefly—to view as evil. Prior to the Second World War Reagan had opposed the greed of private corporations in the film industry. After the war he came increasingly to question the legitimacy of the collective economic activity of unions, although as late as 1959 he returned to SAG briefly and led a labor action over actors' fringe benefits and rights concerning old movies broadcast on television. Reagan's growing skepticism about the labor movement was prompted largely by his inadvertently finding himself involved in the struggle against communism in the late 1940s. While Reagan's later recollections of these activities are less balanced, Cannon (1982, 82–84) shows that although Reagan opposed communists, he was hesitant about naming individuals and, as a manifestation of his growing individualism, also opposed government "witch-hunting." This latter theme gradually broadened in his mind, and Reagan began to fear and warn against the growing power of the federal government. Thus Reagan's early postwar experiences reinforced in his mind the individualistic perspectives of a series of close friends: Hal Gross from his days in Des

Moines and Justin Dart, Dick Powell, and others in California. These persons may have been particularly influential, since Reagan had relied on extrafamilial male mentors (father substitutes) all his life.

By 1954 he was working, through the Music Corporation of America (MCA), for General Electric (GE). Although this work involved his sporadic participation in television films, his main task was spokesperson, both introducing a weekly drama series to a television audience and giving speeches to private groups while touring GE facilities around the country. His income for this period created tax problems, and opposition to the progressive income tax became an important index of his individualism starting in the 1950s (Cannon 1982, 91). Concern about the activities of the federal government increasingly defined the character of his GE speeches. The central theme of these speeches evolved as a result of his refining the moral vision (minimal government coupled with private charity) in light of the questions he received from his audiences so that Reagan focused progressively on endorsing corporate enterprise and warning of government regulation (Cannon 1982, 94). Reagan's adult life thus developed in such a way that the lens of his bifocal cultural bias which had initially been subordinate became increasingly prominent. This change is revealed in Reagan's party affiliation. FDR had been one of Reagan's idols, and his family had been rescued by Roosevelt's New Deal during the Depression. Indeed Reagan voted Democratic through the 1940s. He initially supported Helen Gahagan Douglas against Richard Nixon in 1950, but later shifted over to Nixon. He did not formally change his party affiliation until 1962. But he ran for governor of California as an economically conservative Republican three years later.

Reagan was elected governor of California in 1966. As a consequence of his late entry into the ranks of formal political elites, he had already formed the bulk of the beliefs and values about politics that we associate with his stints as governor and president. While his views had developed and shifted emphasis during his adult life, they were not without substantial elements of stability. So, in spite of an increasingly pronounced individualistic component, Reagan's adult political socialization generally reinforced his early socialization.

Thus Reagan remained in Wills's terms a "company man"—i.e., high-grid high-group (Wills 1987, 282). The "company" changed: the church, the fraternity, Warner Brothers, the Army Air Corps, the SAG, MCA, etc. Reagan was remarkably willing to fit into these organizations as his superiors and various experts suggested. Indeed, on occasion he took dismissal with equanimity (Wills 1987, 284). Even when the "company" was his own gubernatorial or presidential administration, Reagan took direction extremely well, bowing to experts about what to say and do about specific matters. As was the case in the Eureka College strike, Reagan saw his specialized role as providing a moral vision—basically the themes he developed in his speeches for GE. In his view others were responsible for the practical details, and he did not generally care to supervise their work. These characteristics reveal the long-standing hierarchist lens of Reagan's bifocal cultural bias (Will 1985). This lens once appeared prominently in his personal life as well. For instance, at the age of forty-one (thirty-one for Nancy) he and Nancy called to ask her father's permission to marry (Edwards 1987, 430–31). But as Reagan's growing individualism anticipates, his relationships with his own children were much less close (Giles-Sims and Lockhart 2000).

A better-known individualistic lens complemented his hierarchical orientation. While particular experiences of his adult life—celebrity status in Des Moines and later Hollywood, opposing communists in the SAG, distress over federal witch-hunts and tax rates, the individualistic concerns expressed by his audiences on GE speaking tours—developed the individualistic lens of Reagan's bifocal cultural bias, this perspective had a base in Reagan's early socialization from his individualistic father and his mother's opposition to racial discrimination on which to build. So, according to Dallek (1984), the Reagan who opposed improving the lives of the poor through means that increase their dependence on the public programs of an active government was an extension of the child who disdained dependency on an alcoholic father.

These individualistic influences clearly had powerful effects on Reagan's perspective—creating a well-developed shrewdness about his own material self-interest, for instance. Reagan did not, however, live the life of an entrepreneur, nor was he an innovative thinker. The most prominent themes of his mature individualism involved warnings about the growing public regulation of corporations and individuals. Indeed, he repeatedly self-selected himself into hierarchical institutions and showed remarkable hesitancy about calling the shots on most specific matters even when he was the boss. This particular amalgam of hierarchy and individualism is not uncommon. It is similar to that of corporate executives who face an external world of competitive market conditions from preferred home-bases in institutions that are relatively staid hierarchies.

My point in relating selective experiences of Reagan's life is not that all children of alcoholic fathers respond by rejecting dependency generally or that persons who experience labor union corruption become individualists.

Persons' lives involve idiosyncrasies of genetic endowment, social experience, and interaction between them that defy such generalizations. Further, it is difficult to be certain which experiences are formative and why. Nonetheless, I have shown that Reagan acquired a recognizable bifocal cultural bias in early life. From this orientation stem the ontological and value predispositions and institutional preferences of his adult life. Indeed Reagan persistently practiced long-standing patterns of behavior in situations affording alternatives. For instance, Reagan's contribution to his own presidential administration—spokesperson for a moral vision—is remarkably similar to his role in the Eureka College strike fifty years earlier. The following examples show even more clearly that social orientations developed early in life guide important political decisions in maturity.

Mikhail Gorbachev

Mikhail Gorbachev was born in 1931 in the village of Privolnoye in the northern Caucasus near the city of Stavropol.[5] This region had only recently emerged from frontier status. It had been settled largely by liberated Russian serfs in the nineteenth century. These people were independent homesteaders, and the region was known for a relatively individualistic culture in comparison to that of the Russian heartland; indeed, the very word *privol'nyi* means "free" (Schmidt-Häuer 1986, 42–43; Smith 1990, 33–34).

Gorbachev was born into a peasant household during Stalin's campaign to collectivize agriculture. His maternal grandfather, a pivotal figure in his life, was the leader of one of the first collective farms in the region. Gorbachev watched his grandfather adapt to many sharp swings in fortune and circumstance, shifting, for instance, from the status of a relatively successful peasant to a popular official of state agriculture, despite a nasty brush with the NKVD (political police). Gorbachev observed his grandfather practice persuasion in accomplishing many difficult objectives, avoiding in his locale much of the violence that accompanied collectivization elsewhere (Smith 1990). Gorbachev clearly emulated his grandfather's practices in his own life. This is particularly obvious in the capacity he developed for achieving his objectives against the resistance of others without impairing his own prospects in the process (Schmidt-Häuer 1986, 61; Gorbachev 1995, 7–9; Brown 1996, 24–25, 37).

5. My account draws on Brown 1996, Gorbachev 1995, Schmidt-Häuer 1986, and Smith 1990.

Gorbachev's parents—collective farm workers and Communist Party members—were capable but less remarkable than his grandfather in their accomplishments. In personality, Gorbachev followed the example of his self-assured, outspoken, and frequently self-righteous mother, who was more actively involved in Party matters than his shy father was. He appears to have acquired his positive orientation toward hard work and responsibility at least in part in the company of his father, with whom he won national recognition in 1948 for a prodigious wheat harvest (Gorbachev 1995, 38). From this multigenerational tutelage Gorbachev developed ambition, courage, a sense of realism that accepted pragmatic changes in course, skills in organization and leadership, and—particularly from his mother—a remarkable contempt for varying forms of irresponsible behavior, including the use of alcohol. Gorbachev did well in his early schooling, showing particular enjoyment of history and acting. He was also active in the Komsomol, the Party youth organization.

Gorbachev's basic socialization occurred within a hierarchical culture. He accordingly acquired a strong sense of social duty and obedience to rules. He was, however, never imbued with the desirability of blind obedience to one particular authority (Gorbachev 1995, 21; Brown 1996, 32). The portraits of Lenin that his grandfather hung in the house, for instance, had religious icons on their reverse faces, and Gorbachev witnessed his grandfather continue to apply some of the entrepreneurial skills that had made him a successful independent farmer as leader of an agricultural collective. Thus Gorbachev acquired a sense of a hierarchy of duties and an associated instrumental pragmatism. The precepts and experiences of his basic socialization also prepared him for leadership in these hierarchical patterns. From his mother and his acting experience in particular he acquired the self-confidence for leadership. And through emulating the example of his grandfather, he acquired considerable capacity for social diplomacy (Grobachev 1995, 39; Brown 1996, 37).

Gorbachev was clearly a talented young man, but his early education had not been sophisticated. So it appears surprising that he gained admission to prestigious Moscow State University in 1950. His grandfather engaged the local Komsomol organization in his cause, and his extracurricular record—particularly his national recognition as a worker—surely strengthened his application. He was admitted to study law, not a high-status discipline in the late Stalin era, but perhaps a fortunate development in spite of this. Law students were among the few who were permitted access to a variety of Western thinkers on issues such as the origins of the state. Initially university life was difficult for Gorbachev. He had to work hard to catch up academically, and he was desperately poor. But he acclimated quickly.

His university years provide further evidence of his self-assurance, courage, and independence. For instance, he openly criticized aspects of the visit of a distinguished lecturer and defended a Jewish friend at a time when it was particularly dangerous to do so (Smith 1990, 48–49; Brown 1996, 30–31). He also developed his reputation as a leader capable of building consensus. These years reveal as well that he could be a scheming organizational disciplinarian (Smith 1990, 50; Medvedev 1987, 38–39).[6] While still a student he became a full member of the Party and met and married Raisa Titorenko, a talented student who subsequently wrote a provocative dissertation on urban-rural class differences in Soviet life (Schmidt-Häuer 1986, 54–57).

Stalin died while Gorbachev was studying in Moscow, and Khrushchev's 1956 speech denouncing Stalinism came soon after his return to the Stavropol region following graduation. These dual shocks left many in Gorbachev's generation groping for other foundations for their orientations toward social life (Smith 1990, 54–56; Brown 1996, 37–38). Since important aspects of the formal political socialization that they had received during late adolescence now lay in disrepute, his generation became widely noted as being more open, particularly about social and economic change, than the Brezhnev generation. In Gorbachev's case this predicament complemented, once he had weathered the initial disorientation, the curiosity, independence, and pragmatism that he had acquired as a youth. That is, Khrushchev's denunciation of a major source of Gorbachev's political socialization in late adolescence and early adulthood had the—in this case salutary—effect of making him rely more heavily on sound earlier basic socialization for guidance.

Gorbachev was initially disappointed at having to return to the Stavropol region, where he remained for over two decades after his graduation.[7] He

6. Gorbachev argues that he escaped severe reprisal for actions arising from his youthful independence of mind as a result of his "peasant and worker" background (1995, 46). Overall, Medvedev (1987) offers a less encouraging view of Gorbachev's life, particularly his days as a university student. Similarly, Sakwa also makes more of Gorbachev's "ruthlessness," relating that Gromyko supported Gorbachev's bid for general secretary with the line: "This man has a nice smile, but he has iron teeth" (1990, 1). See also Brown 1985 and Murarka 1988.

7. Gorbachev started working at the Stavropol prosecutor's office but, particularly against the background of his maternal grandfather's experience, was put off by the attitudes of his coworkers toward the public (Brown 1996, 36). He switched over to Komsomol work in less than a week (Gorbachev 1995, 53 and 58).

soon acquired a mentor in Fyodor Kulakov, then the Party's first secretary in the region (*krai*) and a relatively open-minded official, who recognized Gorbachev's talent without necessarily being put off by his sometimes unorthodox practices (Gorbachev 1995, 6–7, 73–74). Gorbachev moved through a series of jobs in the Komsomol to positions in agriculture and ended up—after Kulakov moved on to Moscow—in general Party administration as regional first secretary in 1970 (Sakwa 1990, 3). Along the way he acquired a degree in agricultural economics as well as a reputation for both loyalty and innovation. Gorbachev's loyalty was given particularly to the ideals of institutions. Thus he was known as a stringent disciplinarian—a man of unusual integrity—who sought to hold officials accountable to their responsibilities. In spite of his zeal in this regard, however, he was widely recognized as approachable.

Gorbachev's loyalty to the Soviet promise of improving social conditions led him into the pursuit of innovation (Gorbachev 1995, 59; Brown 1996, 44–46). He wanted better results: more production and better living conditions. He initiated and encouraged numerous experiments in this regard, clashing repeatedly with central planners, but creating useful new practices in the process. His visits to Western Europe in the early 1970s, after he became a member of the Party's Central Committee, reinforced his inclination to support decentralization of economic decision making and to experiment with schemes of self-financing and profit motivation in both agricultural and industrial undertakings (Gorbachev 1995, 93–95). This pattern of challenging existing practice in order to better realize ideals, and particularly engaging in this potentially disruptive behavior in a fashion that left his prospects for personal advancement intact, is already visible in Gorbachev's adolescence and likely stems from conscious emulation of his maternal grandfather.

During his tenure as regional first secretary, Gorbachev also selectively sought out and won the patronage of high-level Soviet officials—including Yuri Andropov, Aleksei Kosygin, and Mikhail Suslov—on their frequent visits to the spas of his region (Gorbachev 1995, 10; Brown 1996, 38, 50). These men were not part of Leonid Brezhnev's inner circle, and they shared with Gorbachev a distaste for the growing corruption of the Brezhnev era. Additionally, Andropov in particular shared Gorbachev's perceptions, beginning in the early 1970s, that the Soviet Union was in economic decline and was falling increasingly behind the West (Schmidt-Häuer 1986, 63–65; Smith 1990, 65; Gorbachev 1995, 153). Andropov's preferred solutions to these problems reflected Party orthodoxy, a sharp contrast to the ideas that Gorbachev was gradually developing (Gorbachev 1995, 147).

Gorbachev was chosen to replace Kulakov as the Central Committee Secretary for Agriculture on the latter's death in 1978, thus bringing him back to Moscow. Two years later he entered the Politburo. He initially struggled with Brezhnev and his close associates in this body over agricultural policy. They favored expanding the centrally directed mechanisms of the past rather than adopting the decentralized procedures that Gorbachev proposed. He lost many of these early struggles, and Soviet agriculture did not fare well under his tutelage. Yet he managed to remain in the Politburo, using his position to broaden his contacts among a younger generation of regional Party officials and Moscow intelligentsia. He used these associations to stimulate broader ideas for reform than those the Politburo was then willing to hear.

Andropov became general secretary after Brezhnev's death in 1982, and under his leadership Gorbachev's responsibilities broadened to include the economy generally as well as ideology (Gorbachev 1995, 147). As Andropov's health deteriorated, Gorbachev increasingly filled in for him in a variety of capacities. His broader responsibilities allowed him to further his development of new policy options, an enterprise that led eventually to *perestroika* and *glasnost*. These activities included more travel to the West, particularly a 1983 trip to Canada during which he showed a keen interest in economic incentives (Gorbachev 1995, 149).

Gorbachev did not become general secretary on Andropov's death. The Brezhnev faction remained strong enough to impose Konstantin Chernenko in 1984. Indeed, when Chernenko died a year later, it still required some luck for Gorbachev to be chosen as general secretary in March 1985 (Gorbachev 1995, 163). He was finally in a position to employ more openly and broadly the ideas that he had been developing for a number of years. It seems remarkable, even in retrospect, that he was able to develop and push for these alternative approaches for so long without removing himself from consideration for supreme leadership. The mixtures of persuasive candor and tactfulness as well as ambition and patience that he had learned early from his grandfather certainly served him well, particularly during this final phase of his rise to the top of the Party hierarchy.

Much of Gorbachev's adult professional socialization reinforced the dominant hierarchical lens of the cultural bias that developed from his early socialization. So Gorbachev remained preeminently a hierarchist. But the relative emphasis of rival themes gradually shifted as adult professional socialization built on individualistic themes to which Gorbachev was introduced early on by his grandfather. His loss of faith in Stalinism in early adulthood certainly opened him to rethinking organizational practice, and various visits to the West later reveal him to be reflecting seriously on the appropriate nature of economic institutions. As his conclusions on these matters were revealed in the late 1980s, they involved introducing more individualism into political institutions and the practice of socialist economics (Cook 1993, chap. 4; Gorbachev 1995, 167). Thus features of Gorbachev's early basic socialization—his curiosity and pragmatism—combined with aspects of adult professional socialization—his loss of faith in Stalin's methods along with his loyalty to broad institutional goals—and contributed to a more overtly bifocal cultural bias with an increasingly well defined subordinate lens of individualism.

Helmut Kohl

Helmut Kohl was born in 1930 in Friesenheim, a section of Lugwigshafen, along the Rhine in the Rhineland-Palatinate.[8] His parents were Catholics but tolerant socially and supporters of the political center during the Weimar period. Kohl's father was an official in the state revenue bureaucracy. Depressed yet inflationary economic conditions and the ensuing political instability of the Weimar Republic made the 1930s difficult for the middle class into which Kohl was born. Yet in Kohl's memory the 1930s were better than the period that followed (Maser 1990, 26).

Kohl's father was encouraged neither by Hitler nor the war he brought. He was activated into the reserves and released only in 1944 at the age of fifty-eight after having a heart attack. Kohl remembers his parents listening to Radio London and speaking in hushed tones with their friends about the ravages that had befallen Germany's Jewish population (Maser 1990, 28). Kohl's older brother Walter, an officer in a parachute unit, was killed late in the war. Kohl spent much of the war in and around Lugwigshafen. His schooling was interrupted, and he became involved in efforts to help victims of the Allied bombing raids. He spent the final months of the war, along with other children from Ludwigshafen, in the countryside near Berchtesgaden, the town closest to the Berghof, Hitler's alpine retreat. After the war's end these youngsters were detained briefly by American forces on their re-

---

8. Biographical materials on Helmut Kohl currently available in the United States are not generally of high quality. Among the most useful is Maser 1990.

turn trip to Lugwigshafen. Despite these traumatizing events, Kohl appears to have been a remarkably well adjusted youngster, which Kohl himself attributes to early family socialization (Henscheid 1985, 174).

Kohl resumed his studies in a university preparatory program (*gymnasium*) in the autumn of 1945. His teachers remember him as an intellectual interested in "ivory tower" theories, a democrat, and a "political man" (Maser 1990, 37, 66). In spite of his early membership (at sixteen) in the Christian Democratic Union (CDU) and his work as cofounder of the CDU youth organization in Ludwigshafen, Kohl was disappointed by his first glimpse of Konrad Adenauer (CDU). He feared Adenauer was too old for the tremendous tasks that lay ahead. He was, however, highly enthusiastic after attending a speech by Adenauer's bitter opponent, Kurt Schumacher (Social Democratic Party of Germany—SPD), whose rhetoric ignited his developing political interests.

During his late adolescence Kohl had a number of adult male mentors from Lugwigshafen political circles (including SPD officials—Henscheid 1985, 87), the Catholic Church, and the faculty of his *gymnasium* (Hofmann 1991, 16). He appears as well to have been popular among his fellow students: sincere, open-minded, and fair. His extracurricular skills—he played the accordion and harmonica and was active in soccer and swimming—facilitated his social interaction. In school he was clearly highly motivated, competent, and self-confident. While in *gymnasium* he met Hannelore Renner, his future wife and the daughter of a Protestant engineer whose family had fled the Russian advance in the East. Hannelore, whose father had died after reaching Ludwigshafen, was poor but talented and industrious. She became a translator of French and English for BASF. Kohl graduated in the spring of 1950, showing strengths in history and German and doing less well in mathematics.

In the autumn of 1950 Kohl entered Frankfurt's Wolfgang Goethe University as a student of economics, law, and psychology. He was part of a generation of older students whose lives had been held back by the war and who—as a cohort—are remembered by their professors as remarkably conscientious. Kohl commuted from Lugwigshafen, which meant long hours on the train. Studying in Frankfurt, then, had deleterious consequences on his CDU activities in Ludwigshafen. So the following autumn he transferred to Ruprecht Karls University in Heidelberg, which was much closer to home. In Heidelberg he studied history, public law, and political science and worked vacations as a lapidary for BASF (Hofmann 1985, 14). Studying closer to Lugwigshafen both eased his life as a student and facilitated his active involvement in the Ludwigshafen CDU. Kohl developed a reputation at Heidelberg for having a dual career: university and party.

Kohl's talents and accomplishments in these regards won for him highly selective positions as an assistant in the Alfred Weber Institute for social science at Heidelberg and as a representative in the Rhineland-Palatinate state legislature. He also managed to combine his two careers in his dissertation: "The Political Development of Rhineland Palatinate and the Recovery of the Political Parties After 1945." He completed his degree in 1958, becoming—of all things—a political scientist.

By the age of thirty Kohl had accomplished a great deal, particularly considering the interruption caused by the war. While he has always had encouraging relations with peers, he had clearly displayed himself by thirty to be at home within hierarchical institutions: the family, the church, the *gymnasium,* the institute, and the party. Though he supported liberal democracy and an economy moved by competition and ruled largely by private capital, Kohl was clearly—and had been from the earliest recollections available—a man defined by certain hierarchical attachments. We have here another national political executive with a predominantly hierarchical cultural bias. In his support of democracy and capitalism and in his personal openness and tolerance we find elements of individualism, but it is individualism mediated through and thus restrained by hierarchical institutions.

While continuing his party activities after receiving his degree, Kohl developed as well a related profession as a consultant and lobbyist. For a decade he was employed in such a capacity, specializing in economic and tax policy for the Rhineland-Palatinate Chemical Industry Association. During this decade he also grew increasingly prominent in CDU politics at the state level. In both careers Kohl developed a reputation for teamwork, openness, honesty, and humor. His success in party affairs eventually cut short his consulting career. In 1969 he became *ministerpräsident* (roughly governor) of Rhineland-Palatinate. Thereafter, he focused on the party.

Kohl's party career broadened across three stages: primarily local in the 1950s, increasingly state-level in the 1960s and early 1970s, and federal thereafter. At each stage his career followed a roughly similar pattern (Maser 1990, 110). He began each stage as a modest figure associated with the party in opposition. He gradually rose within the party's hierarchy at successive levels. As he reached the top party ranks at each level he was instrumental in bringing the CDU to power. And his period as chief executive was characterized by considerable energy and accomplishment. Kohl's skills in organizational development and as a political strategist are clearly prodigious. At the state level he also acquired a good deal of policy experience, particularly in reform of schools and other public institutions. He is widely acknowledged as having greatly invigorated Rhineland-Palatinate during his seven years as *ministerpräsident* (Maser 1990, 112).

This record of party building and election winning brought Kohl to Bonn in 1976. At the federal level the CDU was a dispirited party, out of power and rent by numerous conflicts. Combining his political skills with personal characteristics of cleverness, courage, composure, and patience, Kohl performed his "act" once again. Working within the party's alliance was difficult at first. At the federal level the party has a dual—CDU/Christian Social Union (CSU, a largely Bavarian affiliate)—character. CSU leader Franz Josef Strauss clashed repeatedly with Kohl's initiatives. But Kohl gradually succeeded in his efforts. After an unsuccessful try in 1976, Kohl led the CDU to governing and himself to the chancellor's office in 1982.

As chancellor, Kohl remained largely a man of unprovocative positions secured by widely accepted institutions and conventions. He promoted democracy (over extremism of the right and left), the Atlantic Alliance, the social-market economy devised and developed by his CDU predecessors Ludwig Erhard and Konrad Adenauer, enlightened (tolerant) Christianity, the family, and other traditional virtues (Maser 1990, 111). In selected areas Kohl ventured onto less conventional ground. He was an advocate of European unity, built particularly around sound German-French relations and leadership. When unexpected prospects presented themselves, Kohl moved swiftly and boldly, even opportunistically, to unify Germany under his leadership. This was his greatest triumph, but this uncharacteristically bold substantive move also became his greatest trial.

Surprisingly, in the face of the numerous war-time disruptions that afflicted his early life, Kohl appears to have enjoyed the smoothest transition between early basic and adult professional socialization among the three contemporary national leaders I have profiled so far. The agents of adult professional socialization provided a narrower, more intense focus on requirements for his success in certain political institutions. However, while adult professional socialization further sharpened Kohl's impressive political skills, it did so largely through refinement rather than redefinition of the preferences stemming from his basic socialization. Kohl has apparently retained his peculiar mixture of hierarchy and individualism his entire life. His individualism appeared in his broad political preferences: his support of the democratic, social-market middle, as well as in his open-minded political entrepreneurship. His hierarchist orientation was revealed most clearly in the nature of his institutional affiliations. He clearly relished a high-grid, high-group social context. Kohl exuded the hierarchical values of safety and security in these choices and in his decisions and personality generally. His was, to be sure, an inclusive and merit-based hierarchy that revealed itself as well in his political style. Kohl was a valuable organization man or team player whose most important contributions were largely procedural; he was remarkably good at bringing people together in constructive ways. He made astute decisions about the application of his skills, and through this process Kohl built improved institutions and won elections.

In contrast, his vision of desirable political objectives was hardly novel. Rather, it was typically either inherited from his predecessors (Erhard and market socialism) or arrived at serendipitously (unification). Kohl generally deferred to what are conventionally seen as the requirements of the established institutions of which he was a part. This is a common preference for hierarchists, who following Edmund Burke, perceive existing institutions as embodying the "wisdom of the ages" and think that the rational capacities of individuals are modest by comparison.

Yoshida Shigeru

Yoshida Shigeru[9] was born in 1878 in Yokosuka near Tokyo.[10] Many details of his early childhood are obscure. Yoshida, to the degree that he knew them himself, was generally reticent on the topic. His natural father, Takeuchi Tsuna, was an entrepreneur, a political activist, and a member of the first Japanese Diet (1890). He had thirteen other children and was jailed for his political activity shortly before Yoshida was born. The precise identity of Yoshida's mother is unknown; she is thought to have been a geisha. Yoshida was adopted almost immediately after his birth by a childless friend of his father's, Yoshido Kenzo.

Yoshido Kenzo had become extraordinarily wealthy, primarily by procuring Western weaponry for the government in the 1870s and 1880s. So as Dower (1988, 18) points out, Yoshida Shigeru's adoption improved his material existence and brought him into an atmosphere that was entrepreneurial, international, Anglophile, and Confucian. When Kenzo died at a relatively early age, Shigeru inherited a substantial fortune. He was reared

9. The obvious Japanese counterpart for Reagan, Gorbachev, and Kohl is Nakasone Yasuhiro rather than Yoshida Shigeru. Biographical materials on Nakasone in English are scarce, however; and I was unable to put together an account of sufficient depth.
10. This account draws heavily on Dower 1988.

further by Kenzo's wife, Yoshida Kotoko, the granddaughter of a prominent
Confucian scholar, on their estate in Oiso. Kotoko was highly self-reliant,
dignified, strict, proud, and capable, but she lacked, it appears, a mother's
warmth (Dower 1988, 20–21).

Yoshida's formal education began in a rural boarding school of Chinese
learning. Thereafter, he attended an academy in Tokyo run by the ethics
tutor of the crown prince. These institutions introduced Yoshida to a considerable range of topics, and he was impressed by both the abstractions of
Western thought and the intuitive humanistic wisdom of Chinese literature.

Late-nineteenth-century Japanese social life generally and Yoshida's rearing through his teenage years in particular were both predominantly hierarchical. Yet the peculiarities of Yoshida's early life were such that, in Dower's
words, " 'family,' which carries such a heavy burden in most personal and
social histories pertaining to Japan, seems of dubious value when applied to
Yoshida" (1988, 26). His extraordinarily limited relationship with his natural parents, his unexpectedly brief relationship with his adoptive father, the
lack of warmth of his adoptive mother and his years at boarding school left
him feeling orphaned. In his own words:

> No home to which to return
> And no parents from whom to receive love
> The heart of this orphan student
> How pitiful it is.[11]

Additionally, Yoshida's adolescence came during a period in which there
was a sudden veneration of the " 'individualistic' entrepreneur whose indus-
triousness was conducive to the creation of a strong state" (Dower 1988,
24). Yoshida's natural and adoptive fathers were among these men, and
Yoshida, who carried the nickname "One Man," was known for his "maverick streak" or independence throughout the entirety of his political career.
Thus, for instance, Yoshida went out of his way to visit Shinto shrines during the Occupation, when the religion was associated with a disreputable
militarism, but was baptized Joseph Thomas More on his death, and buried
as a Catholic (Dower 1988, 305–6).

In his later teens Yoshida experienced the first of several periods of aim-
lessness. This one included a brief stint in business school and a year spent

11. From a poem Yoshida wrote for the magazine of his rural boarding school. Quoted in
Dower 1988, 25.

in illness at home in Oiso. He continued his education in 1897 at the prestigious Peers' School, which prepared the elite for public service. His instructors there included leading military figures, who taught that the Japanese empire should dominate Asia. Yoshida progressed from this school, run by Prince Konoe Atsumaro, into the prince's college for diplomats. The college did not long survive the prince's death in 1904, and Yoshida completed his education in law at Tokyo Imperial University in 1906. Among his peers at the university were many who would later be his governmental colleagues. Yoshida's academic record was modest, but his great wealth and personal idiosyncrasies supported a vividly unconventional lifestyle that gave him considerable visibility.

After graduation Yoshida passed the foreign service entry examination with a modest score. He improved his chances of future influence in 1909, however, by marrying Makino Yukiko, the eldest daughter of Makino Nobuaki, later a foreign minister and close adviser to the emperor.[12]

While he gradually acquired some generally undistinguished European and foreign ministry service, the bulk of Yoshida's prewar experience and the center of his interests lay in Japan's imperial ambitions in Manchuria and neighboring regions. Through the 1920s Yoshida was known to favor expansion into China, and into the spheres of influence in China of the other imperial powers, even more strongly than his superiors did. His Anglophile reputation during this period stemmed more from his appreciation for British "elite hauteur and rigid class stratification" (Dower 1988, 37–38) than from his perceptions of common British-Japanese interests. Across the 1930s, however, Yoshida's version of *realpolitik* demanded growing efforts to cooperate with the British on the basis of perceived common interest. Thus his Anglophile position became increasingly pronounced, and the distance separating him from the more ambitious military, particularly army, leaders widened.

Yoshida thus opposed the early stages of what became the Second World War on the Pacific rim, and he further opposed extending the conflict to include the United States. He became a central figure in an elite antiwar group and was arrested in the spring of 1945 as a result of his activities. The opposition of this group was based, not on any principled rejection of imperialism, but rather on the view that current policy did not represent an

---

12. Yoshida's capacity to achieve such a favorable marriage was probably based on his great wealth. His unconventional behavior shows up even on this occasion. He missed his wedding reception as a result of his hospitalization for venereal disease (Dower 1988, 30).

effective means of achieving desirable national imperialistic aims. Indeed, Yoshida viewed Japan's predicament as stemming from a "militarist-communist conspiracy" (quoted in Dower 1988, 277).

Yoshida had been in retirement from official positions for nearly a decade by the time the war ended, and at sixty-seven he appeared an unlikely person to lead Japan's postwar resurgence. His stint in jail served him well in this regard, however, since the likelier candidates among his competitors had been purged by the Americans for their connections with the wartime regime. Yoshida's efforts were guided by several objectives that further reveal his adherence to a hierarchist cultural bias that developed in his youth.

First and perhaps most important, he was concerned to preserve the emperor. In his public activities he labored to resuscitate related traditions as well. His high-group perspective placed great importance on these symbols of the social collective. Second, he was anxious to repress the political left that he perceived as having serious revolutionary potential. In this regard he shared with his colleagues a surprisingly strong belief—characteristic of hierarchy—that Japan was balanced insecurely on the brink of social chaos. Yoshida's characteristic high-grid commitment to one right way required a degree of social order at odds with nurturing a liberal society. Third, he wanted to reconstruct the close connections among big business, government bureaucracies, and conservative politicians that Japan's military defeat and the early phases of the American Occupation had to some degree dismantled. And fourth, he wished to return Japan to partnership among the great powers. This last goal was increasingly hampered over time by Yoshida's caution about rearmament and his lack of enthusiasm for a military orientation toward containing China (Dower 1988, 275–77). Yoshida repeatedly tried to persuade the United States to shift the emphasis of its anticommunist efforts in Asia from military to economic activities.

In the course of the eight years (1946–54) during which Yoshida guided Japanese recovery from the Second World War, he was—with rare exceptions—routinely hostile to not just the Japanese socialist left but even to liberals. While he was not a civil libertarian (Dower 1988, 363–64), Yoshida did appreciate those facets of individualism relating most directly to entrepreneurial success. But he was particularly supportive—in a fashion similar to Bismarck's, which we shall encounter in Chapter 4—of entrepreneurial talents if the broad objectives to which they were instrumentally linked were shaped by public bureaucrats who took a national as opposed to a corporate or even industry view of circumstances. Thus while appreciating entrepreneurial contributions to the social collective, he was not enthusiastic about the Smithian view that social objectives are best attained through the exercise of personal self-interest constrained only by market competition. Rather, Yoshida personified the Japanese hierarchical perspective, in which according to Thurow (1992), economic relations are simply another means of social control and are appropriately directed at least in broad outline by society's highest elites.

In matters such as Yoshida's respect for entrepreneurial talent, his recognition of the utility of economic prowess to support social institutions such as empire more subtly and effectively than military domination, and his irrepressible "maverick streak" that periodically led to embarrassment among his colleagues, we catch glimpses in his maturity of an individualism that originated in his early socialization. But these aspects of his cultural bias are enfolded in a larger structure of hierarchical perceptions and preferences, which is also a product of the basic socialization of his youth. In spite of numerous abrupt career shifts—frequently prompted by the irritation of superiors with his independence and frankness—Yoshida retained remarkable steadfastness of cultural orientation across his life.

IMPLICATIONS

These four examples support the suggestions that I introduced earlier about the capacity of grid-group theory to explain beliefs, values, and practical political preferences. First, they show that basic and largely early socialization can produce persons easily recognizable in terms of the beliefs and values of grid-group theory's cultural biases or bifocal composites of these biases. Easy early acquisition is facilitated by grid-group theory's focus on fundamental concerns: Does the social environment present opportunities or threats? Are humans relatively equal or unequal? Is centralized expertise preferable to grassroots consensus? Although it is possible to grow up without acquiring identification with a political party, it is virtually impossible for persons to avoid acquiring at least implicit views on such fundamental matters. Nonetheless, modifications in perspective sometimes occur in later life, particularly among those holding bifocal cultural biases. Indeed, bifocal cultural biases facilitate traversing the discontinuities that contingencies of later life occasionally create. For instance, Reagan did not become an individualist in middle life; rather he applied his existing individualism more broadly. Prior to the mid-1950s he made little use of the individualistic lens of his cultural bias in the public sphere. But a series of events—becoming a celebrity, struggling with the influences of communism and government witch-hunting in the SAG, coping with tax problems and the individualistic expectations behind the questions raised by his GE audiences—brought him increasingly to apply an individualistic lens in the sphere of public life.

Second, these examples are consistent with my view that basic socialization can continue to guide matters such as career choices and institutional or policy preferences, even those of mature political elites. All four of the national leaders whom I have profiled clearly applied as mature adults cultural preferences acquired early in life. For instance, Yoshida, the most thoroughly hierarchical of these statesmen, chose to spend his professional life in an imperial hierarchy. Further, he viewed low-grid egalitarians as an immediate threat to social order. Indeed, he valued low-grid individualists almost exclusively for their entrepreneurial capacities, feeling most comfortable when these capacities were integrated into a corporatist-like structure that assured opportunities for state experts to channel them to the service of the social collective.

Third, multiple mechanisms contribute to the influence of early socialization into later life, particularly for persons whose basic socialization produces bifocal cultural biases. For one, the issues on which grid-group theory focuses are fundamental, identity-constituting concerns that are unlikely to shift sharply with maturation (Teske 1997, 143). For instance, from relatively early in his career Gorbachev perceived more scope for employing incentives to tap the latent managerial capacities of at least some workers in local enterprises than did many other party officials. For another, political elites characteristically self-select themselves for the professional positions of their adult lives. All four of the political executives profiled here, for instance, applied varying but substantial hierarchist influences in early basic socialization in choosing political careers in hierarchical executive institutions. None spent any significant time as a mature adult in developing a career as a legislative representative, a direction that both individualists and egalitarians would find more appealing. Kohl's parliamentary presence was always a result of his position in the CDU hierarchy. Thus in broad outline their adult professional socialization was a consequence of and reinforced basic socialization. Finally, the cultural biases resulting from basic socialization predispose persons to perceive even potentially disruptive contingencies of adult life in predictable ways consistent with their long-standing patterns of selective attention and interpretation. Thus Yoshida's remarkable concern about a weak Japanese left should not surprise us. Most of the contingencies that adults experience are sufficiently complex and ambiguous to allow persons to interpret them according to their long-standing cognitive patterns. Reagan experienced several sharp life changes as a result of contingencies; yet he was able to successfully apply the "company man" orientation that he had learned in early life repeatedly across these experiences.

Sharply disruptive contingencies in adult life may even reinforce the influence of some aspects of early basic socialization. Khrushchev's 1956 denunciation of Stalinism, by repudiating important aspects of the formal political socialization that Gorbachev had received in late adolescence, reinforced the instrumental pragmatism that he had acquired from early family experiences. Gorbachev went on, like Madison, to alter significant societal institutions so that they reflected his values more thoroughly. It is possible, of course, that meeting harsh contingencies in adult life may sometimes seriously disrupt the effects of basic socialization, leading persons to adopt cultural orientations for which their early lives offer no support. But we have not encountered examples of this phenomenon among the lives of these national leaders.

If political elites, who experience extensive and intensive overt political socialization as adults, can nonetheless be guided in their professional lives by social preferences arising from early basic socialization, the importance of early experience for explaining the adult cultural orientations of ordinary citizens, whose adult political socialization is likely to be more limited and diffuse, may be even greater. Certainly later episodes of basic socialization in the workplace and the family may impart lessons relevant to basic social relations preferences, and these lessons may sometimes contradict those of earlier socialization. But the broad, deep basic socialization of early life would appear to have considerable capacity for shaping later predispositions by fostering certain identity-defining characteristics, guiding self-selection into particular social niches, and establishing patterns of selective attention to and interpretation of complex and ambiguous social contexts.

CULTURAL CONFLICT IN SOCIETY

Machiavelli argues in *The Prince* that politics inevitably poses decisions difficult in the sense that, in order to support some values, political elites must sacrifice other values. Berlin (1982) alerts us that conflicts between values characterize the political aspects of life generally, not just the public lives of political elites. And the most obvious way in which grid-group theory's cultures appear in political life is through orientations that reveal distinctive patterns of value support. Indeed, it is largely through the presence of multiple cultures, each with its distinctive constrained value preferences, that societies experience choices and conflict among values and their associated practical political objectives. Hierarchists (and the adherents of other ways of life as well) perceive the social world through selective patterns of attention and interpretation that produce strong support for some values, moderate support for other values, and rejection as reprehensible of still other matters that the adherents of rival cultures view as values.

For instance, Yoshida, who had a strongly hierarchist bifocal cultural bias (HI), placed great value on a centrally controlled and highly stratified social order. He placed less emphasis on national prosperity, which he saw as desirable primarily if it were derived from corporatist oversight through which central state executives assured that economic development supported rather than subverted his preferred social design. In general, Yoshida did not perceive liberty, in either the freedom-from-external-constraint version championed by individualists or the self-development sense preferred by egalitarians, as a value but rather as a socially disruptive influence. And for Yoshida, equality of condition was completely reprehensible.

Ronald Reagan shared Yoshida's distaste for equality of condition. Otherwise, Reagan, who as a mature adult had a much better developed individualistic face to his bifocal cultural bias (IH), represented a sharp contrast to Yoshida. He placed a high priority on national prosperity and sought to achieve it by freeing the initiative of private enterprise from what he perceived as stifling state regulation. Indeed, he championed the individualistic conception of liberty more generally, particularly as it pertains to property rights. So his conception of social order was less confining. Thus when forced to choose, Reagan and Yoshida had opposing preferences in situations which juxtaposed options that constrained business enterprises (for the purpose of realizing a broader social order conceived by state officials) and alternatives that allowed enterprises greater freedom of action (while sacrificing corporatist planning for social order in the process). Grid-group theory shows that these different preferences were a consequence of distinct beliefs, values, and associated practical purposes that are attributable to rival cultures.

For instance, grid-group theory's three socially interactive cultures each provide rival rankings for a set of prominent political values. Consider the following values: respect for traditionally sanctioned expertise, status differentials, social order, economic prosperity, economic efficiency, liberty (freedom from external constraint), liberty (self-development), equality of condition, and (uncoerced) consensus. This listing is constructed so that the first three entries appeal primarily to hierarchists, the next three primarily to individualists, and the last three primarily to egalitarians. However, the values of one culture that are located adjacent to another culture's values are shared to some degree by the latter culture. For instance, hierarchists share an interest in economic prosperity with individualists, who in turn, share an interest in social order with hierarchists.[13] Some of these values, while endorsed by one culture, are rejected by another: e.g., egalitarians reject the status differentials prized by hierarchists, who in turn reject the equality of condition prized by egalitarians. We can expect adherents of various cultures to favor different institutional and policy decisions in predictable ways consistent with supporting the particular rankings of these values associated with their cultures (e.g., Reagan favoring markets free from government intervention and Yoshida preferring expert-led corporatism). The rival rankings then give us thumbnail sketches of the practical objectives of various cultures. Thus rational behavior for each culture entails deriving different efficient means (institutions) for realizing distinctive high-priority value clusters.[14] I present an expanded version of this conception of culturally constrained rationalities in Chapter 3. I think that this approach offers greater scope for improving distinctions among the motivational bases considered by theories of rational action than more elegant schemata, such as the one offered by Margolis (1982), which appear daunting to apply to actual political life.

13. This holds true as well for variations of the first (respect for traditional practices) and last (consensus) values in the list for which the cultures of hierarchy and egalitarianism share some sympathy.

14. Marcus, Sullivan, Theiss-Morse, and Wood (1995) employ a related but narrower formulation that links the acquisition of different values acquired in early life to instrumental rationality in order to explain why persons support or reject civil liberties.

THREE

CULTURE CREATES STRUCTURE:
EXPLAINING CROSS-SOCIETAL INSTITUTIONAL DIFFERENCES

Hobbes, Locke, and other state-of-nature theorists raise in our imagination a time before republics and kingdoms when persons could form social institutions from scratch on the basis of rational self-interest or related criteria these theorists hold to be unvarying across time and circumstance. Actual humans have rarely, if ever, faced such opportunities (Lukes 1973). Building institutions nearly always amounts to modifying existing social structures, mindful of specific objectives rooted in peculiarities of historical accident and cultural orientation. Consequently, persons disagree on the characteristics social institutions should have. Adherents of rival cultures strive to form and maintain disparate institutions that embody their distinctive beliefs and values. In this sense it is reasonable to say that culture creates (institutional) structure, although other factors—particularly existing institutional design and the character of historical contingencies—also contribute importantly to institutional innovations. Institutions also help to sustain cultures, because the beliefs and values they embody shape the views of persons who work within them (March and Olsen 1989) and are transmitted to new generations as institutions contribute to socialization (Rohrschneider 1994). In this chapter, however, I focus on the less frequently examined influence of distinctive cultures in shaping cross-societal institutional differences.

A THEORY OF RATIONAL ACTION

Berlin argues that values are unfortunately related to one another in such a way that they cannot all be realized simultaneously; pursuit of one may require neglecting or violating another (Berlin 1998; Gray 1996; Walzer 1995; Berger 1997). For Berlin, values are also distinct in the sense that they are not reducible to any meaningful common denominator. Rather, efforts to make such reductions produce concepts such as subjective utility (self-interest), which, as Macaulay (1852, 299) showed, can become vacuous. Instrumental rationality provides an appropriate goal-seeking orientation, but the differing perspectives and priorities of various persons need to be distinguished and explained. Why do humans interpret the world differently? Why do they seek different goals? Questions such as these lie at the heart of the social sciences (Searle 1995, xii; Eckstein 1996 and 1997). Grid-group theory's conception of culture offers a means for distinguishing and explaining interconnected patterns of constrained ontologies, value priorities, and institutional preferences.

Rival Ontologies

As Gell-Mann (1994) suggests, the basic elements of cultural guidance come from experience. Some experience is acquired firsthand. But consciousness and language allow humans to acquire experience indirectly, through stories, for example, and the precepts associated with them. Different experiences produce varying beliefs about how a complex and ambiguous world works. Grid-group theory's three socially interactive cultures portray distinctive but predictable worlds. Individualists perceive bounty and resilience; egalitarians view a delicate environment subject to easy degradation; and hierarchists see a combination of these views (a tolerant/perverse environment) with accompanying sharp limits on the appropriateness of various human activities. In contrast, fatalists see only randomness. One factor that contributes to contrasting ontologies is that experience varies with place and time. Persons living in temperate climates enjoy a natural environment more bountiful than those living in the arctic, where, unsurprisingly, individualistic cultures are unknown.[1] Additionally, social environments can change rapidly; a particular urban region may provide supportive neighborhoods for families in the 1950s yet be racked by random violence in the 1980s (Wilson 1987). As this environmental change occurs, fatalism is apt to become a more prominent culture among the region's residents. The complexity of human environments also contributes to rival ontologies. Efforts to determine whether climate statistics indicate short-term random fluctuations or global warming or what one's adversaries or even colleagues are up to produce data open to conflicting interpretations. Complexity thus fosters ambiguity.

Conceptions of our fellow humans, who are also complex, varying, and ambiguous, provide another crucial ontological element. These conceptions derive, at least in part, from general beliefs about how the world works. Individualists fit their conceptions to their view of a bountiful environment and take humans to be rational, equally capable in broad capacities, and self-interested—able to master their own fates in this cornucopian setting. Since egalitarians and individualists perceive human environments differently, their conceptions of humans are distinct as well. Close cooperation and voluntary sharing are essential for survival in a world perpetually perched on the brink of destruction, so egalitarians see humans as naturally benign creatures, roughly equal in basic capacities and needs. Hierarchists, for whom discerning crucial limits between tolerant and perverse environments is so important, perceive humans as unequal in these important capacities as well as in the severity of their moral flaws. Fatalists perceive capricious humans who fit well with nature's randomness.

A person's grid and group positions are derived from their conceptions of how the world works and what humans are like (Thompson, Ellis, and Wildavsky 1990, 1–68). Conceptions of human inequality, rooted in perceptions of tricky environments, locate persons in high-grid positions. Conceptions of natural human cooperativeness, arising from perceptions of perpetual environmental danger, locate persons in high-group positions. Thus high-grid, high-group hierarchists rely on the capacities of experts in particular matters to keep ordinary persons and society generally clear of danger zones. Conceptions of human equality, promoted by perceptions of either environmental bounty (making most differences in capacities unim-

---

1. Even among marmots, such variations prompt behavioral differences. See Masters 1978.

portant) or scarcity (emphasizing roughly equivalent needs) engender low-grid positions. Conceptions of individual human viability, fostered by beliefs of at least intermittent environmental bounty, produce low-group positions. So low-grid, low-group individualists think that persons can be the masters of their own fates. Thus grid and group interact to produce rival cultures, each supporting distinctive clusters of values.

Distinctive Constrained Value Clusters

In part, the distinctive value clusters of rival cultures differ in the identity of their constituent elements. Hierarchists, for instance, do not value liberty or toleration of other persons' autonomy as individualists do; individualists do not value equality of condition as egalitarians do; and egalitarians do not value specialized expertise as hierarchists do. (See Table 1, section A, for this and other examples.) So one culture pursues as a value what another may despise as knavery and vice versa. This is what we should expect from ways of life that disagree on how the world works and what humans are like. But stark differences such as these account for only a portion of the distinctiveness of cultural value clusters.

Another contributing factor is that even when cultures share certain values, or more precisely the terms used to express these values, they frequently have rival specific conceptions of what the values entail. So for hierarchists, order is having everyone fit into a situation according to the centralized planning of experts. This is order as central direction in Table 1, section B. This conception of order surely has its place. As television football commentators point out, when even a few folks are not on the same page of the play book with everyone else, disaster frequently follows.

Individualists are horrified by this conception of order, seeing in it the near total loss of the unique talents of most persons. Instead, they cherish the "order" that individual choices among rational self-interested persons produce under what we could generally call market circumstances. I call this sort of order market coordination (see Table 1, section B). Such a conception includes, not only Smith's free markets for goods and services, but also Mill's marketplace of ideas and Schumpeter's (1950) free elections among multiple parties. But hierarchists view markets such as these as chaotic; there is no expert in control. These are forums in which many counterpoised persons count roughly equally, and this runs counter to hierarchists' beliefs in the inequality of human capacities and their accompanying preferences for reliance on expert knowledge.

Table 1   Core Cultural Value Clusters

	Hierarchy	Individualism	Egalitarianism
Section A: Distinctive values	expertise	liberty	equality of respect
	deference	economic efficiency	equality of condition
	honor	procedural fairness	humility
Section B: Distinctive meanings	order as central direction	order as market coordination	order as voluntary consensus
	duty to social collective	duty to contractual relations	duty to "own" group consensus
Section C: Distinctive rankings	expertise	liberty	equality of respect
	order	economic efficiency	equality of condition
	duty	personal economic success[a]	voluntary consensus
	deference	procedural fairness	social solidarity
	stratification	order (from limited government coercion)	sharing
	harmony	autonomy	humility
	honor		
	economic development		

[a] Leading to societal economic growth.

Egalitarians are skeptical of both of these conceptions and, to the degree that they recognize order as a value, find it in whatever the group accepts consensually. I call this order through voluntary consensus (see Table 1, section B); egalitarians are more likely to refer to it as consensus than order. For hierarchists, this is an even more upsetting conception of order than that of individualists. Individualists at least do not hold order hostage to the will of nearly every person—no matter how silly or perverse. For hierarchists, seeking order through consensus among relatively incapable and flawed persons will only assure disaster. Individualists perceive in the egalitarian conception of order a needless and costly repression of individuality and initiative that will stifle economic growth and related forms of social progress. So while all three of grid-group theory's socially interactive cultures can be said to value order, they have distinctive and conflicting understandings of what order is. As Table 1, section B, indicates, a similar argument could be made in the instance of duty as a social value.

A third difference among the value clusters of various cultures arises from disparities in the rankings that the adherents of rival cultures give even to those values that they share. (See Table 1, section C.) For instance, among hierarchists order is roughly coequal with expertise at the apex of their rank-orderings. Neither individualists nor egalitarians place similar priority on order. Thus the difficult choices with which political life confronts persons may force hierarchists to sacrifice personal economic success, even personal honor, to centrally determined social order; whereas individualists would hold the opposite preference. Egalitarians share with individualists a lack of priority on order, but egalitarians are not favorably disposed toward exceptional personal economic success. Thus in a similar preference-revealing situation, egalitarians would likely sacrifice both order and exceptional economic success to the maintenance of human equality in both its tangible and intangible aspects. The close warm human relationships that develop among the members of egalitarian groups would be destroyed by both hierarchical conceptions of order and individualistic concerns with exceptional economic success. Both of these latter cultures view egalitarians' sweeping support of harmonious equality as unrealistic. According to individualists, humans are inherently estranged and naturally competitive, and hierarchists perceive humans as inherently unequal. So neither of these stratifying cultures places any value on equality of condition among humans; individualists follow a more limited conception of equality of respect.

Table 1, section C, portrays distinctive rank-orderings of the values that lie at the heart of grid-group theory's three socially interactive cultures.[2] These rank-orderings are not meant to be exhaustive, but the shortness of these lists reflects more than arbitrary decisions to leave off certain lower-ranking values. As Wildavsky (1987, 8) puts it, grid-group theory generates miles of preferences from inches of facts. The theory reveals a system of beliefs that guides the social preferences of many ordinary humans. Such a

---

2. I have less confidence in the rank-orderings for egalitarians in Table 1, section C, than in those of the other two cultures. In terms of its central values egalitarianism is a narrower culture than either of the others. This characteristic contributes to its being somewhat less realistic on the macrosocial stage. Particularly across a variety of social contexts, it is possible to distinguish the egalitarian values that I have ranked in Table 1, section C, but in any given social context, two of these values might be operationalized very similarly, thus creating ranking problems.

system has to be fairly simple. Persons of average intelligence have to be able to keep it in mind. They have to be able to apply it quickly in a variety of different social circumstances. They need to be able to teach it to their children. Hence, their central normative lodestars must be relatively few.

These distinctive value rankings, along with the beliefs from which they stem, provide us with a grasp on the processes of social preference and cultural identity formation. In this regard they supplement rational choice's focus on preference implementation. Grid-group theory gives us three rival, time-honored (Hume 1951, 172–76) and widely socially embedded (Sen 1977; Mansbridge 1990a and 1990b) value bases for rational action. Yet action that is rational from the standpoint of the rank-ordering of hierarchy may not be rational from the standpoint of the rank-ordering of individualism. So considering distinct instrumental rationalities, based in rival value clusters, appears preferable to labeling social patterns that do not fit with economic-man preferences as "nonrational norms" (Elster 1989a, 1989b, and 1989c). Ferejohn's (1991) terminology of multiple "thick" rationalities is also preferable, although I use the terminology "culturally constrained rationalities" in part to indicate that I do not accept Ferejohn's associated privileging of some ends over others.

Even within the value clusters of particular cultures, however, pursuit of some values may foreclose opportunities for realizing others. Some of the resulting decisions about which to realize may entail, as Johnston (1991) and Monroe (1991a) show, "unresolved dilemmas" rather than admitting optimization. If, for instance, one restaurant offers what I judge to be superior food and atmosphere at prices comparable to a competitor, I can patronize the former—optimizing with no regrets. Contrast the mother who holds her newborn on her lap while she enters an academic paper on her computer (Monroe 1995, 10). She will have regrets associated with conflicting conceptions of her identity whether she devotes herself more fully to her child or her research program. So too, returning to Table 1, the identities of hierarchical political elites may suffer from the disruption of social harmony that results from the necessity of their having to foster greater economic development, possibly even accepting some reliance on impersonal markets, in order to sustain societal integrity (order) in the face of foreign imperial threats. The poignancy of such dilemmas in political life stems from the association of the competing values with actors' identities.[3] Build-

3. While I agree with Monroe (1995) on the importance of identity, she refers to personal identity, while I speak of cultural identity—clearly adhering to a particular culture. I view cultural identity as a more feasible tool for students of comparative politics, since it presumably comes in fewer varieties than personality. For more on relations between personality and culture, see Greenstein 1992.

ing whatever social institutions are required for the realization of their identity-providing values will likely be among the actors' highest political priorities.

Culturally Distinct Institutional Preferences

Distinctive constrained value clusters provide the adherents of different cultures with rival purposes and practical interests. That is, they serve a function similar to, though collectively more comprehensive and differentiated than, the economic-man assumptions commonly employed in rational choice theory (Monroe 1991a) by identifying the high-priority normative ends of the distinctive rationalities that the adherents of various cultures seek to realize (Wildavsky 1994; Coughlin and Lockhart 1998; Lockhart and Wildavsky 1998; Lockhart and Coughlin 1992).[4] Since most persistent value realization efforts involve building and maintaining institutions, we recognize differences among cultures most obviously in their distinctive institutional preferences. Thus, starting from the culturally constrained value rank-orderings in section C of Table 1, we can translate values into preferences for distinctive institutional designs.

In examining how the value clusters associated with grid-group theory's three socially interactive cultures support distinctive institutional preferences, we need to keep several caveats in mind. First, in specific social circumstances some of the values that I have identified might be more precisely expressed in related terminology. For instance, the value sets for both individualism and egalitarianism include an explicit criterion for just distribution: procedural fairness, and equality of condition (Fishkin 1983, chap. 3; Hochschild 1981, chap. 3). The value of deference that I have included in hierarchists' value cluster might, in the context of distributive justice issues, be more precisely expressed by a criterion of merit, as in Aristotle's view that a person's allotment of a good should be proportional to that person's virtue. Second, I have purposely tried to use terms that, while distinguishing the three cultures, are not so specific that they ignore differences among the adherents of a particular culture. For example, a few egalitarians demand absolute equality of some goods—e.g., income (Carens 1981). But most egalitarians want to allow differential distribution of many goods based on

4. The elements of individualism's value cluster are similar to, but somewhat broader than the objectives normally derived by economic-man assumptions. Also, Marcus, Sullivan, Theiss-Morse, and Wood (1995) employ a schema similar to that of grid-group theory but allowing less constraint of distinctive value clusters.

concerns of need (e.g., medical care) or even incentives. What egalitarians have in common is preferring greater equality of condition than either individualists or hierarchists who support distinctive bases of social stratification. Thus in comparison to hierarchists and individualists, they strive to reduce certain existing inequalities of condition. Third, these value clusters are not exhaustive. In particular social circumstances hierarchists might become concerned about productive efficiency, a value normally associated with individualism. But it is unlikely that hierarchists would ever sacrifice honor, or particularly order or expertise, to efficiency. More generally, other values that could reasonably be added to these rank-orderings would fit with, in a sense be deducible (in a particular social context) from, the more basic values that do appear.

Hierarchists' beliefs in a tolerant/perverse environment make expert knowledge crucial for them. The social collective's reliance on expertise is facilitated by the presence among unequal humans of exceptionally capable persons. Determining the nature of a social order that fits with how the world works (particularly by avoiding blundering beyond the boundaries separating tolerant and perverse environments) falls naturally to relevant experts who lead vertically arrayed institutions focused on education and social control. The Roman Catholic Church, especially in its heyday, provides an exemplar of this institutional formation imperative: spreading the word (mass) and monitoring the compliance of ordinary persons with that word (confession). Such institutions foster social harmony in which most persons find a way to contribute to a social order devised by the most capable.

For hierarchists, each person's particular expertise creates, not only a niche that is relatively secure because it is socially useful, but a duty to contribute one's unique capacities to the social collective, which is more important than any of its members.[5] All derive honor from the proper performance of their duties (part of which is deference to the superior expertise of others), but just as persons differ in the types and amounts of their talents, so too does the status associated with the various duties that draw on these talents. Thus society's honors should be stratified in a way that parallels the inequalities perceived to distinguish persons. The basis for this stratification may be crude and explicit (ethnicity or gender) or subtle and

5. The importance of the (generally organic) collective usually arises from some conception of transcendental purpose that can be achieved only by the whole (e.g., doing God's will on earth for European feudalism or reaching the communist period of history for the early Soviet Union).

sophisticated (intelligence—Young 1959). For hierarchists, such stratification is good because, as Plato and Aristotle noted, it places persons where they belong. It is socially destructive and, as Montesquieu indicated, a violation of personal honor to occupy a social position inappropriate for one's inherent nature (1900, 2:32 [bk. 4, chap. 2]).

Individualists, in contrast, value liberty over all else. This preference fits with their conception of nature as benign and bountiful and with humans as rationally self-interested creatures with roughly similar broad capacities. Individuals choose to engage in different activities. In the process, as Madison (*Federalist 10*) pointed out, they define and individuate themselves, and according to J. S. Mill (*On Liberty*), they concomitantly provide society with a never ending supply of innovative suggestions, some of which foster social progress. As Locke (*Second Treatise*) suggested, the self-interest of individuals is focused on material acquisition. Personal economic success is a virtue that results at the societal level in economic growth. Persons armed with liberty-supporting rights have produced unprecedented degrees of this vision of social progress in several Western societies. Their vision is centered on personal liberty, efficiency-driven technological development, and economic prosperity—a combination of values uniquely associated with individualism (Olson 1993). Collectively, these values provide the central tenets of the institutional design preferences of individualists.

Hierarchists frequently hold a closely related concern with economic development, and particularly when they are spurred by severe historical contingencies, hierarchists are capable of remarkable feats of social mobilization, such as Stalin's industrialization drive (Lindblom 1977) or the development efforts launched by the Meiji Restoration (Johnson 1982). So hierarchists may sponsor more political and economic development than Mill was inclined to grant. But hierarchists are routinely skeptical of the ability of the market to achieve economic gains; where an individualist sees liberty based on the exercise of individual rights and economic efficiency based on the market, the hierarchist sees chaos. Hierarchical development is guided by a contrasting institutional formation imperative: a master plan devised by socially recognized experts. From the hierarchist's perspective, a market-based social process, driven by countless decisions of persons exercising liberty, is too prone to conflict. Individualists find virtue in the allocative efficiency that they attribute to this mechanism and view markets as orderly primarily because they are efficient. For hierarchists, market relations are inherently conflictual and thus destructive of social harmony. Hierarchists simply perceive many humans as too incapable or morally flawed to use liberty constructively.

Although individualistic markets stratify persons by outcome, individualists argue that this process is fair because the rules are the same for everyone (Fishkin 1983). The resulting stratification thus represents, for them, benign variations in personal preferences (some choosing to be investment bankers, while others are more intrigued with sculpture) rather than inherent inequalities of broad capacities. For individualists, a person's duties are to herself and those with whom she has voluntarily contracted. The sense of duty to the social collective characteristic of the hierarchist is too broad, vague, and confining to fit with individualistic conceptions of human nature. Individualists generally acknowledge that the self-interested nature of humans requires coercive public institutions, similar to those employed by hierarchists, to assure that personal behavior is lawful and that society has protection from external threats. But in contrast to hierarchists, individualists believe that government should be limited. They prefer to accomplish as much as possible through what they perceive as voluntary markets rather than coercive governmental institutions.

As their grid and group positions suggest, egalitarians resemble individualists in some respects and to hierarchists in others. For instance, egalitarians generally share the hierarchists' sense that social order requires everyone to have a similar orientation toward particular matters. But egalitarians share with individualists a distaste for external authority, so rather than imposing uniformity through central coercive institutions as hierarchists do, egalitarians prefer that the members of their groups reach consensus voluntarily. Thus egalitarians place little emphasis on expertise or efficiency; their particular combination of grid and group produces a distinctive institutional formation imperative based on their broad conception of human equality. Egalitarians support relative equality of material conditions among persons. Further, they advocate equal respect. It is from this latter preference that their practice of seeking consensus flows. Like Rousseau (*Social Contract*), egalitarians believe that even if only a small minority disagrees with the rest of the group, overriding their views denies them equal respect and will eventually pervert society by creating an arrogant majority and a resentful and tacitly noncompliant minority.

Egalitarians see an orderliness in consensus that contrasts sharply with what they perceive as the tyranny of expert central direction or the impersonality of the market. In contrast to the individualistic view of humans as materialistic, egalitarians see humans as concerned primarily with the quality of their relations with other group members. We should expect this among persons who perceive the natural and extragroup social environments as prone to destruction; it is exclusively within the group that support is to be found. Accordingly, egalitarians think that persons should willingly share the modest bounty that can safely be gleaned from external environments with other group members. Egalitarians thus recognize a form of duty: the humility required for the voluntary self-abnegation of one's idiosyncratic personal concerns for the benefit of the group (Titmuss 1971). This duty is based on love of one's comrades. Hierarchists and individualists counter that humility offers little to recommend it. In actual social life egalitarians, like individualists, frequently compromise with hierarchy and accept central public institutions in order to achieve specific objectives. The most notable contemporary example of this phenomenon is social democracy. When egalitarians join hands with hierarchists in constructing welfare states, the former sacrifice their distaste for coercion in order to achieve greater equality of condition (Wildavsky 1985).

Collectively, the institutional formation imperatives of these three socially interactive cultures might be summarized and contrasted by visualizing a triangle whose three angles represent distinctive cultural lodestars. One angle represents the "office" of liberty-inspired individualists, who seek to constrain the size of the state and limit its activities. They strive to produce what Lovejoy (1961) calls counterpoise institutions. These include various civil and political rights, Smith's economic markets driven by private capital, Madison's separation of powers, Mill's marketplace of ideas, and Schumpeter's (1950) competitive political parties. These institutions rest on skepticism about centralizing power and authority among self-interested creatures. More positively, these institutions are valued for fostering liberty by those who perceive human environments as beneficent and humans as capable. So long as the societal "playing field" remains roughly level, individualists think that these institutions leave equal and capable persons free to master their own fates. The "base" of hierarchists dedicated to expertise and social harmony occupies another angle. Their preference for a larger, more active state devoted to security and paternalism rests on their belief that there is a single right way of doing everything. Hierarchists strive to construct the centralized bureaucracies and related institutions (e.g., sectoral "peak" associations) through which the most capable persons can organize a harmonious common life. The third angle provides the "home" of egalitarians dedicated to increasing interpersonal equality. They work to achieve broadly equal membership in society by supporting socioeconomic rights and participatory institutions—among citizens, workers, consumers, and others—which strive to accord roughly equal respect and circumstances to as many persons as possible.

Adherents of each of these cultures seek to extend the influence of their respective institutions as thoroughly as possible throughout society. Their respective fortunes and thus the trajectory of institutional formation in society varies across time, hinging in large measure on the character of the historical contingencies that their societies encounter. As we examine below, for instance, external security threats lend credence to hierarchical calls for centralized, expert-led societal institutions. Thus hierarchists are advantaged over the adherents of the low-grid cultures in societies which experience such threats frequently.

Social reality is messier than abstract theorizing. All three socially interactive cultures coexist and engage in simultaneous efforts to realize their values by shaping the institutions of the societies that all three form. Each of the rival ways of life makes socially essential contributions to the multicultural societies which they comprise. Yet in particular societal contexts one of the cultures may contribute more to societal viability than others (Lockhart and Franzwa 1994). So across time one or perhaps two cultures may be more effective at organizing society in its image than the other(s), or perhaps one culture succeeds in one particular realm of social life while another triumphs in another social context. The resulting institutionalization represents a mixture, certainly across institutions and sometimes even in the character of a single institution (e.g., central government through the American separation of powers). But it is possible, as we shall see, to read the results for clear-cut evidence of the differential success of the institutional preferences of rival cultures.

CULTURE AS A CAUSE OF CROSS-SOCIETAL SOCIAL POLICY DIFFERENCES

My argument so far in this chapter has involved human purposes. I have contended that the constrained beliefs and values of rival cultures foster preferences for distinctive institutional designs. I now offer three illustrations of my causal argument that cross-societal institutional differences reflect variations in the relative influence of rival cultures among relevant organized societal elites. The first, involving Esping-Andersen's (1990) typology of welfare-state regimes, goes beyond the societies on which this study focuses, but is simply too good an example to pass up. His schema will also provide a useful frame of reference in Part Two. The second and third illustrations draw on the social programs and related public institutions of the Soviet Union and Japan.

Three Types of Welfare-State Regimes

Esping-Andersen (1990, 27–28) distinguishes three types of welfare-state regimes in terms of their overall objectives. I want to draw on his typology to specify distinct, culturally constrained institutional preferences focused particularly on social policy. One of Esping-Andersen's types, the "liberal" regime, is characterized by relatively narrow social insurance programs and thus comparatively heavy reliance on means-tested public assistance (Smeeding, Torrey, and Rein 1988, 11; Heidenheimer, Heclo, and Adams 1990, 249). This regime does little to mitigate the commodification of labor; indeed it champions market relations, stigmatizing public assistance and providing extensive hurdles for the effective use of social insurance. This regime reflects the reluctance of societies in which the individualistic culture is powerful to accept a welfare state. Unsurprisingly, Esping-Andersen's prime example of this regime is the United States. He includes other Anglo-emigrant societies—Canada and Australia—in this category as well.

Esping-Andersen's "corporatist" regime appears in societies—France, Germany, Italy, and Austria—in which market liberalism never became preeminent and traditional feudal rights to subsistence were thus more easily transformed by hierarchical elites into socioeconomic rights supported by relatively inclusive social insurance programs. This regime distinguishes sharply, however, among beneficiaries on the basis of social status. The influence of hierarchy, frequently stemming from church as well as state (Inglehart 1997), is noticeable as well in implicit conceptions of family life and the place of women in society. For instance, these societies provide relatively generous child allowances, but they are far less committed to the provision of childcare services.

A third "social-democratic" regime is found among Scandinavian societies. Its distinctive character is found in an exceptionally strong commitment to full employment, reinforced with child care and related services, as well as generous social insurance programs. In these societies manual workers and middle-class professionals share social insurance programs that Esping-Andersen terms "solidaristic, universalistic and de-commodifying" (1990,

28). This regime seeks both to develop the full potential of all persons and to bind these persons together into a solidaristic whole. Thus, it is much more distinctly egalitarian in its central purposes than either of the other regimes.

More recently, Esping-Andersen (1996) has shown how the societies in which these three welfare-state regimes are found have further adapted to the socioeconomic challenges of the late 1980s and early 1990s. The United States has followed a "neoliberal" design that Esping-Andersen calls wage erosion. That is, an increasing proportion of workers labor for modest wages and little in the way of benefits such as medical-care insurance. The West-Central European societies have followed what he portrays as a "labor reduction" route, aiming to maintain opportunities for mainstream male workers by earlier retirement for current workers. The Scandinavian route has stressed active labor market policies, seeking to sustain solidarity and relative equality of condition through training and public-sector employment, particularly for women and other less-traditional labor market participants.

These three recent policies are also recognizable, respectively, in terms of individualistic, hierarchical, and egalitarian institutional formation imperatives. In conjunction with the earlier welfare-state regime typology, they offer clear examples of the social policy approaches apt to characterize the angle areas of the "imperatives" triangle introduced in the previous section. Individualistic social policy is market-based, emphasizing liberty for capable persons and striving to minimize reliance on the public programs that adherents of other cultures perceive as necessary for coping with the gaps in and inadequacies of market participation. In contrast, hierarchists eagerly employ significant public social insurance that maintains status differentials but mitigates these market shortcomings. Egalitarians may be even more ambitious than hierarchists in their social policy aspirations, but they prefer to draw on different public program designs, emphasizing social insurance that seeks to reduce the stratification fostered by market interaction.

Varying historical contingencies are apt to facilitate the approaches of rival cultures and so help to determine contrasting social policy trajectories. German hierarchical preferences for generous but differentiating social programs, for instance, have been reinforced if not forged by the nearly continuous external security threats that German-speaking regions have faced for centuries. Inglehart (1997) argues that exceptional (against societal history) postwar prosperity has reinforced the Scandinavian preference for increasingly inclusive and redistributive social programs. Relative American isolation from external security threats has likely made individual self-reliance appear more feasible and cultivated a preference for relatively modest social programs. Esping-Andersen's (1996) study carries the suggestion that recent historical contingencies have prompted societally dominant cultures to develop new programs that support their preferred ways of life in altered circumstances—what Eckstein (1988, 793–94) calls "pattern-maintaining change"—rather than revising the relative prominence of rival cultures and thus redirecting the trajectory of social policy development from one angle of the "imperatives" triangle to another. We examine culture's contribution to political change in later chapters, finding more variety. But as Esping-Andersen's work suggests, the roots of relative cultural dominance in particular societies are deep; and even when subjected to considerable pressure, sharp institutional change is relatively rare.

This quick characterization of regime types in terms of the contrasting institutional design preferences of rival cultures offers an example of how culture might contribute to explaining cross-societal social policy variation. It is yet another instance of my using theory to interpret evidence, not a systematic effort at confirmation. Yet the fit is encouraging. The liberal regime appears in the society best known for the strength of individualism (Lipset 1990, 1996). The corporatist regime appears in Germany, a society that until the 1960s was as well known for hierarchy as the United States is for individualism (Dahrendorf 1967). And the most egalitarian of the three welfare-state regimes, the social democratic, appears in Scandinavia among societies in which egalitarians are exceptionally influential (Grendstad 1999). Various institutional factors facilitate these associations, but these factors—like the welfare-state regimes themselves—may frequently be the results of the relative influence of rival cultural preferences.[6]

Imperfect correlations between distinct institutional designs and varia-

6. Surveys and related studies of the relative frequency of grid-group theory's three socially interactive cultures are in their early stages. The broadest to date is Grendstad's (1999) analysis of twelve European societies. No similar study on the United States exists (but see Coughlin and Lockhart 1998 and Ellis and Thompson 1997). An encouraging feature of Grendstad's recent work is that it reinforces characterizations that other scholars have offered: exceptionally high levels of fatalism in Mediterranean societies (Banfield 1958), exceptionally high levels of egalitarianism in Scandinavia (Inglehart 1997), and increasing individualism in the Federal Republic (Baker, Dalton, and Hildebrandt 1981; Rohrschneider 1994). Yet the character of public institutions is presumably influenced more by the relative frequency of various perspectives among political elites rather than across societal populations generally. There are to date no surveys or related studies on the relative frequency of grid-group theory's socially interactive cultures among societal elites. In Part Two of this study, I rely on affiliations with political party factions and interest groups as indices of relative frequency and organization.

tions in the relative influence of rival cultures in society are also found in cross-societal statistics on public sector size. Table 2 shows public sector expenditures as a proportion of GDP at three junctures bracketing the 1980s for eight European societies and Australia, Canada, and the United States. The 1991/92 means clearly distinguish the three welfare-state regimes. An explanation of this pattern of cross-societal variation that relied solely on the relative influence of rival cultures would certainly be incomplete. But it would, nonetheless, offer a quick and reasonable accounting. The liberal state represents individualistic resistance to extensive public activity stemming from the values of liberty and self-reliance. In contrast, the corporatist state embodies hierarchy's predisposition for securing society from a variety of threats through public programs. Finally, the social-democratic state evinces an even more extensive public sector, suggesting the realization of egalitarian aspirations to achieve greater equality of condition.

Data focused on "national effort"—a term developed by Wilensky (1975) to denote the proportion of gross national (or domestic) product (GNP or GDP) devoted to social programs—as an index of welfare-state regime type are less sensitive on this last point. Table 3 compares the proportion of GDP

Table 2   Public Expenditures as a Percentage of GDP[a]

	1975	1981	1991/92
Sweden	49.0	64.2	59.8
Denmark	47.6	53.8[b]	57.2
Finland	36.6	39.0	56.2
Norway	46.6	48.0	52.9
			The 1991/92 group mean is 56.5.
Italy	41.6	45.0	51.3
France	43.1	48.5	48.5
Austria	44.2	48.2	45.7
Germany	47.4	47.8	44.4
			The 1991/92 group mean is 47.5.
Canada	40.6	40.2	47.9
Australia	32.5	31.0	36.6
United States	36.0	35.7	36.4
			The 1991/92 group mean is 40.3.[c]

[a] Data for 1975 and 1981 are from OECD 1985. Data for 1991/92 are from OECD 1994a. Data for Australia, Austria, Canada, Denmark, Norway, Sweden, and the United States are from 1991. Data for Finland, France, Germany, and Italy are from 1992.

[b] Data are from 1979.

[c] Lipset (1990) questions whether Canada belongs in this group as Esping-Andersen suggests.

Table 3   National Effort: Social Policy Expenditures as a Percentage of GDP[a]

	1975	1981	1990/92
Sweden	26.8	33.3	31.5
Denmark	32.4	33.3[b]	40.2
Finland	23.3	25.9	29.3
Norway	26.2	27.0	35.4
Italy	26.0	28.9	30.6
France	24.2	29.4	33.1
Austria	24.5	27.7	33.1
Germany	32.6	29.1	29.1
Canada	21.8	21.0	22.1
Australia	18.8	18.9	21.9
United States	20.8	20.7	24.5

[a] Data for 1975 and 1981 are from OECD (1985). Data for 1990/92 are from OECD (1995). In a few instances I have supplemented OECD (1995) with data from the OECD's annual Economic Surveys series of specific societies. See, for example, OECD 1994b. Data for France and Germany are from 1990. Data from Norway are from 1991. Data for Australia, Austria, Canada, Denmark, Finland, Italy, Sweden and the United States are from 1992.

[b] Data are from 1979.

that is spent on social programs at the same three junctures for these eleven societies. These data distinguish the liberal welfare states sharply from the other two categories. But as Esping-Andersen forewarns, the other two welfare-state regimes are less clearly distinguished by the size of their social policy expenditures than by the specific ways in which these expenditures are applied (e.g., child allowances as opposed to child care).

It would be ridiculous to deny that institutional variations contribute to public social program spending differences between liberal regimes and the other two categories. But the differences in spending levels are sharp. It seems unlikely that institutional variations responsible for spending differences this large occur inadvertently. Rather, they are more likely to represent clear differences in the relative societal influence of distinct orientations and purposes. Yet Wilensky's primary explanatory factor for the level of national effort (the age of social security programs) is an institutional one, and thus ignores cross-societal differences in orientation or purpose (1975, 135–37). In his view Germany is a welfare state spending leader and the United States a spending laggard because the former pioneered in developing these programs while the United States was one of the last industrial societies to adopt them. Assuming nearly inevitable incremental program expansion, Wilensky concludes that the age of social programs heavily influences spending levels.

All explanations leave something more to be explained, but given the importance of the timing of program adoption in Wilensky's schema, the question of why Germany developed social programs long before the United States seems to be too crucial a point to ignore. As we shall see in subsequent chapters, both historical contingencies and cultural preferences contribute to the age of social programs in these two societies. In Germany, hierarchical state officials responded to certain social hazards associated with industrialization by enthusiastically developing social programs that fit well with their general endorsement of state paternalism for dealing with the varying problems of what they perceived as unequal members of society. In the United States, however, dominant individualistic elites successfully fought the development of related programs, minimally until the onset of the Great Depression, because such programs were at odds with their preference for relying almost exclusively on market institutions for regulating economic relations among what they perceived as equal persons.

Soviet Consumer Price Subsidies

Tucker contends that the original Soviet political elite held what he calls a "composite revolutionary culture, an amalgam of ideal and real cultural patterns" (1987, 58—see also Malia 1994). In my terminology they exhibited bifocal EH cultural biases through which long-term egalitarian goals were regularly "supported" in practice through hierarchical means. These EH bifocal cultural biases share some ground with the perspectives that Free and Cantril (1967) report for some of their American respondents. The Americans whom Free and Cantril examine frequently have individualistic ideals of Lockean limited government. However, in practice they often favor extensive public social programs. Thus in everyday life their practical orientation tends to predominate, producing bifocal cultural biases in the form of HI (or perhaps some instances of EI). Similarly, early Soviet elites' practical experience with governing helped to transform their bifocal cultural biases from EH to HE. So across the first couple of decades of Soviet experience, while the initially instrumental hierarchical practices of the Soviet era were crystallized through institutionalization and continued to shape social life, the original egalitarian revolutionary objectives became, in the absence of similar institutional embodiment, increasingly ethereal. An attitude that accepted hierarchical institutions as comprising a desirable social order in themselves progressively took hold.[7]

How Soviet leaders perceived their citizenry appears to have been a crucial factor in producing this transformation. In contrast to the encouraging vision of these citizens in Lenin's revolutionary statements (Madison 1968, 50), early Soviet leaders found the citizenry alienated, selfish, and uncooperative. This discovery sealed the fate of the Soviet Revolution in terms of its dominant cultural bias.[8] It set as the Revolution's major practical objective an inherently hierarchical program of educating persons characterized by varying degrees of social irresponsibility, transforming them into stalwart self-motivated contributors to the social collective (Figes 1997; Tucker 1987, 57; Volkogonov 1994).

Indeed, the Soviet Union became an exceptionally centralized hierarchy. While the cultural transformation of its political elite just discussed contributed to this outcome, the characteristic was likely overdetermined. That is, exceptional institutional and policy-process centralization was probably the product of multiple distinct explanatory factors, any one of which might have been sufficient on its own. The Soviet Union confronted a series of daunting circumstances—civil war, international estrangement, and the Second World War. Even in the highly individualistic United States, the societal threats of the 1930s and 1940s contributed to greater hierarchical centralization.

I want to focus here on a social policy design feature that derives from the highly centralized decision making and—sometimes—closely coordinated institutional interaction that a combination of Soviet HE bifocal cultural biases and perpetual security concerns produced. High degrees of centralization allowed for considerable integration among policies concerning employment, wages, prices, income maintenance, and social services. So, for instance, even in the early years Soviet leaders subsidized rents, the prices of basic foods, and some other essential consumer products. By setting costs of these necessities very low, Soviet leaders offset some, though surely not all, of the problems posed by weaknesses in their public income maintenance programs and social services. This policy structure is an obvious embodiment of a remarkable degree of high-group influence that became

7. Trotsky and Nikolai Bukharin, who resisted aspects of this shift, characterized it as a move to Soviet "Bonapartism" (Tucker 1987, 69).

8. However, some reactions to this discovery were egalitarian. The concept "class enemies" was expanded to encompass anyone providing any inconvenience to Party officials (Tucker 1987, 70).

progressively more hierarchical over time. Individualists would shrink from providing such a broad range of consumer goods without recourse to markets that would prompt greater productive efficiency and likely consumer satisfaction as well. Egalitarians would be skeptical about the high degree of paternalism represented by such a system. Only an exceptional degree of societal dominance by hierarchists would produce support for this approach, which likely represents the social policy apex of the hierarchical angle to the "imperatives" triangle that I introduced above.

Indeed, consumer price subsidies became progressively more prominent across time, growing particularly during Brezhnev's rule from the mid-1960s to the early 1980s. (See Table 4.) This was a period characterized by both greater routinization and inclusion than previous Soviet history and increasing hierarchical ossification and corruption. In contrast to the practices of previous leaders, Brezhnev directed additional amounts of social consumption spending more at need than at work performance. Some American analysts of the Soviet Union argue that Brezhnev fostered an implicit social contract (Cook 1993). That is, Soviet leaders would provide an increasingly abundant and secure life for ordinary persons. In return, Communist Party leaders demanded the unchallenged right to direct society. McAuley (1982, 149) contends that consumer price subsidies held an important place in the Party's program of guiding less capable persons. Soviet reliance on broad need-based subsidies represented hierarchical state support for what are called "merit wants" in market economies. That is, the Party encouraged low-income consumers to purchase more complete nutrition and make other more encouraging consumption choices than many would have made in the absence of subsidies.

Further, after the 1960s the Soviets increasingly viewed employment,

Table 4 Food Subsidies and Social Consumption Expenditures

Year	Total social consumption (in billions of rubles)	Food subsidies (in billions of rubles)	Food subsidies (as a percentage of social consumption)
1970	69.1	14.3	21
1975	95.0	17.2	18
1980	120.1	25.2	21
1985	141.6	56.0	40
1990	192.3[a]	66.0	34

SOURCE: McAuley 1982, 152, 155, and 1979, 324; Ashland 1991b, 25.

[a] Data are for 1988.

wages, prices, income maintenance, and social services as complementary facets of a broad integrated approach to human material welfare. This Soviet approach represents the antithesis of the small, relatively inactive state preferred by individualists. Through this Soviet orientation, an asymmetrical and exceptionally centralized version of corporatism (Cook 1993, 12–15), assuring full employment in a stratified labor force was the primary means for realizing the economic welfare of the citizenry. Coordinating wages and prices in order to assure that employment had this intended effect became integral aspects of this broad but coherent objective.[9] Some social services—education, medical care, child care—were also integral to this perspective. In contrast, most income maintenance programs, generally the central components of Western social policies, were designed only to plug narrow niches in the Soviet schema. They were insufficient for achieving this limited objective in numerous cases, so even with consumer price subsidies, many elderly Soviets needed to work to supplement their modest pensions.

A Fiscally Modest, Economically Interventionist Japanese State

In some respects Japan has the ultimate small state among advanced industrial societies. Table 5 contrasts Japan in terms of public expenditures as a percentage of GDP with the United States, the quintessential example of small-state liberalism, and the Federal Republic of Germany, a characteristic example of societal corporatism (Abelshauser 1984). Not only does the German state dwarf the Japanese, the American state is also larger. Further, the Liberal Democratic Party, which has governed for the vast majority of the postwar era, is well known as the "conservative" party of business, thus suggesting that the LDP is "liberal" in a Smithian, economic conservative sense.

Yet as Johnson (1982) and others (Katzenstein 1977) relate, the Japanese state, while shifting its particular practices across time, has followed varying strategies of what in the United States would widely be considered as too

9. From the perspective of market liberalism, the results of such ambitious social engineering were mixed. Wage increases during this period were especially large for those at the bottom of the scale, so some of the poorest workers acquired a modest measure of economic security (Cook 1993, 33–40). Yet diluting the relationship between wages and productivity exacerbated a variety of economic difficulties. Additionally, McAuley (1979, 301, and 1982, 168) suggests that expanding consumer price subsidies merely changed the basis of social stratification from work performance to other, less worthy considerations—social class, urban residency, etc.

Table 5 Public Expenditures as a Percentage of GDP[a]

	1960	1965	1970	1975	1981	1986	1991
Germany	31.4	35.3	37.3	47.4	47.8	43.3	44.4[b]
Japan	17.0	18.6	19.4	26.3	30.4	27.4	25.4[c]
United States	28.1	28.5	33.0	36.0	35.7	35.4	36.4

[a] Most data are from OECD 1985. Data for 1986 are from OECD 1995. Date for 1991/1992 are from OECD 1994a.

[b] Data are for 1992.

[c] In 1991 Japan had a huge public sector surplus. Public sector revenues represented 34.4 percent of GDP. The Federal Republic of Germany had a modest surplus, and the United States had a sizeable public sector deficit, revenues amounting to 32.2 percent of GDP.

interventionist an industrial policy. The Ministries of Finance and International Trade and Industry (MITI) have realized the preferences of Prime Minister Yoshida for sequentially guiding various sectors of Japanese industry to a position that, in the 1980s, could reasonably be called global leadership in value-added exports. That is, Japan imported raw materials and combined clever direction by central-state executives, experienced corporate management, and skilled labor to export huge quantities of sophisticated manufactured goods.

So in terms of state expenditures as a proportion of GDP, Japan has a smaller state than the United States.[10] Yet in terms of industrial policy and related programs, the Japanese state has been even more active than the Federal Republic's. Thus the "conservatism" of Japanese political elites and the implications of this concept for social programs need to be clarified.

In the contemporary United States the term "conservative" has at least two well-developed meanings in political contexts. One of these might be amplified as economic conservatism. This persuasion is represented by Milton Friedman, among others. Persons with these views fit well within grid-group theory's individualistic culture. Friedman (1962), for instance, wishes to rely as extensively as possible—far more than we do now—on what he sees as voluntary market mechanisms and less on inherently coercive state programs. Friedman's preferences in this regard are supported by his beliefs in bountiful social environments and humans as masters of their own fates

10. A couple of caveats are appropriate here. First, by relying heavily on the United States for international military security, Japan has enjoyed modest military expenditures during the postwar era. Second, as we shall see in Chapter 8, Japan's potentially expensive program of public pensions for the elderly was still "immature" and thus inexpensive into the early 1980s.

consistent with those that grid-group theory attributes to the institutional formation imperatives of individualists.

A distinctive sense of the term "conservative" involves what might be specified more clearly as social conservatism. This viewpoint is represented by Patrick Buchanan, among others. Conservatives of this sort fit well within grid-group theory's hierarchical culture. In contrast to Friedman, Buchanan perceives the state as an important moral resource (Bennet 1995). Law represents a crucial means for teaching persons how to behave appropriately, so—from Buchanan's perspective—it is ridiculous that law should forbid prayer in the public schools. In even sharper contrast with Friedman, it is a calamity that law allows employers to shift jobs overseas so easily, leaving workers with no means for earning a living. For Buchanan, there is nothing voluntary about the resulting unemployment. In his view, a larger, more active state—through which leaders teach less capable persons appropriate forms of behavior—is supported by more fundamental conceptions of unequal humans and troublesome human environments similar to those that grid-group theory portrays as underlying the hierarchical institutional formation imperative. In the United States, conservatives of these two sorts currently populate distinct factions of the Republican Party.

When Americans, even in academic works, describe the Japanese as conservative, they are generally understood as referring to economic conservatism. This is understandable, given the association of the LDP with business and the concern shared by prominent national executives and, less systematically, LDP Diet representatives with holding down the size of public budgets. Nonetheless, this inference is at best only partially correct. Contemporary Japanese central-state executives and a good proportion of the leading figures in the LDP are likely to be adherents of a version of social conservatism (i.e., hold predominantly hierarchical cultural biases) and only possibly economically conservative thereafter (have hybrid cultural biases with a subsidiary individualistic face). Pempel (1982, 160–62) presents portions of a speech by former labor minister Hara Kenzaburo that will help to illustrate this point.

In this 1972 speech to young persons Hara stated: "Old people's homes are assemblies of self-centered people with no sense of gratitude" (Pempel 1989, 160). Further, Hara identified "the residents of old-age homes as a 'stagnant pool' of egoists" (161). Were it not for the last word of this passage, Hara might be interpreted as a libertarian extremist. But Hara is arguing a central hierarchical tenet: that all persons have a responsibility to contribute in their own particular ways to the social collective rather than to ride free on the contributions of others. In the case of the ordinary elderly persons whom Hara is castigating, this responsibility may amount to little more than living in a sufficiently prudent fashion so that public resources which are required for other more important purposes are not redirected needlessly to support them. Hara is upset largely because he perceives higher priorities for public resources than the support of persons who, he believes, have lived indulgently and are consequently dependent in their old age. The higher priorities that Hara perceives as jeopardized by needless public support of elderly persons include fostering greater national economic development and, in the course of so doing, increasing Japan's international status and influence as well as making it easier for persons to acquire the resources necessary for realizing their responsibility for living independently. For Hara, persons who have made insufficient use of the existing socially provided opportunities for supporting themselves show a lack of gratitude to the social collective.

Hara's perspective employs terms that Americans are apt to interpret as individualistic. Verba et al. (1987, 75–83) offer help in this regard. Using elite sample data acquired about 1980, they show that, when asked whether persons generally (exempting the elderly and the handicapped) should have to take care of themselves, Japanese elites across the conventional (American) liberal-conservative political spectrum agree more regularly than their Swedish and American counterparts. Japanese Socialists agree with this statement more regularly than do American Democrats (73). So far, it is easy to interpret pervasive Japanese conservatism in an economic or individualistic sense.

But when Verba et al. ask whether government should guarantee the jobs that allow persons to take care of themselves, Japanese elites across the political spectrum are moderately to highly favorable (1987, 75). Japanese Liberal Democratic respondents are only slightly less positive than American Democratic respondents. Japanese social conservatives are thus more positive than Swedish and American (predominantly) economic conservatives. This task of job provision represents one portion of the higher priorities toward which Hara wished to direct resources. For him, an important responsibility of society's leaders is to provide the resources that ordinary persons need to carry out their own responsibilities. This perspective reveals a different and more hesitant orientation toward conventional public social programs than that of German hierarchists.

Relatedly, on questions such as whether government should work to substantially reduce the gap between the incomes of the rich and the poor or whether it is fair to tax the rich in order to help the poor, all Japanese respondents—from business to labor—are in a fairly narrow range from mildly to enthusiastically positive (Verba et al. 1987, 78). This pattern of elite opinion is sharply different from that of U.S. respondents, who vary more on both these questions and are more frequently negative. These distinctive patterns reveal how the orientation of high-group cultures toward the welfare of group members differs from that of individualists. Among the adherents of hierarchy, ordinary members of society are responsible for contributing to the social collective in various ways, but society's elites have a reciprocal obligation to facilitate these contributions. U.S. respondents drawn from groups apt to be relatively individualistic (farm, business, and Republican elites) do not share this latter conviction.[11] Their perceptions of human social environments and human nature support a view of each person as capable of independently mastering her own fate.

Across the political spectrum (including farm, Liberal Democratic, and business sectors) Japanese elites also generally react more favorably to suggestions of a limit on income and more equal earnings than their Swedish and American counterparts do (Verba et al. 1987, 81).[12] Finally, when asked whether the interests of employers and employees are inherently opposed, Japanese elites across the political spectrum react with a tighter pattern of modestly more optimistic responses than their Swedish counterparts and a considerably more optimistic, though no tighter, pattern than the American elites (83). This is exactly what we should expect from the elites of various social sectors in a society in which hierarchy is influential across most sectors. Rather than perceiving antagonistic classes, as their Swedish counterparts clearly do, Japanese Socialist elites on one hand and farm, Liberal Democratic, and business elites on the other are both more inclined to see employers and employees as contributing to the same overarching social collective in complementary ways. They recognize, of course, conflicts of interest, but they perceive much common ground and thus bases for cooperation as well.

Thus the relatively small size of the Japanese state (in terms of the proportion of GDP that it consumes) does not indicate acceptance of American notions that industry (or other segments of society) should operate indepen-

11. For instance, see Dobrzynski 1996, 4, particularly the responses to question 6 in the box labeled "The Corporate Role in Public Life."

12. The only exceptions in this regard are that Swedish labor and Social Democratic elites react more favorably to suggestions of roughly equal earnings. Such wage solidarity has long been a central goal of the Swedish Social Democratic Party and much of Swedish labor.

dently from oversight by central-state executives. Japan has made extensive and, in some periods, extremely effective use of close state-industry collaboration, and the advocates of modest public budgets in Japan are generally hierarchists. Yet in other societies hierarchists frequently favor embellishing, not only the activities and status of public institutions (matters which the Japanese also favor), but also their budgets.

Japanese "exceptionalism" in this regard is one of the consequences of late development. For most of the period since the Meiji Restoration Japanese leaders—particularly central-state executives—have felt great pressure to develop (economically, technologically, and—until 1945— militarily). One implication of this focus on development has been an imperative to place as many resources as possible in the hands of those best able to use them for the purposes of national development. The various forms of cooperation between central-state executives and industry leaders facilitate this objective by directing resources to industries that central-state executives view as exceptionally promising for societal economic development. A financially modest public sector contributes as well. It leaves a greater proportion of GDP in the hands of business executives. While central-state executives may, from the Japanese perspective, have superior ideas as to the most appropriate investment opportunities at particular junctures, business executives are best able to implement the specifics of broad national plans.

In Chapter 8, I distinguish the social policy preferences of two factions of contemporary Japanese hierarchy. I call the faction discussed in the previous paragraph traditional. That is, it represents a long-standing, Japanese, late-developer perspective particularly common among central-state executives. For these traditional Japanese hierarchists, an extremely ambitious industrial policy that assures sufficient employment for household support is the social policy of choice. A more recently evolved Japanese hierarchical perspective, common among national elected officials, supports a different orientation toward social policy, which I call conventional. By this I mean that its social policy views are conventional and familiar from the hierarchical perspectives found in many other societies. Like hierarchists prominent among the corporatist welfare states discussed above, conventional Japanese hierarchists support comprehensive pensions which distinguish among beneficiaries according to their social status. As I discuss in later chapters, these two institutionally distinguished forms of contemporary Japanese hierarchy mark a limit on the capacity of culturally derived institutional formation imperatives to predict specific institutional designs.

IMPLICATIONS

Culture is not the only contributor to institutional design. Socially disruptive historical contingencies, such as the Russian Revolution, affect the timing of institutional development initiatives and, as in the instance of the Meiji Restoration, frequently contribute to fostering new institutional design preferences that shift the trajectory of subsequent institutional development measures for decades. Institutionalists (e.g., Hall 1986; Katzenstein 1984 and 1985; March and Olsen 1989; Skocpol 1992; and Steinmo, Thelen, and Longstreth 1992) argue that institutional actors' motives arise endogenously—as a result of what I have termed institutional maintenance imperatives—rather than from exogenous sources. Thus these actors orient themselves in order to act appropriately in light of the meanings of certain roles and duties that are defined by the standard operating procedures of the institutions in which they spend their adult professional lives. This is, of course, frequently true, and this perspective likely provides a sound explanation for the activities of many political actors much of the time. But acts of human agency that cannot be adequately explained in this manner contribute much to shaping society. In these latter situations elites sometimes let go of existing institutions, replacing them with distinctive alternatives, or at least alter existing arrangements despite high institutional costs. Persons who choose such alternatives rarely act from their current institutional roles or duties alone.

So, while institutional analysis can explain much routine political activity, any schema that relies only on those preferences of adult political actors stemming from their professional institutional contexts cannot adequately explain certain—perhaps relatively infrequent but nonetheless important—institutional formation and development steps. The explicitly political realm of public policy formation appears to be permeable to institutional design preferences that arise in early life, generally apart from institutions comprising the formal political system. As I suggested in Chapter 2, these preferences are subsequently transferred to political life as persons apply themselves in the formal political domain. Such broad basic preferences are likely to be insufficient to provide all the refined guidance that political actors need in complex institutional contexts, but they nonetheless provide powerful guidance on fundamental issues.

If the institutional pressures of adult life dominated the formation of preferences about institutional design, then where a person stood (her policy position) on various issues would hinge on where she sat (her institutional niche). Certainly institutional niches contribute much to explaining many political preferences and conflict among them (Allison 1971; Halperin 1972). But as we saw in Chapter 2, Gorbachev spent his adult life following the professional career of Fyodor Kulakov, his regional mentor and predecessor as Central Committee Secretary for Agriculture. The two men had similar sequences of institutional positions. Yet from early in his career Gorbachev sought to ease central economic controls and foster local managerial responsibility. He had a long-standing cultural bias distinct from those of many of his colleagues that transcended both the similarities and differences of their adult institutional experience. Thus the values that persons think, frequently on the basis of early learning about appropriate ways of living, it is desirable to realize sometimes influence their institutional design preferences even in the difficult decisions of later professional life.

Moynihan (1973) suggests that politics breaks most men. By this he means that political actors often fail to shape the institutions of their adult lives to fit their beliefs and values. The 1994 example of former Senate majority leader George J. Mitchell forgoing a Supreme Court position in a futile attempt to enact a national health insurance program is a case in point. For some persons self-selection into institutions that are largely compatible with their cultures mitigates these difficulties. Nonetheless, for some, institutional formation imperatives, developed apart from their activity in the professional institutions of adult life, prompt efforts to reshape these institutions. These efforts may only occasionally produce sharp institutional discontinuities inexplicable from a perspective that focuses on the adult institutional socialization of elites. But these occasional instances can place societies on new trajectories. Thus a focus on cultural orientations, not only helps to explain some cross-societal institutional differences, but also provides insight—as the next chapter shows—into how and why political change occurs within societies.

FOUR

CULTURAL MECHANISMS OF POLITICAL CHANGE

If a person's culture arises from experience with the world, then new experiences may alter a person's cultural biases, and shifts in cultural biases may lead to political change. Thompson, Ellis, and Wildavsky (1990, 69–93) discuss how shifting historical contingencies can alter cultural biases in terms of "surprises": that is to say, in terms of experiences which indicate that the world no longer working in the way the subject's cultural bias predicts (for example, the belief that hard work will be rewarded). For instance, in response to the Great Depression and the Second World War Roosevelt built a substantial national government in little over a decade. Some persons who had previously held individualistic cultural biases and had thus been skeptical of large active government supported these changes, given the new circumstances they addressed. Although many persons did not change their views, some persons who had considered themselves self-reliant came to recognize that the altered context of the Depression left them increasingly dependent on help from new, more active public institutions. As their beliefs about the social environment changed, so too did their views of humans and their institutional preferences. As Richard Nixon later remarked: "I am now a Keynesian" (Silk 1972, 14).

This is the sort of change, Eckstein (1988, 796) insists, that political culture theory virtually precludes. Two points are pertinent to a clarification of differences between his views and mine. First, as we examine below, this is probably neither the most common nor the most powerful way that culture contributes to political change. Other mechanisms, more compatible with first-wave political culture theory, account for most of culture's contributions to political change. So these two versions of political culture theory are not as seriously at odds as they might seem. But grid-group theorists do emphasize the lifelong character of socialization and think that extraordinary events in later life may alter some effects of earlier socialization. For grid-group theorists, culture is in part a conception of how the world works that supports certain forms of social behavior as both moral and prudent. When experience provides seemingly clear signals that the world no longer works the way it was once perceived to do, we should not be surprised if some persons—particularly those with bifocal cultural biases—apply their culture(s) differently (Lockhart 1999, 875–76).

Second, Eckstein (1988)—like others (Elster 1989a, 1989b, and 1989c; Inglehart 1997; Rogowski 1974)—portrays political culture theory as a rival to rational choice theory, so he is concerned to emphasize the differences between them, including the stress that political culture theory places on the lasting effects of early socialization. Grid-group theorists have been inclined to see rational choice theory and their own as complementary. Grid-group theory explains how social preferences are formed; while rational choice theory explains how persons go about realizing what they prefer (Becker 1976; Wildavsky 1994; Lockhart and Wildavsky 1998; Lockhart and Coughlin 1992). In this view, explaining preferences does not involve competition between self-interest and culture, but rather among cultures, each of which relies on instrumental rationality. Everyone is self-interested in some sense, but rival cultures define both the self and its appropriate values or interests differently. So rival cultures exhibit distinctive conceptions of the self, each having a constrained perspective of what interests it is appropriate to seek.

Thus while the "surprise" (i.e., sharp changes in life experience) mechanism offers a means for clarifying both grid-group theory and how culture might generate political change, I do not carry it further here. I think that it only rarely translates easily into societal-level political change. As we shall see below, the New Deal is better explained by an alternative mechanism. In actual political life cultures contribute to change more by adjusting their institutions so that they continue to support their distinctive ways of life in altered circumstances than by transforming themselves into other cultures. Across this study, then, I consider three other cultural mechanisms of political change. First, in Chapter 2, I introduced bifocal cultural biases. In Chapter 3, I discussed an example of these compound cultural biases contributing to political change: the EH-shifting-to-HE cultural biases of the early Soviet elites.

My primary focus in this chapter rests on two other, more common mechanisms to which grid-group theory's conception of multicultural societies is particularly sensitive. The first of these two involves shifting patterns of cultural coalitions. Each of grid-group theory's three distinctive socially interactive cultures shares values with the other two. Both individualism and egalitarianism support personal rights against state authority. Both individualism and hierarchy admit social stratification, albeit on different grounds. And both egalitarianism and hierarchy care deeply about the welfare of the social collective. These shared values provide bases for intercultural coalitions. But each of these rival cultures is also at odds with the others over conflicting beliefs and values. Thus political coalitions between any two of these three cultures may break down. Since the adherents of rival cultures prefer distinctive institutional designs, political institutions are apt to change if the character of the cultural coalition that dominates society shifts. The second of these two mechanisms concerns how historical contingencies may sharpen conflicts between cultures. In these situations the adherents of rival cultures may revise existing institutions or develop new institutions in the process of defending enduring beliefs and values in changing circumstances (Eckstein 1988, 793–94).

EXAMPLES

Historical contingency and culture both contribute to political change through these latter two mechanisms; yet their contributions are distinct. Adherents of various cultures alter their institutions to meet changing social circumstances. Frequently these social changes are initiated by purposive human activities. But many social upheavals, such as wars or economic depressions, are unanticipated and unintended rather than purposeful consequences of social action (Jervis 1997). These contingencies prompt political change by threatening the values of particular cultures or affording new opportunities for their realization. And in responding to change by altering their institutions, the elites of rival cultures shape the character of that political change by tailoring those institutional innovations to the support of particular clusters of constrained values, that is, by applying distinctive institutional formation imperatives. I invoke again the "imperatives" triangle that I introduced in Chapter 3. Its three angles provide characterizations of the general institutional and social policy preferences of grid-group theory's three socially interactive cultures. We can expect the adherents of each of these cultures to push institutional innovation as far in these preferred directions as the circumstances afforded by various historical contingencies allow. Which culture(s) may be favored by future contingencies is uncertain, but the direction of institutional development in which particular cultures seek to take societies is clear.

Shifting American Cultural Coalitions

Early I-E Oscillation with I-H

Some portions of American political history provide exceptionally clear examples of oscillation between various cultural coalitions. Hartz (1955) correctly identified individualism as the dominant culture in the United States, but he exaggerated its standing. Individualists, while prominent, are not alone (Ellis 1993; Smith 1993). Rather, they provide the stable element of coalitions that for a time oscillated back and forth between egalitarians and hierarchists (Lockhart 1997, 96–99; 1999, 877–80).

For example, as Bailyn (1967, 302–3) relates, in 1760 social stratification arising from hierarchical and individualistic sources was widely practiced and accepted among the colonial societies of North America.[1] But by the mid-1760s increasing English regulation of the American colonies made allies out of such persons as the Whig individualist Samuel Langdon and the egalitarian Thomas Paine. Under these circumstances of increased external regulation many individualists shifted toward emphasizing a democratic public action face, compatible with egalitarianism, that is familiar from McClosky and Zaller (1984), Hirschman (1982), and Huntington (1981).

---

1. The following brief sketch of American political life from the early 1760s through the mid-1830s is illustrative. I draw on Bailyn 1967, Elkins and McKitrick 1994, Hofstadter 1958, Lee 1994, Lutz 1980, Main 1964, Schlesinger 1945, Wills 1978, and Wood 1969.

North American Whigs had grown up under the benign neglect that Britain had generally bestowed on its colonies prior to incurring the expenses of the French and Indian War and had become accustomed to regulating their own social lives. The imposition of new British regulations served as a trigger for an I-E coalition by bringing individualists initially to question these British actions and eventually to join egalitarians in maintaining that institutions which acted so high-handedly were thoroughly corrupt. This was basically a coalition of low-grid cultures reacting against distant, and indifferent, authorities. The government they created, under the Articles of Confederation, was minimal and highly decentralized. In addition to waging an unsurprisingly poorly managed but successful revolution against British authority, this coalition fostered new political institutions in several of the resulting states that emphasized local control through an active citizenry operating governments with limited powers and constrained ambitions.

But individualism has another aspect, one concerned with the acquisition and development of material resources and the need to establish a state sufficiently powerful to secure them (McClosky and Zaller 1984; Hirschman 1982; Huntington 1981).[2] It shares these institutional preferences less with egalitarianism than with hierarchy. In the decade following the Revolution a series of historical contingencies such as Shay's Rebellion created new circumstances that alarmed many—but not all (Beard 1965)—individualists. Perceptions of "desperate debtors" (Hamilton, *Federalist 6*) using remarkably egalitarian state legislatures to successfully attack some forms of property thus provided the trigger for an I-H coalition. The preceding I-E coalition had so undone social stratification that these propertied interests felt endangered, and increasing numbers of individualists thought that government needed less to represent ordinary humans than to filter out their crasser influences (Ellis 1993, 63–67). The constitutional convention of 1787 illustrates the movement of these individualists back toward a coalition with hierarchists like Alexander Hamilton and Gouverneur Morris. This Federalist coalition built a substantially more powerful, centralized, and active national government than that of the Articles.

Like the fashion in which the persistent opposition to authority of the previous I-E coalition had gradually made many individualists increasingly concerned about stable rules for securing property and thus receptive to the

---

2. Schlesinger (1986, 40–43) shows Tocqueville distinguishing these two faces of individualism.

Federalist coalition, routine Federalist practices of economic favoritism and exclusion—franchises, concessions, charters etc.—and the glorification of public authority gradually prompted some individualists to shift again toward closer relations with egalitarians. This shift reached a crucial juncture in the election of 1800, which brought the Democratic-Republican victory of Thomas Jefferson and the resurgence of an I-E coalition. So the trigger in this instance lies in the very success of the preceding I-H coalition's efforts to achieve greater social stratification through various practices of favoritism. The Jeffersonian phase of this coalition was not as ambitious in destroying the Federalist state as many of its supporters had hoped, and "Jeffersonian" inclinations were actually relaxed for a time after 1812, but a countervailing (I-H) coalition was not able to regain control. The anti-authority character of the Jeffersonian period was reasserted by Andrew Jackson's presidency (1929–37), which marked another high point in terms of antistatist collaboration between individualists and egalitarians. The Jacksonian coalition engaged in at least modest state smashing, eliminating the Bank of the United States and reducing the activities and resources of the national government generally.

As Ellis and Wildavsky (1989, 221–22) show, James Madison was a bellwether of the coalition dynamics of this period. An individualist, Madison was counted among the revolutionaries of the 1770s. But he realized the limitations of the Articles and became—along with Hamilton—a leading figure in the Federalist movement. Thereafter, he shifted into the Democratic-Republican ranks, and his presidency—at least until the shattering experience of the War of 1812—followed the Jeffersonian pattern.[3]

So as the cultural composition of the dominant coalition shifted, the character of American national political institutions changed, reflecting the different shared values and practical interests of the various combinations of

---

3. Two different coalition patterns characterize a pair of later periods of American political development: the late 1830s–early 1890s (relative individualistic dominance), and the middle 1890s–early 1990s (H-I oscillating with relative individualistic dominance). Across this extended history Elazar's (1984) subcultures can be translated into grid-group theory's categories (Thompson, Ellis, and Wildavsky 1990, 233–45): individualism as individualism, moralism as egalitarianism, and traditionalism as a version of hierarchy. Making these translations carries two benefits. First, it offers a compelling solution for the dispute over how Elazar's subcultures interrelate (Sharkansky 1969; Haight 1976; Wirt 1980; Elazar 1980; and see also Lieske 1993). Second, grid-group theory's categories enable us to get Whigs such as Daniel Webster out of the high-group but low-grid moralism subculture and into a more broadly titled high-group high-grid (hierarchical) culture where they belong (Howe 1974). Locating Whigs is also a problem for Greenstone (1982 and 1986), who sees only competing versions of liberalism outside the South.

cultures. The I-E Revolutionary and Jeffersonian/Jacksonian coalitions attacked central political authority, whereas the intervening Federalist (I-H) coalition reasserted it. This period offers particularly clear oscillation because the trigger mechanisms for the I-E and I-H coalitions were the extravagances of the British imperial and, then, American Federalist hierarchists in the 1760s and 1790s, which united individualists and egalitarians, and in the early 1780s, the extravagances of the egalitarians, which united individualists and hierarchists.

An American "Grand Coalition"

Individualistic oscillation between egalitarians and hierarchists across the late eighteenth and early nineteenth centuries comes too early in American history to have any relevance for modern social programs. Accordingly, I want to discuss an additional example of shifting coalition partners that is closely associated with American social program development. As late as the early 1930s the United States had not followed other industrial societies in developing national public social insurance programs. Social insurance had developed at the state level, generally focusing on the social hazard of unemployment.[4] These programs were not present in all states, and they varied widely among states with coverage typically leaving substantial holes in their limited safety nets. Social insurance sponsored by the national government was or had been categorical, focusing on merchant seamen (Starr 1982) or Union Civil War veterans (Skocpol 1992) rather than the population generally. These programs served persons who had undertaken unusual risks while providing services to the social collective. The Union veterans program had been the largest of these efforts. It had expanded in part through graft that had diluted ties between benefits and veteran status. So in spite of efforts by some Progressives (Seager 1910) to use these pensions as the basis for the development of more general social insurance, Civil War pensions succumbed to the broader pressures associated with the Progressive movement for responsible government, whose procedures were impartial laws rather than practices of favoritism among cronies.

Lipset (1996 and 1990) attributes the exceptional reluctance of the United States to develop public social insurance programs to the dominance of its individualistic culture. Adherents of this culture see social programs as contrary to their basic beliefs in a bountiful social environment and roughly equal broad human capacities and thus as destructive of their cen-

4. State-level public assistance programs for widows were also common (Skocpol 1992).

tral values of liberty and autonomy. However, individualism's influence was reduced in the 1930s by the effects of a historical contingency—the Great Depression. After 1929, the Depression began to produce a social environment in which the market practices that individualists had applied with considerable success throughout much of American history were no longer achieving outcomes that were generally acceptable. Staunch individualists often interpreted the Depression as an expanded version of the normal business cycle that would soon play itself out. President Hoover, for instance, had been hesitant in his own programmatic responses to the Depression, and throughout much of the 1930s he traveled the country giving popular speeches that criticized Roosevelt's policies as counterproductive and socially dangerous overreactions (Abbott 1991, 236).

Adherents of the high-group cultures perceived the matter differently. Both hierarchists and egalitarians saw clear signs that the social collective was beset with severe difficulties requiring the activation of central response capacities. Further, both hierarchists and egalitarians had experienced high degrees of dissatisfaction in the long stretches during which the individualistic culture had enjoyed social dominance since the Civil War. Depression conditions brought prospects for increased influence for these rival high-group ways of life.

First, the Depression helped to mobilize greater numbers of egalitarians and hierarchists for voting and other forms of political action. Adherents of these rival cultures frequently disagreed on what remedies were appropriate. Nonetheless, the Depression mobilized cultures that perceived significant social problems in Depression conditions and were more inclined than individualists to use public resources to solve these problems.

Second, the severity of Depression conditions prompted efforts among some members of all three socially interactive cultures to form a loose coalition that could support related perceptions of the social problem and agree on some acceptable mechanisms for its solution. These predispositions provided exceptional coalition-building opportunities for leaders with HI bifocal cultural biases such as Franklin D. Roosevelt and those whom he gathered around him (Lustig 1982; Schlesinger 1957, 1959a, and 1959b; Fusfeld 1956; Greer 1958; Rossiter 1949; Crothers 1996). Persons with these cultural biases were particularly capable of fostering cross-cultural cooperation, since their HI orientation made them sufficiently willing to extend public distribution to those suffering social dislocation to calm some egalitarians and sufficiently sensitive about acceptable distributive procedures (e.g., public employment rather than cash disbursements and social

insurance rather than public charity) to win the approval of many hierarchists. Under circumstances of a poorly performing market economy even
some individualists, particularly those with bifocal cultural biases (e.g., IH
and IE), could support this coalition as well.

Depression conditions thus prompted the longest-lived, though not the
only (Coyle and Wildavsky 1987), coalition involving substantial elements
of all three socially interactive cultures in American political life. This
"grand coalition" had its limits. Many individualists never came to believe
that market capitalism was imperiled and thus saw no need to work more
closely with those who favored a larger, more economically active state.
Some egalitarians clung to their traditional preferences for local initiatives
and/or insisted on more direct forms of aid (cash, food etc.) to the unemployed than New Deal measures generally offered (Weir, Orloff, and Skocpol 1988). Even among hierarchists some held back, concerned for instance
about the relatively race-blind orientation of New Deal public employment
programs. Yet significant portions of both high-group cultures and various
bifocal combinations between these cultures and individualism contributed
to this coalition.

A tiered structure facilitated the formation and maintenance of this loose
grand coalition. The members of Roosevelt's "brain trust" and their earlier
mentors (e.g., among the former, Adolph Berle, Sumner Slicter, and Rexford
Tugwell; among the latter, Herbert Croly, Henry Carter Adams, Richard T.
Ely, and John R. Commons) were predominantly HI "bifocals" (Tugwell
1992). Further, many of the persons Roosevelt brought into his rapidly expanding national government shared this culture. This was as true for persons he lured away from the hierarchies of private corporations (e.g.,
Raymond Moley) as for those who came from experience with some of
the more active state-level governments (e.g., Arthur Altmeyer). While this
coalition leadership was interested in improving economic circumstances
for persons in the lower reaches of the socioeconomic order, it was *not*
egalitarian. Rather, it sought a more inclusive, stable, prosperous yet differentiated economic order by focusing on efforts to achieve and maintain
higher levels of aggregate demand.

On the other hand, the grass roots of the coalition were much more
strongly egalitarian. For many of these persons Roosevelt's policies were
revered for helping competent persons cope with exceptionally difficult circumstances beyond their control. Others saw much of Roosevelt's programmatic response as too little and too late (e.g., modest social security
payments that began for a few in 1940), but nonetheless as better than

available alternatives. Roosevelt thus benefited from a substantial egalitarian contingent among the "foot soldiers" of his coalition.

Without the impetus of the Depression, however, it is unlikely that rival cultures would have been sufficiently motivated to cooperate with one another. Particularly for bifocal individualists, serious market instability was surely a prerequisite for their willingness to accede to a larger, more economically active state. And Depression conditions both raised hierarchists' fears of social chaos and emboldened them to overcome their differences with individualists and take a leading role in creating new state institutions aimed at assuring social order. The severity of the plight Depression conditions posed for many average persons inclined egalitarians to lend their support to initiatives that strengthened capitalism and a central state that they could not realistically hope to dominate as well as to accept programs that relieved the poor less immediately and less directly than they would have preferred.

As a consequence of this coalition's efforts to deal with a serious historical contingency, the United States developed a much larger, more active central government in the course of a decade. In essence, the United States became less exceptional in the character of its nationally prominent cultures and the political institutions that these cultures fostered. Bolstered by a second contingency, the Second World War, this coalition maintained considerable influence into the early 1970s. Thereafter, in the absence of subsequent societal shocks of this magnitude, this coalition dissipated, and individualism began to recover its customary dominant position in American political life. Thus since 1980 active government has once again been widely labeled as a problem, not a solution, and American social programs have accordingly been under siege.

Before moving to German examples, I want to draw attention to four facilitating factors that recur among the coalitions I examine in this study. First come shared values. Certainly rival cultures have conflicting values as well, and shared values are not a sufficient basis for coalition formation. But shared hierarchical and individualistic fears for the security of property in the 1780s as well as shared hierarchical and egalitarian concerns arising from the economic insecurity that threatened many citizens during the Great Depression facilitated cross-cultural cooperation. Second is the severity of the historical contingencies that foster the coalitions with which I am concerned. Hierarchists, egalitarians, and some individualists all saw the Depression as a threat to society. Third, the cultures that form coalitions frequently make different specialized contributions. In the instance of the

Depression, policy formulation and introduction lay almost exclusively in the hands of persons with HI bifocal cultural biases. Yet given the limited practical choice between these initiatives and the much more individualistic alternative represented by the status quo ante, many egalitarians contributed crucial electoral support to Roosevelt's HI administration. Fourth, persons—especially leaders—with bifocal cultural biases may be particularly helpful in the process of coalition formation. They share some perspectives and purposes with the adherents of two distinct cultures and thus have bases for empathizing with and persuading multiple constituencies. I periodically highlight one or more of these four factors in the coalition instances that I examine below in this and subsequent chapters.

Germany: Cultural Conflict and Shifting Coalitions

Clashing Cultures Produce Social Policy Innovation

During the mid-nineteenth century German society confronted the complex constellation of social dislocations—industrialization, urbanization, the development of the nuclear family, etc.—that we recognize as the industrial revolution. The consequences of this contingency attracted the attention of all three of the socially interactive cultures. Two of these cultures—hierarchy and individualism—were relatively closely allied in a "blood and iron" coalition dominated by the former. While there were certainly differences and disagreements between these coalition partners, they are not as important for this study as the conflict between them and the socialist egalitarians, particularly the Social Democratic Party of Germany (SPD).

By the late 1870s, German socialists had organized some workers and were establishing various institutions, such as self-help societies (Rimlinger 1971), for coping with various social hazards as well as calling for the creation of a social order that would serve workers' interests more effectively. Most workers remained outside the socialist movement. But the socialists' strength grew, as did their public profile. They organized demonstrations and related activities that focused attention on the plight of workers and their families as well as on socialist ideas for rectifying these circumstances.

In some respects these activities—agitation as Bismarck and his colleagues perceived them—challenged the most basic principles of Imperial Germany's ruling class (Snyder 1967; Taylor 1955). These circles were predominantly hierarchical. They believed in pervasive human inequality. For them, only those favored by birth and thus acquiring education and travel had the expertise necessary for guiding the social collective.

Socialist suggestions about a new social order, however vague in form, thus challenged Imperial Germany's rules about who was fit to make decisions on broad social and political questions. Bismarck's circle might recognize and appreciate the talents of a skilled worker, but they were not inclined to acknowledge that these talents extended to any but the most limited participation in questions of societal governance. So the historical contingency that fostered the development of an organized working class, with an agenda demanding more political influence for ordinary persons, also structured a nearly irreconcilable conflict between this egalitarian culture and the dominant hierarchical culture of this era.

Accordingly, Bismarck's response to socialist agitation was strong and repressive. New legislation prohibiting various activities in which the socialists engaged was promulgated, and the police and other state-security groups enforced it enthusiastically, indeed, up to and past the point of violence in the streets. Thus during the 1870s and 1880s the issue of social governance fostered extensive conflict between German egalitarians and hierarchists.

This is precisely the sort of conflict that we should expect between hierarchists and egalitarians. According to grid-group theory, egalitarians think that all persons should participate roughly equally in making the rules that govern their collective lives, and hierarchists believe that only a few persons have the capacities for participating productively in guiding the social collective. However, the implications of industrialization for workers also included issues of collective welfare. Grid-group theory predicts that these latter issues will provide common ground between the high-group cultures of egalitarianism and hierarchy.[5] This potential was not lost on Bismarck. While he was hesitant about cooperating directly with the socialists on any issue, Bismarck was concerned that the progressive marginalization of the working class, attributable to industrialization, was having seriously deleterious effects on the national unity that would be necessary for Germany to survive a struggle with the other great powers. Moreover, his vision of the limitations of ordinary persons and of his own role as societal caretaker created both sympathy for the problems of industrial workers and a sense of his obligation to mitigate these difficulties. These thoughts were reinforced by his perception that the state's easing of workers' burdens might

5. Relations between egalitarians and individualists reverse both of these patterns. Although individualists generally join egalitarians in their struggles with hierarchists over the extension of the franchise and other civil-political rights, they usually resist egalitarian and hierarchistic efforts to support socioeconomic rights with various sorts of public social programs.

help to shift workers' loyalties from what he saw as the false doctrine of socialism to the expertise of the hierarchical state, thus increasing social unity.

Bismarck and his colleagues, then, developed a second front in their struggle with the socialists: the pioneering creation of the sorts of social insurance programs that define the modern welfare state. Bismarck's efforts represent a fine example of Simon's (1955) concept of problem-driven search. The constellation of problems to be solved were those entailed by wage dependency and vulnerability, particularly as they related to certain social hazards of the life cycle. Some of these events could be predicted for individuals (e.g., aging). While this was not possible for other events (e.g., industrial accidents), reasonable predictions for classes of workers could be derived. Search focused first on a general mechanism for coping with these social hazards. Bismarck drew on a variety of scattered practices, extant particularly in Germany's mining regions (Leichter 1979, 119; Rimlinger 1971, 113), in further developing the concept of social insurance funded by employer and employee contributions. He favored adding state contributions to this insurance, but this aspect of his program ran into difficulty from (individualistic) liberals in the Reichstag. The basic mechanism of social insurance was then fashioned into several distinct proposals designed to cope with specific social hazards afflicting industrial workers. Medical-care insurance for industrial workers, encompassing both coverage for medical expenses and modest living allowances during periods of convalescence, became the first modern social program in 1883. This was followed by accident insurance for industrial workers in 1884. Pensions for those elderly who had worked in industrial occupations completed Bismarck's innovations in this area in 1889.

Bismarck's institutional innovation shared some elements with traditional hierarchical efforts to cope with the material problems of the poor, but it also opened new territory. His programs were traditional in that they were designed by an elite for masses held to be incompetent to participate in their formulation. Further, they were designed to cement the loyalties of these masses to the political institutions and society dominated by this elite, in some cases to draw these loyalties away from the socialists. In these senses Bismarck's social programs were revised versions of the feudal subsistence rights of the poor (Tawney 1926). But the programs were pioneering in other respects. They were designed specifically for social hazards that developed as integral aspects of the social changes of industrialization. Moreover, these social insurance programs were funded through the productive activities of their beneficiaries. This deviated sharply from previous church and public efforts to cope with poverty that had characteristically considered the poor to be incapable of doing much to help themselves (Katzenstein 1987, 172). Once social programs began drawing their funds from the efforts of future beneficiaries, egalitarians found it easier to support an expanded array of rights for these obviously responsible persons.

So Bismarck adhered closely to Simon's (1955) search guidelines. He started from the nature of the problem: a series of social hazards afflicting particularly the lives of industrial workers. He then drew on both traditional responses to related problems as well as the salient recent experiences of others confronting similar situations to construct an innovative mechanism (social insurance) to better cope with the new circumstances of industrial life. Yet the implications of this innovation vastly exceeded Bismarck's intentions of using it as a tool for capturing and holding working-class loyalties. This was the case largely because Bismarck's innovation could be adapted by another culture, becoming an integral element of a rival institutional formation imperative. In its egalitarian form social insurance realizes socioeconomic rights, and these rights are linked with other civil-political rights (Marshall 1963) in order to arm ordinary persons with the full range of rights that egalitarians argue enable citizens to participate in contemporary society as relative equals.

Additionally, as egalitarianism has developed since Bismarck, the conflict between hierarchy and egalitarianism in Europe has been transformed for lengthy periods in some societies into a coalition that forms one of the distinctive political institutions of the twentieth century: social democracy. In forming this derivative of Bismarck's innovations, hierarchists come to accept varying forms of social equality (e.g., a range of civil liberties, including equality before the law and universal extension of the franchise). Egalitarians, in turn, generally limit their interest in reducing socioeconomic differences among persons to those most likely to suffer severe deprivation in the absence of public social provision, a maximin concern.[6] So the tool that Bismarck developed subsequently fostered changes far beyond what he had intended, or even imagined.

6. Differences in the willingness of egalitarians to compromise and their need to do so vary among societies. For instance, in Sweden where egalitarianism is exceptionally broadly and deeply represented, it has supported more extensive efforts at labor solidarity, designed to shift both the upper and lower extremes of the wage distribution toward the middle, than have generally been feasible elsewhere. See Furniss and Tilton 1977.

Nevertheless, we have in Bismarck's programmatic responses to socialist agitation a dramatic example of a conflict between cultures producing political change in the form of prominent new political institutions. In the twentieth century, social insurance revolutionized views of public responsibilities in Germany and other advanced societies. The funds employed in various social insurance programs have come collectively to represent the largest single category of public sector expenditures in virtually all such societies.

A Shifting Cultural Coalition

German experience also offers an exceptionally important example of shifting coalition partners (Lockhart 1997, 91–92; 1999, 880–83). Rogowski (1974, 3–17) uses the transformation of Germany from a seemingly highly authoritarian (i.e., hierarchical) society in late 1930s to a stable democracy (i.e., far more individualistic and/or egalitarian) in the early 1970s effectively against first-wave political culture theorists. If, as these theorists argue, culture develops early and is impervious to rapid change (Eckstein 1988), then the transformation of Germany from enthusiastically Nazi to a stable democracy in the span of roughly three decades would appear to relegate culture to the sidelines as an important explanatory variable. Rogowski opts instead for rational choice theory, which portrays humans as adept at shifting their preferences quickly in pursuit of their interests. If political culture theories are to reacquire significance in the explanation of social phenomena, they must deal more effectively with this instance than they have in the past. Grid-group theory has the capacity for showing how culture contributes importantly to explaining this German transition.

The speed and thoroughness of Germany's transformation from a hierarchistic to an individualistic society (Dahrendorf 1967; Grendstad 1999) is remarkable. Historical contingencies prompted the shifting cultural coalition that produced it, but a particular cultural composition was required in order for these contingencies to work out as they did. The crucial point to which grid-group theory alerts us is that, as in the American examples discussed above, there was no single national culture in Germany. In spite of a history of hierarchical dominance, the cultures of egalitarianism and individualism were reasonably well developed in Germany by the late 1930s. The former, for instance, provided the basis for a working-class socialist movement, and the latter appeared most noticeably among entrepreneurs who had long been the lesser partners in the ruling H-I "blood and iron" coalition.[7] These low-grid cultures had been discredited by association with the social and economic turbulence of the Weimar period. But the hierarchical faction dominant in the late 1930s was the upstart Nazi Party, which was not well respected by more traditional factions of the H-I coalition. After achieving considerable mass popularity through reestablishing social stability and economic prosperity (central virtues for hierarchists and individualists, respectively), the Nazis also became widely discredited by leading Germany to the brink of destruction in the Second World War. This war left the regions that initially formed the Federal Republic dominated by Western societies that worked selectively with German elites to build more individualistic institutions.

Thus one historical contingency, the unusual openness to external influence created by Germany's wartime destruction, interacted with another, the presence of a significant indigenous individualistic culture with which representatives of the West could work, and facilitated a reversal in the relative influence of the partners in the long-standing German governing coalition. German individualists were encouraged and emboldened by Western colleagues and set about constructing institutions more congenial to their cultural biases: a competitive representative political system that respected civil-political rights and a form of market capitalism (a "social market") that acknowledged and respected certain socioeconomic rights. Simultaneously, German hierarchists frequently found that some of their values and the institutions that realized them were discouraged by the Western allies. During the formal Occupation, a coalition of Western and German individualists dominated western Germany, reshaping its institutions in accordance with their values. As the Federal Republic acquired autonomy, it became increasingly clear that indigenous German individualists had replaced hierarchists as the preeminent partners in the governing coalition.[8]

Rogowski's argument emphasizes a paucity of generational differences in citizen support for this new coalition and its institutions (1974, 9). Others have since acquired evidence of intergenerational change. For instance,

7. In comparison to more liberal societies, the political defeat of German liberals in 1848 slowed the development of German individualism, with predictable effects on issues of public life such as whether persons should be viewed as citizens or as subjects (Dahrendorf 1967, 387). See also Zapf 1986, 129.

8. As Padgett (1989, 125) shows, egalitarians have become more influential since the late 1960s, and varying cultural coalitions dominate predictable policy areas: corporatist issues involve the Christian Democratic Union (CDU) and SPD in a loose H-E coalition, market issues involve the CDU and the Free Democratic Party (FDP) in a loose H-I coalition, and individual rights issues involve the SPD and the FDP in a loose E-I coalition.

using participation in political discussion as an index of democratic allegiance, Baker, Dalton, and Hildebrandt show that although participation in
political discussion increased for all Germans between 1953 and 1972, there
were also sharp and growing intergenerational differences (1981, 45–52;
see also Pulzer 1989). Engaging in political discussion, for example, is more
common among later generations (Baker, Dalton, and Hildebrandt 1981,
47).

Even given the limitations of the data available in the mid-1970s, Rogowski overlooks the capacity of total defeat in total war to shake an adult's
confidence in existing beliefs. If following a particular pattern of social relations leads persons to severe experiences, some—particularly those with bifocal cultural biases—may shift the culture they apply in certain domains of
social life. Particularly across the Federal Republic's early decades, then, it
is reasonable to interpret the growing support for individualistic institutions
(Conradt 1980; Conradt 1978, 49; Dalton 1989, 100–104) as the combined
result of cultural shifting among older persons, particularly those with bifocal cultural biases, and increasing proportions of individualistic and egalitarian cultural biases developing among younger persons socialized under
the sharply different circumstances of the Federal Republic.

Grid-group theory thus offers an interpretation of German responses to
shifting events from the 1930s through the 1970s that does not force culturalists into strained and unconvincing improvisation. First, concerning coalition dynamics, grid-group theory focuses on an externally prompted and
supported transposition of the two cultures forming Germany's long-standing dominant coalition. Historical contingencies of the early cold war period facilitated the activities of individualists in western Germany and
hindered their hierarchical counterparts. So instead of relying on the process
about which Rogowski is understandably skeptical (e.g., an entire society
of hierarchists rapidly reorienting and adopting individualism), the initial
transformation of the Federal Republic was accomplished by emboldened
indigenous individualists replacing hierarchists in numerous positions
throughout the governing coalition. Thus what had once been an H-I coalition became an I-H coalition. Across time, the new institutions that this
coalition constructed socialized (thus gaining the allegiance of) increasing
proportions of the population.

Second, concerning persons with bifocal cultural biases such as Konrad
Adenauer (IH), the influential historical contingencies of the early postwar
period encouraged HI and IH bifocals to apply their individualistic faces
more extensively in public life. These contingencies provided considerable

scope for realizing individualistic ambitions but more limited avenues for achieving hierarchical aspirations. Additionally, over time these contingencies triggered shifts in relevant analogies. Hierarchy became increasingly associated with the German defeat and the stagnant East. Individualism, in contrast, became progressively associated with growing prosperity and the ascendant, constructively interventionist (e.g., Marshall Plan) West. These circumstances encouraged a growing tendency among West Germans with bifocal (particularly IH or HI) cultural biases to apply their individualism more widely in public life.

Rohrschneider's recent (1994) study of the members of Berlin's new united parliament (MPs) provides additional evidence of external forces collaborating with indigenous ways of life to reshape the Federal Republic's overall political culture. He further suggests that related changes occurred in eastern Germany. Rohrschneider finds, for instance, that MPs from the West conceive of democracy differently than those from the East do. So his work supports the contention that institutions influence basic political values. But it does not follow, as institutionalists (March and Olsen 1989) might argue, that culture is residual. The institutions that socialized Rohrschneider's MPs—largely to allegiance in the West and to opposition in the East where few current Berlin MPs have close ties to the former German Democratic Republic (GDR)—were constructed through processes involving considerable extrasocietal influence designed to realize particular beliefs and values.

External powers shaped the institutions of the Federal Republic and the GDR in the images of particular realizations of individualism and hierarchy. Western societies, particularly the United States, whose dominant culture disapproves of hierarchy, constructed, with sympathetic Germans, a parliamentary market system in the Federal Republic. In the GDR the Soviets imposed specific hierarchical institutions embodying the Soviet belief in a society led by an expert elite toward an improved historical era. While the relatively egalitarian Eastern MPs in the current Berlin parliament generally resist this hierarchical vision, they nonetheless adopt its associated (highgroup) Marxist egalitarianism in their conceptions of democracy. In contrast to the individual rights version of democracy favored by Berlin MPs from the West, Eastern MPs adhere to conceptions of democracy relying heavily on plebiscitary procedures and relatively equal material distribution. The united Federal Republic thus offers strong evidence in support of the symbiosis between culture and structure for which I have argued. External and indigenous adherents of the cultures of individualism and hierarchy created and sustained new political institutions in the Federal Republic and the GDR, respectively, and these institutions, in turn, helped to acculturate those who lived within them.

IMPLICATIONS

Political change thus arises through cultures rather than in spite of them. In some instances, historical contingencies pose difficulties so compelling that rival cultures perceive them as threatening for related reasons. Under these circumstances, new political institutions may develop from the formation of coalitions between cultures which are normally rivals. Social security is such an institution (Altmeyer 1968). Institutions that arise from intercultural coalitions are typically designed to deal with a limited range of concerns that the cooperating cultures share, and are not apt to represent an ideal response from the perspective of any single culture. So social security did not incorporate medical-care provisions (too provocative to individualists) similar to those of many other societies, and none of the three socially interactive cultures that contributed to social security's initiation viewed the program as ideal. Individualists would have preferred public efforts to stimulate private annuities. Egalitarians would have preferred greater redistributive effects. Even hierarchists, while probably more satisfied with the program than the other two cultures, would have favored benefit formulas with less sharply redistributive effects.

What these cultures acquired in social security was quite different. Experience at the state level, particularly in Wisconsin, suggested that, in order to be successful in the United States, social insurance had to exhibit program design features that catered to individualistic beliefs and values. In combination, these features (e.g., effort- and results-based pensions, personal "accounts," introduction of pensions several years after initiating the collection of "contributions," etc.) meant that the program did nothing to relieve the immediate problems of Depression-era elderly who had lost their savings in bank failures and who found employment difficult or impossible to acquire. Providing immediate help to these persons was an important objective for both egalitarians and hierarchists. Particularly from the standpoint of egalitarians, a program that began to provide small pensions to a few persons in 1942 (later moved up to 1940) was irrelevant as a response to the crisis that the Depression represented, whatever the program's long-term virtues might be. Thus the need to adjust policy design in order to obtain the approval of an independent Congress and judiciary in which individualists were still influential required that the program which in the long-term has surely been the most significant piece of New Deal legislation began operations only at the very end of the Depression. Other more short-lived programs bore the brunt of coping with Depression conditions.

When policy innovation arises from conflict between or among cultures, it frequently offers more straightforward evidence of culture contributing to political change. Bismarck's introduction of modern public social policy in the 1880s is about as clear an example of this process as can be imagined, sharply revealing the pattern-maintenance response that is often clouded by the complexities of compromises among coalition members. Bismarck's hierarchical colleagues furthered their conflict with egalitarian socialists, not only through repressive measures, but by developing a new form of social program which they hoped would create sufficient commitment among the working class to the existing hierarchical state that workers would lose their interest in socialist promises. The changes that Bismarck fostered were in fact much larger than those he anticipated because the socialists subsequently appropriated his policy innovation for their own purposes.

CULTURE, INSTITUTIONS, RATIONALITY, AND PROMPTING CHANGE

While cultures produce political innovation, they work in conjunction with other factors that also contribute to political change. According to grid-group theory, culture arises from perceptions concerning how the world works. Cultures exhibit constancy in their basic beliefs and values. But as historical contingencies alter the world that persons confront, adherents of rival cultures react to their varying perceptions of these changes with institutional innovations designed to perpetuate the support of their beliefs and values under these new circumstances. Historical contingencies are unpredictable by definition. And while rival cultures contribute to political change through a process guided by distinctive beliefs and values that favor some institutional designs and preclude others, various outcome details of particular problem-driven search processes likely remain indeterminate.

Institutionalists argue that policy responses to historical contingencies are shaped by institutions; thus analysis should focus on the activities of formal organizations. Institutional activities are certainly highly visible. On a national political stage cultures routinely act through institutions to achieve their objectives, and the effectiveness with which rival cultures organize their efforts to realize contrasting beliefs and values has much do to with their relative practical success. So an interest in culture does not discredit the valuable analysis of institutions.

It is certainly true, for instance, that the practical efforts to achieve Bismarck's social insurance innovations or Roosevelt's introduction of the social security program were undertaken by persons who, for the most part, carried out their duties by portraying particular institutional roles and were constrained in various ways by their institutions' missions and standard operating procedures. The different institutional resources that supported these persons' efforts were important to the realization of these programs. But decisions to apply the resources of these institutions to the tasks of realizing sharp program innovations reflect an influence that transcends institutional norms. Little about the trajectory of German national political institutional development across the 1870s socialized German officials to produce the innovation of social insurance in the 1880s. Indeed, the trend in both parliament and the bureaucracy had been one of gradually growing individualistic influence (Katzenstein 1987). Bismarck's social programs were a response to both exigency and opportunity that arose as a consequence of his earlier basic socialization about the character of a healthy society and the obligations of societal leaders (Katzenstein 1987, 172). Similarly, there was little about the trajectory of American national political institutions in the 1920s that socialized American officials to produce social security in 1935. Indeed, the 1920s had witnessed a general withdrawal from the more statist approaches associated with the Progressive era and American involvement in the First World War. Rather, a societal crisis brought to power new leaders whose basic socialization had imbued them with views on social responsibility and appropriate institutions different from those held by former President Hoover.

Rational choice theorists might argue that Bismarck and Roosevelt only acted on their interests in furthering certain policy innovations. But how were these interests recognized? Eduard Bernstein and Herbert Hoover adopted different opposing interests in these respective instances.[9] Invoking interests is helpful if we are concerned with the specifics of practical implementation efforts: who gets what and why. But attributions to interests does

9. Eduard Bernstein was a prominent figure in the Social Democratic Party of Germany.

little to help us explain why persons want what they do and, accordingly, reshape institutions to serve new objectives rather than familiar concerns (Becker 1976, 133). Simply identifying the interests that persons hold does not explain their reasons for fidelity to these interests rather than alternatives preferred by others. To understand where interests originate and why persons hold some rather than others, we need to employ cultures that organize human experience into rival coherent perceptual patterns and give distinctive constrained directions to human purposes (Eckstein 1996). So institutional analysis and rational choice theory carry us over only part of the ground required for explaining human social interaction. For the most part, institutional analysis helps us to explain a common but fairly narrow range of preference formation which is dictated by existing institutional design (i.e., by institutional maintenance imperatives). But to explain why persons alter the design of existing institutions or create new ones (i.e., employ different institutional formation imperatives), we need a broader conception of preference formation that focuses on the cultures that arm humans with differing, often rival, values and associated practical interests.

Thus a focus on institutions alone will likely fail to explain sharp changes in the broad objectives that guide institutional activities. Why did Roosevelt create new public institutions in response to the Depression and redirect the activities of some existing institutions? Why did Hoover perceive these changes in institutional trajectory as unnecessary, even counterproductive? Why did the leaders of populist egalitarian groups favor programs offering more immediate forms of aid for the victims of the Depression than Roosevelt was willing to develop? A focus on culture provides compelling answers to these questions, linking institutional preferences to deeper beliefs about the way the world works and human nature as well as to the values that result from varying views on these matters—such as looking out for the less capable, fostering liberty among equals, and achieving greater equality of respect and circumstance. Adherents of rival cultures thus have distinctive sets of high-priority values and strive to build different institutions in order to realize these purposes. So when historical contingencies help move a society from a period of individualistic dominance to another directed by a hierarchically led grand coalition among grid-group theory's three socially interactive cultures, the character of political institutions changes as well.

PART **TWO**

INTRODUCTION TO PART TWO

In Part One, I introduced the rival and culturally constrained rationalities of Douglas-Wildavsky grid-group theory. I argued that these rationalities rest on distinctive responses to basic human issues (e.g., are humans equal or unequal), and that the fundamental character of these issues facilitates the acquisition and persistent use of these rationalities across various stages of persons' lives. I illustrated as well how and why the adherents of rival cultures strive to realize contrasting institutional designs. Finally, I demonstrated that changes in the relations among and the relative influence of societal cultures can, in conjunction with shifting historical contingencies, produce change in a society's political institutions.

If, as I contend, the adherents of rival cultures favor distinctive institutional designs, and if rival cultures are found in sharply varying proportions among the political elites of different societies, then we ought to find evidence of the institutional differences that grid-group theory predicts when we compare societies. The character of the social policies of these societies at a given juncture offers a "snapshot" of these differences, but by studying significant social program decisions, we can examine the processes by which the relative influence of rival cultures helps to shape programs differently. Part Two of this study represents such an exercise. In the next four chapters I examine decisions on pensions in the United States (1983), the Federal Republic of Germany (1989), and Japan (1985) and on consumer price subsidies in the Soviet Union (1987–91). These decisions all fulfill Cook's (1993, 6–7) criteria for a "pressured decision point." That is, these decisions require political leaders to make difficult choices that reveal their value priorities.

These case studies are organized around the following six questions:

1. What is the relative influence of the various cultures (hierarchist, individualistic and egalitarian) among relevant portions of the society's political elite, both historically and during the period of the decision in question, and what are the most salient (general and social policy) institutional manifestations of this influence?

2. What historical contingencies give rise to the particular "pressured decision point" (Cook 1993) in question, and how do rival cultures perceive these contingencies as posing distinctive threats or opportunities?

3. What policy options are seriously considered, and to what degree do they reveal the rival, culturally constrained rationalities and institutional formation imperatives that I have associated with grid-group theory's three socially interactive cultures?

4. To what degree do societal elites rely on increasing program revenues as opposed to reducing program benefits in order to resolve the financial difficulties confronting the public social program in question?

5. How explicitly and straightforwardly does the resulting societal decision deal with the long-term financial costs of social programs for the elderly?

6. What cultural mechanism(s) of political change does this decision illustrate and how does the society's resulting social policy trajectory reveal changes in the relative influence of various cultures?

Collectively, my responses to these questions show how variations in the relative influence of rival cultures among relevant organized societal elites help to shape social policy decisions. Question 1 elicits salient background information regarding the relative influence of rival cultures in each society, particularly among its political elite, and the institutional manifestations of this influence, especially the relative degree of social program support at the outset of the 1980s. The other five questions draw on the distinctive features of grid-group theory. Question 2 examines how the disparate patterns of selective social attention and interpretation that rival cultures employ construe different threats or opportunities in the same historical contingencies.

Question 3 focuses on what I have called the purposive process. I examine the degree to which prominent elites who hold the beliefs and values of any of grid-group theory's three socially interactive cultures also prefer and strive to construct the institutional designs that I have associated with their cultures. I identify rival elite factions in terms of their culture through data distinct from the decisions that I examine in this study.

Questions 4 and 5 focus on aspects of decision outcomes. Question 4 deals with the degree to which societies rely on increased revenues as opposed to benefit reductions to resolve these 1980s public social policy problems. Question 5 examines how explicitly and straightforwardly the resulting societal decisions deal with the long-term financial costs of social programs for the elderly. Question 6 inquires about the mechanisms of political change that these decisions illustrate as well as how the resulting shifts in social policy trajectories reveal changes in the influence of rival cultures.

Table 6 shows that the Federal Republic faced the most difficult situation in terms of the elderly as a percentage of the working population during the

Table 6   Relative Severity of Selected Aspects of Societal Social Policy Situations

	Japan	Federal Republic of Germany	United States	Soviet Union
Elderly population (as a percentage of the population aged 15–65)[a]				
1990	16.6	22.5	18.7	13.9
2020	33.7	33.2	25.0	(downward trend)
Relevant public program net financial liabilities (as a percentage of the 1990 GDP)[b]	200	160	43	(likely more than Japan)

[a] Adapted from Davis 1995, 45, and Shoup 1981, 62.

[b] Adapted from Davis 1995, 48. "Net liabilities" = [existing program entitlements + future entitlements] − [current assets + future dedicated taxes].

1980s. Yet Japan is predicted to edge Germany out for the top spot in 2020. Different sources portray modest variations on this picture, but I think the overall situation is clear. Among these four cases Germany faced the heaviest burden posed by the elderly in the 1980s, and Japan and Germany confronted—and still confront—the most difficult futures in this regard. Table 6 also indicates that the United States had, by far, the most enviable situation in terms of future net financial liabilities associated with these programs.

These four societies differ, not only in the contingencies they confronted, but also in the situations they facilitated. For instance, through their social programs and tax policies they created varying incentives for retirement. Germany does the most to encourage retirement, and the Soviet Union did the least. The United States and Japan fall into a middle ground and are relatively similar in this regard (Gruber and Wise 1999, 5–6; Shoup 1981).

So, from the perspective of the 1980s, the United States faced a less daunting future worker/beneficiary ratio than either Japan or Germany. Further, its net financial liabilities for the programs in question were modest in comparison to the other three. This relatively favorable situation was the result, not only of external contingencies, but also of policies intended to make retirement less enticing than in, say, Germany.

In the case studies that follow I examine two distinct processes. One involves my tracing human purposes. I focus on this process in the section of each case study titled "Options Considered and Their Association With Distinct Rationalities." In tracing this process, I examine the degree to which persons who adhere to the contrasting beliefs and disparate constrained value clusters of grid-group theory's rival cultures develop strong preferences for and strive—in varying degrees under different circumstances—to construct the distinctive institutional designs that I have associated with these cultures. I conclude that they do engage in the efforts that the theory predicts, although I recognize that other factors (e.g., different adult institutional experiences) also influence their institutional preferences. Overall, the controversial societal decisions that I examine below are clearly aptly portrayed as conflicts among rival, culturally constrained rationalities.

In the course of examining social policy decision outcomes, I trace as well another, independent causal process. I examine the degree to which variations in the influence—i.e., the relative strivings to construct distinctive institutional designs—of rival cultures shape decision outcomes differently. I focus on this process in the sections of each case study titled "Relative Reliance on Benefit Reductions as Opposed to Revenue Increases" and "Explicitness of the Focus on Long-Term Financial Costs." In this process, my dependent variable in the previous paragraph becomes incorporated in my primary independent variable for predicting and explaining decision outcomes. I find that, at least within the context of "pressured decision points" (Cook 1993, 6), the relative influence of rival, culturally constrained institutional preferences among the relevant members of societal elites is important for predicting and explaining significant aspects of decision outcomes. This conclusion does not necessarily follow from my argument about human purposes, since the world might frequently, and clearly sometimes does, work so that what persons want is of little consequence in determining what they get (Skocpol 1979). Yet the complexity of these decisions is immense, and other variables also contribute to their outcomes. For instance, the character of the historical contingencies that societies confront may strengthen one culture at the expense of another. Further, a variety of institutional variables (e.g., the differing organizational effectiveness of various elite factions) also influence decision outcomes. Additionally, interaction occurs among these variables, and (at least seemingly) random factors difficult to specify in advance influence decision outcomes (Jervis 1997). Indeed, the complexity of these decisions is sufficient that I doubt that any remotely parsimonious combination of variables is capable of predicting their outcomes exhaustively. Nonetheless, as we shall see, culture performs well as a predictor of some important decision outcome characteristics.

Tracing these two processes requires indices for the variables involved. When analyzing the purposive process linking the beliefs and values of rival cultures to distinctive design preferences, I rely on beliefs about humans as well as their environments and values—as specified in Chapter 3—as indices of my independent variables. I examine the beliefs and values of major political actors and others associated with them. I use both societal visions, what—in Chapter 3—I called general institutional formation imperatives, and social policy design preferences as indices of my dependent variable.

When analyzing the causal process linking the relative influence of rival cultures among relevant, organized societal elites to decision outcome characteristics, I use the relative prominence and cultural adherence of major actors as well as the relative frequency of the adherents of rival cultures among prominent elites as my independent variables. I draw on selected organizational affiliations (e.g., particularly factions of political parties and interest groups) as indices of relative frequency. I grant that organizations such as these represent both incomplete (not involving all relevant elite members of a culture) and—more important—imperfect (containing the elite adherents of multiple cultures) cultural indices. Nonetheless, it is generally possible to characterize the parliamentary members of one party (or recognizable factions thereof) as more or less individualistic (or hierarchical) than those of another, although even this is easier in some societies (e.g., the Federal Republic) than in others (e.g., the United States). I employ the selected aspects of social policy decision outcomes that I specified in questions 4 and 5 as my dependent variables (i.e., relative reliance on revenue increases or benefit reductions and the explicitness with which long-term financial costs are confronted).

FIVE

REINING IN AMERICAN SOCIAL SECURITY EXPANSION, 1983

RELATIVE CULTURAL INFLUENCE AND INSTITUTIONAL CONSEQUENCES

Although variations exist across region (Ellis 1993) and time (Wood 1969), the United States has had an exceptional political culture from its inception (Hartz 1955; Devine 1972). In comparison to most other societies, hierarchy has been relatively weak in America, whereas the low-grid cultures, egalitarianism and particularly individualism, have been exceptionally influential. Turner (1962) argues that American individualism was encouraged early on and maintained for a lengthy period thereafter by the presence of the frontier. In Wills's (1987, 94) view, frontier life was more commonly egalitarian than individualistic, the settler who could build a barn on his own being rare. Lockhart (1991) shows that the American experience illustrates how a society in which individualism is prominent will deal with a frontier. Other societies have frontiers, but rival ways of life adopt distinctive approaches to frontiers as they do with most other phenomena. The

American frontier facilitated certain practices that supported the low-grid cultures by fostering widespread ownership of land, the conventional eighteenth-century prerequisite for the franchise. Thus American colonists were able to realize the theories of Europe's liberal thinkers more thoroughly than the societies of Europe. For this opportunity to be realized, however, advocates of liberal thought had to be present.

Unlike Canada, early European communities in what became the United States were formed by persons fleeing differing aspects of hierarchy, although their specific motives varied (Lipset 1990). In New England, Puritans dominated early on and formed congregational or relatively egalitarian communities that practiced faiths then discouraged in England. The middle-Atlantic region had from the outset a somewhat more commercial (individualistic) orientation. The southern areas were more hierarchical, initially dominated by persons (e.g., second sons of landed families) for whom the English hierarchy offered no secure niche (Ellis 1993; Abbott 1991). Traces of these original regional differences remain into the present (Lieske 1993); yet the differences did not preclude the development of related political practices in the middle eighteenth century. While property qualifications varied across the colonies, all the colonies had legislatures that were elected by property-holding adult males from districts that were roughly equal in population and revised as the population shifted westward. Thus in a setting offering land ownership to large proportions of the population, the different political practices of these three rival cultures achieved some convergence in colonial legislatures that operated roughly through the practice of republican virtue and were—by the standards of their time—broadly representative.

This accommodation was eventually upset by a series of events, such as the Stamp Act, that prompted the Revolution, which pitted a coalition of individualists and egalitarians against British hierarchists and their North American allies. Hierarchy's influence in America was then further undercut by the defeat of the English in the Revolutionary War and in the exodus of many Tories to Canada and England before, during, and after this conflict. Thus America's exceptional political culture originates in a migration, consisting disproportionately of the adherents of low-grid cultures, from Europe to America, unusual indigenous conditions that favored the inclusion of many adherents of all three socially interactive cultures in similar governing institutions legitimizing beliefs shared by these low-grid cultures, and the defeat and partial exodus of hierarchists as a result of the Revolution.

Individualism has retained its early preeminence across time. A factor crucial to this culture's success has been the ability of its numerous adherents to maintain a position in the entire series of shifting cultural coalitions that have dominated American political life. In the decade following the Revolution events such as Shay's Rebellion turned many individualists away from their coalition with egalitarians in search of an alternative that provided a more predictable social order generally and better protection of property rights in particular. These individualists formed the Federalist coalition with remaining hierarchists (e.g., Hamilton), a coalition that constructed a new constitution. While hierarchists achieved some significant victories in this process, Madison and his fellow individualists were highly successful in crafting a document that is clearly individualistic in broad outline (Lovejoy 1961). Egalitarian antifederalists generally opposed this attempt to build a more powerful central government that would shift influence away from the limited state and local governments dominant under the Articles of Confederation. But the politics of national self-interest of the Federalists overwhelmed egalitarians clinging to local practices of republican virtue (Dworetz 1990).

The institutionalization of individualism in this fundamental document facilitated its subsequent exceptional influence in American political life. Yet the cycle of individualistic oscillation between coalitions with egalitarians and hierarchists that I discussed in Chapter 4 dissipated after the Jacksonian era as two conditions supporting these coalitions collapsed.[1] First, American hierarchists were greatly weakened by the Civil War, which separated southern hierarchists from their Whig brethren (Howe 1974) in the North. The defeat of the Confederacy further weakened the institutions through which hierarchy had influenced American political life. Hierarchists would not command the political resources to entice general coalition partners for over a quarter-century. Second, egalitarian coalitions with individualists were progressively foreclosed in the aftermath of the Civil War inasmuch as egalitarians increasingly favored a larger, more active state as a means for coping

---

1. That American political life has involved distinct periods is well recognized (Shafer 1993; Jillson 1993; Sklar 1991; Silbey 1991; Hahn 1991). Some analysts have perceived the process of period change in terms of cycles (Schlesinger 1986; Namenwirth 1973; Resnick and Thomas 1990; Huntington 1981; Skowronek 1993). But the cycles of different authors vary in duration and are either silent or unpersuasive concerning the internal mechanisms or external forces that maintain the regularities they perceive. Still others have found tensions that contribute to oscillation in American political life (Greenstone 1982, 1986; Hirschman 1982; McClosky and Zaller 1984). My own thoughts about shifting cultural coalitions share ground with many of these views but I suggest further that movement does not simply retrace familiar paths as the terms "cycle" and "oscillation" imply. Rather, as I relate below, distinct patterns of coalition dynamics occur in different historical periods.

with the problems industrialization posed for farmers and urban workers. In both the Revolutionary and Jacksonian periods egalitarians generally perceived government favoritism as the primary cause of social inequality (Ellis 1993). Thus egalitarians had shared a preference with individualists for a small, relatively inactive state. But after the Civil War egalitarians increasingly viewed the growing political influence of private industrial wealth as the central source of social inequality. This influence could be countered only through a larger, more active democratic state that responded to numbers rather than wealth. So egalitarians lost an important aspect of their common ground with individualists, who favored laissez-faire with increasing fervor. Thus from the late 1830s through the early 1890s the United States experienced a distinct second period of relative individualistic dominance.

Three rounds of a new coalition pattern occurred during the first three-quarters or so of the twentieth century. The Progressive, the New Deal, and the Great Society coalitions all arose from initiatives prompted by what adherents of the high-group cultures viewed as individualistic excesses. In all three instances hierarchists mobilized to rescue what they perceived as the public interest and were joined by some hybrid individualists who shared a sense that private wealth had exceeded the bounds of responsible behavior. The Progressive movement, while enjoying some egalitarian grass-roots support, was the purest H-I coalition of the three. By creating a federal civil service, it increased the capacities of the central government (Skowronek 1982). Further, it provided a series of increasingly symbolic federal agencies to reassure the public that watchdogs were alert for various forms of individualistic malfeasance. The momentum behind this coalition dissipated in the First World War, and the 1920s represented a return to relative individualistic dominance similar to that of the late nineteenth century.

The Depression prompted the second of these coalitions. This time the stimulus was so severe that the New Deal could be called a "grand coalition" (i.e., including significant portions of all three socially interactive cultures). Egalitarians, however, contributed to this coalition almost exclusively in the capacity of "foot soldiers." This coalition unraveled somewhat in the aftermath of the exertions required by the Second World War, and another period of relative individualistic dominance followed in the 1950s. Lyndon B. Johnson's Great Society coalition, arising in part from the "rediscovery" of poverty (Harrington 1958), had a much more prominent egalitarian composition and agenda. It was the shortest-lived of the three and has suffered the greatest destruction as individualists have become increasingly influential across the final decades of the twentieth century.

Fittingly for a society in which individualism has been highly influential, American political structure is exceptionally decentralized. This structure predates but has been sustained by the Constitution of 1787. This document addresses the basic elements of an individualistic state: internal order and external defense, support of contracts, and a currency system (Friedman 1962). It shields various propertied elites from possible excesses at the hands of popular majorities through a complex system of vertical and horizontal checks and balances reflecting hesitancy about putting power into the hands of self-interested creatures.[2] This structure leaves significant activities in the hands of state and local governments and relies on an existing body of custom for most domestic law and order problems including the rules securing property. Additionally, through its initial amendments the Constitution illustrates the individualism of its founders by preserving a relatively large sphere—vigorously defended into the present—for private life into which the government should not intrude.

Throughout the nineteenth century the most influential aspect of this decentralization was the vertical (federal) element whereby significant powers are divided between the national and state-level governments. Thus as Lowi (1984) suggests, there was—in contrast to the situation in several European societies—no *Staat* that reform movements could succeed by dominating. In this century, as the national government has grown more influential, the horizontal aspect of decentralization has become increasingly prominent. Decentralization at this level involves, not only the multiple branches of government with their distinct personnel, varying terms of office, and counterpoised powers, but also an unusually loosely structured executive branch and a meaningfully bicameral legislature (Lijphart 1984) with relatively independent committees, since political parties have historically weak interest-aggregating capacities. Patterns of interaction among these decentralized political institutions are frequently uncoordinated and conflictual. Results from the 1996 general election suggest that many voters prefer divided government, perhaps even gridlock, to a unified government apt to damage

2. While this constitutional structure remains successful with respect to the imposition of policies with significant widespread effects that particularly concerned Madison (e.g., the imposition of an established religion), constitutional checks and balances have shown little resistance to initiatives backed by groups eyeing concentrated benefits but imposing limited costs, further moderated through wide diffusion, on others. See Wilson 1973, chap. 16.

some interests as a consequence of its relatively unfettered ability to act in support of others.

National social programs have arisen slowly and hesitantly in the United States in stages associated with the three major H-I coalitions of the twentieth-century. First, came the prerequisite state-building efforts of the Progressives. This stage created a national government capable of managing social programs competently.[3] The Progressives enabled the second-stage New Dealers, faced with the Great Depression, to produce a selectively focused welfare state (Skocpol 1987—mostly short-term stimulators of aggregate demand in addition to a long-term program of social insurance pensions for the elderly) in the 1930s. The success of social insurance for the elderly, in turn, facilitated Johnson's third-stage selective expansion of public assistance in the late 1960s.

In spite of these successes, the United States develops social programs hesitantly at best. Wilensky (1975) characterizes it as generally "laggard;" while Skocpol (1987) terms it "selective" on the basis of its failure to develop national health insurance and child allowances. As we saw in Chapter 3, the United States is Esping-Andersen's (1990) exemplar of the liberal (individualistic) welfare state, the most limited of his three welfare-state regimes. Those social insurance programs that do exist are narrow (e.g., Medicare, not national health insurance), and public assistance is increasingly limited through retrenchment (e.g., the demise of Aid to Families with Dependent Children).

Beyond slowness and hesitancy, another hallmark associated with social policy development in a highly individualistic environment is lack of close coordination among different social programs. Skepticism concerning the entire enterprise of public social provision produces narrow programs designed to address particularly compelling aspects of distinct social hazards. The resulting programs leave gaps or inconsistencies among their coverages for different afflictions. For example, elderly Americans with chronic disabling conditions that are not sufficiently acute to warrant the hospitalization and physician treatment covered by Medicare are eligible for public monies to cover nursing home expenses only if they are sufficiently destitute to qualify for public assistance (Medicaid). The separate jurisdictions and piece-

---

3. Yet this hierarchist-led coalition also eliminated a program of pensions for Union veterans that had survived the long stretch of relative individualistic dominance in the late nineteenth century, rather than transforming it into a national program of pensions for the elderly. So this first stage of state development ironically entailed social program retrenchment (Skocpol 1992).

meal approach associated with social program development in an individualistic social environment cumulate in programs with distinct and nonoverlapping prerequisites. Consequently, vulnerable citizens frequently fall through the cracks.

REVISING SOCIAL SECURITY'S REVENUES AND BENEFITS IN 1983

Nature of the Problem and Implications for Various Cultures

Recognition of certain Old Age and Survivors' Insurance (OASI or "social security") funding problems developed in the mid-1970s. The OASI's difficulties arose from two distinct sets of problems. The long-term problems stemmed from changes in longevity and fertility among Americans. When social security was introduced in 1935, Americans were not living much past the program's retirement age of sixty-five. By the early 1980s they were living roughly a decade longer. So pensioners were typically drawing much more heavily on the program's trust fund than had been anticipated decades earlier. Additionally, the "baby boom" from the late 1940s through the early 1960s was followed by sharply reduced birthrates in the late 1960s and 1970s. Thus after 2010 the number of social security beneficiaries will rise sharply, but the number of workers will not. Under these anticipated circumstances long-term program expenditures will exceed program revenues unless benefits are scaled back, taxes are raised, or some combination of the two occurs.

Short-term problems surfaced in the early 1980s. While increasing longevity had contributed to the urgency of this crisis as well, the immediate causes were three other factors. First, OASI reached "maturity" during the 1970s. The program's requirements for prior contributions along with its incremental extension to various segments of the work force produced a situation for several decades after its 1935 adoption in which vastly more persons were involved as contributors than as beneficiaries. By the mid-1970s, however, no large groups of workers had entered the program for some time, and many who had entered through its various earlier expansion steps were reaching retirement. Second, the automatic cost-of-living adjustments (COLAs) that Congress had enacted in 1972 generated sharp benefit increases during the highly inflationary years of the late 1970s. Third, the late 1970s were plagued, not only by inflation, but by relatively high unem-

ployment as well (i.e., stagflation). High levels of unemployment constrained OASI's revenues.[4]

Several presidential commissions had studied these distinct problems, and
President Carter had responded with packages of tax increases coming on
line at various points in the future as well as modest cuts of some benefits
effective in the late 1970s. But rapidly deteriorating economic conditions in
the late 1970s and early 1980s reinforced fears about the long term and
prompted a crisis in the short term. For instance, under the circumstances
prevailing in the early 1980s, the OASI trust fund was predicted to run out
in July 1983. This created what Cook (1993, 6–7) calls a "pressured decision point;" that is, an urgent important decision that would reveal much
about the beliefs, values, and policy priorities of national political elites.

From the perspective of the loose, virtually policy-specific H-E coalition
that had spearheaded social security through sometimes dramatic benefit
increases and related development increments during the preceding decade,
these contingencies represented problems to be resolved by continuing the
approach of the recent past and relying largely—though not exclusively—on
increased program revenues. Yet this was not a viable political course in the
early 1980s. Ronald Reagan had come to Washington bearing the message
that extensive government programs were the problem, not the solution.
The president and his ascendant individualistic allies in the Congress viewed
social security's difficulties as a golden opportunity to reshape America's
largest public program by sharply reducing its benefits. Against this social
context, the increasing problems for funding the social security program
represented a threat to the H-E coalition's policy preferences and an opportunity for individualists to shift the program in the direction of their social
policy ideals.

Options Considered and Their Association with Distinct Rationalities

Relatively pure individualists had accepted social security grudgingly at
best.[5] In the face of the Great Depression a program of limited pensions that

4. In spite of relatively high levels of unemployment, the size of the work force was actually
growing as a result of women and baby boomers entering the labor market in large numbers.
Increased numbers of workers raised OASI revenues. But the number of retirees grew sharply
as well. Further, wages (and thus social security taxes) did not keep up with inflation (and
inflation-adjusted social security benefits). See Schwarz 1988, chap. 3, and Light 1995, 88.
Other factors also contributed to this situation. For instance, prior to 1972 OASI calculations
had been based on a "level-wage" assumption, meaning that the trust fund's future income
had been calculated on the basis of current wage rates. When wages rose, surpluses accrued to
the account. This practice was discontinued as a result of introducing COLAs.

5. Light (1995) provides the most thorough single source for these events. What follows
here emphasizes the beliefs, values, and institutional preferences of rival cultures.

fostered demand for goods and services as well as helped to secure the lives of long-term workers was hard for all but the most zealous individualists to oppose. But across the intervening half-century social security grew in breadth and depth of coverage.[6] Innovations of the early 1970s in particular relaxed linkages between benefits and wages (the so-called equity principle), directing the program more obviously to need (the adequacy principle). By the early 1980s individualists generally thought that the program had gotten out of hand. A few, including White House staff members, wanted to terminate it (Light 1995, 89, 105–6, 130, 218). More commonly, they preferred to scale the program back sharply so that it reflected more clearly a public-private partnership: what they referred to as a stable "three-legged stool" formed by OASI pensions, personal savings, and private pensions (Light 1995, 89).

Among the prominent elites holding this perspective were a number of political figures—mostly but not exclusively Republicans—whose high-profile views on a broad range of other public issues identified them as individualistic.[7] They included President Ronald Reagan and several of his allies, most prominently; Richard Darman, a Republican, Deputy White House Chief of Staff, and member of the smaller informal group that succeeded President Reagan's National Commission on Social Security Reform (hereafter, the National Commission); Representative William Archer (R, Tex.), a member of the House Ways and Means Committee and of the National Commission; Senator William Armstrong (R, Colo.), chairman of the Social Security Subcommittee of the Senate Finance Committee and a member of the National Commission; Robert Beck, a Republican, member of the National Commission and chairperson of the Business Roundtable Social Security Task Force; Alexander Trowbridge, a Democrat, member of the National Commission and president of the National Association of Manufacturers; and Joe Waggoner, a former member of Congress (D, La.) and member of the National Commission.

6. Yet benefits are hardly luxurious once the cost of living is taken into account (Light 1995, 87).

7. Ideally, identification of elites as the adherents of various cultures would be based on survey data designed to measure their grid and group positions, but unfortunately such data do not exist. These data would be ideal both in terms of focusing on precisely what we want to know and also by virtue of being sharply distinct from the dependent variable of what I have called the purposive process: social policy preferences. Ideal data are often unavailable to the social sciences, and most social science efforts work with suboptimal substitutes, as I do here. Nonetheless, the beliefs and values I use as independent variables afford similar face validity and distancing from the dependent variable. Their major drawback is that they are not always derived for each "respondent" independently. Thus I am less certain how accurately they reflect the views of each member of a social collectivity such as a party faction.

As Light (1995, 35–39) shows, individualists such as these perceive poverty as a personal rather than a social problem. They view persons as capable and the social environment as full of opportunity. Individualists believe that there is always work available for anyone willing to work. They reject most claims that supportive public policies are necessary to alleviate poverty. In addition, they value liberty and are inclined to view the increasing payroll tax that has funded social security as a progressively more egregious suppresser of entrepreneurial freedom of action. In their view, program taxes have translated into suboptimal job creation. Similarly, as social security has matured, its administration has become more extensive. Thus, for individualists, the program has become a prime example of the growing public bureaucracy that they perceive as smothering individual initiative.

With the exception of national defense (at least against the context of the cold war), these individualists preferred a more limited public sector than the one that the United States had in the early 1980s. Further, they wished to shift a portion of those public responsibilities of which they approved from the national to state-level governments. Their societal ideal involved a smaller, less active and more decentralized government that was inevitably weaker vis-à-vis market and other private interactions among persons and thus less threatening to their Lockean "negative" conception of liberty. For Reagan and others associated with him, a government active in the domestic realm was the obstacle, not the solution, to a revitalized America.

In terms of social policy preferences, these American individualists preferred to solve the 1980s OASI funding crisis through benefit reductions. As we shall see, however, frontal assaults in the form of immediate benefit cuts did not prove feasible. Instead most individualists settled for longer-term, less direct methods. These included delaying or limiting future COLA increases and raising the future retirement age in conjunction with reducing future benefits, especially those associated with early retirement.[8]

Arrayed against these individualists was a loose high-group coalition, dominated by persons with hierarchical views, but including as well persons with egalitarian beliefs and values. Once again, these designations are facilitated in the instance of these active participants by their high-profile views on a broad range of other public issues. The hierarchical figures included Senator Daniel Patrick Moynihan (D, N.Y.), a member of the National

---

8. Similar proposals are now (2000) routinely offered by the program's friends rather than its critics. In the years since 1983, individualists have increasingly looked to publicly sanctioned individual retirement accounts of various sorts (Weinstein 1998; Friedman 1999).

Commission and the smaller informal group that succeeded it; Robert Ball, a Democrat, former Social Security Commissioner and member of the National Commission and the succeeding group; and Robert Myers, a Democrat, former Social Security Chief Actuary and Executive Director of the National Commission. More egalitarian figures included Representative Thomas P. O'Neill (D, Mass.), then Speaker of the House of Representatives; Lane Kirkland, a Democrat, president of the American Federation of Labor/Congress of Industrial Organizations (AFL/CIO) and member of the National Commission; and Representative Claude Pepper (D, Fla.), chairman of the House Aging Committee and member of the National Commission.

Light (1995, 35–39) shows that members of coalitions like this one tend to see poverty, particularly poverty among the elderly, as a social problem that, while not obviating individual responsibility, nonetheless transcends it. They think that income inequality produces a situation in which saving substantial sums is difficult if not impossible for many workers, that inflationary times undercut the efforts of many of those who do save, and that the most poorly paid have the least access to private pensions. In addition, they view growing public policy expenditures as stimulating the economy, thus creating new employment opportunities. Further, the hierarchical and egalitarian members of this coalition were less concerned by, frequently even favorably inclined toward, the growth of sophisticated public bureaucracies which offered prospects for assuring a minimum level of welfare or greater socioeconomic equality.[9]

Both the hierarchical and egalitarian factions of this loose coalition perceived societal ideals in terms of a much larger and more active public sector than did their individualistic counterparts. The hierarchists among them included some of the most sophisticated statists of the postwar United States, persons who believed in using their expertise to build central public bureaucracies and related institutions that would help to orchestrate social harmony. The egalitarians included persons well known for supporting rights and participatory opportunities designed to improve the lives of weak and vulnerable members of society by supporting greater equality of condition and respect.

9. Different bases for egalitarian and hierarchical support of public social policy bureaucracies are even more obvious in the related policy area of public assistance. Here egalitarians (Wilson 1987) perceive a more sophisticated and active state as better able to provide more inclusive and thus less stigmatizing support for sound persons caught in difficult circumstances, whereas hierarchists (Mead 1986 and Glazer 1988) call for increasingly sophisticated social programs that provide more effective means of educating and socially controlling problematic persons.

Generally, members of this loose H-E coalition had supported OASI's shifts across the 1970s toward an adequacy or need criterion and were also inclined to solve OASI's 1980s funding crisis by increasing revenues. Explicit immediate tax increases were about as impractical in the early 1980s as were immediate benefit cuts. So, like their individualistic counterparts, members of the H-E coalition relied largely on subtle, back-loaded or narrowly focused means for generating new revenues. These strategies included moving forward the effective dates of future tax increases already legislated, perhaps in conjunction with additional future tax increases; drawing on general revenues; bringing previously uncovered workers—primarily federal and other public employees as well as some nonprofit sector workers—into the social security system; and making various changes in accounting procedures (e.g., allowing borrowing among the various social security trust funds—OASI, Disability Insurance, and Hospital Insurance).

Arrayed between the staunch individualists and this H-E coalition were some IH "bifocals" or "wistful" individualists such as Senator Robert Dole (R, Kans.), chairman of the Senate Finance Committee and member of the National Commission and the group that succeeded it; Representative Barber Conable (R, N.Y.), the ranking Republican on the House Ways and Means Committee and a member of the National Commission and the succeeding group; Alan Greenspan, a Republican, former chairman of the Council of Economic Advisors, and chairman of the National Commission and member of the smaller informal group that succeeded it; Representative J. J. Pickle (D, Tex.), chairman of the Social Security Subcommittee of the House Ways and Means Committee; and Representative Dan Rostenkowski (D, Ill.), chairman of the House Ways and Means Committee.

Persons with these IH bifocal cultural biases contributed significantly to resolving social security's funding crisis. They were more willing than the individualists whom I profiled earlier to compromise with hierarchists and egalitarians. They held bifocal perspectives similar to those portrayed by Free and Cantril (1967—see also Feldman and Zaller 1992). One lens of their cultural biases, arising from the pervasive influence of individualistic precepts in American society and dominant in abstract thought, had a favorable view of the individualistic, small-state vision. Ideally, these persons preferred a smaller, less active and more decentralized state. For instance, Dole supported this individualistic orientation toward many public policy matters (e.g., his opposition to the large, complicated, quasi-public bureaucracy entailed by President Clinton's 1994 national health insurance initiative). But another lens of their cultural biases, arising from their own firsthand experiences, was more realistic and thus alerted them, for instance, that ordinary citizens are ill suited to withstand the constant deluge of advertising urging them to spend their incomes, that aggregate demand would likely fall if this were not the case, and that substantial private pensions are limited to relatively high status workers, etc. (Sanger 1997). Thus, these wistful individualists were more willing than their relatively pure individualistic counterparts to compromise ideals that fit imperfectly with their views of reality.

These rival social policy preferences are revealed most clearly among prominent political elites such as those discussed above. But they appeared as well among various interest groups. The individualistic societal ideal involving a smaller, less active and more decentralized government was supported in the resolution of the 1980s social security funding crisis by several powerful business interests. Most prominent among these were various associations such as the National Federation of Independent Business, the Business Roundtable, the National Association of Manufacturers, and—less thoroughly individualistic—the Chamber of Commerce. The individualistic vision appealed to these groups at least in part because of its promise of fostering greater individual initiative, reducing payroll taxes and other regulations perceived as stifling entrepreneurial activity, and reversing the trend of growing public bureaucracies. These groups generally favored resolving social security's problems by cutting benefits. Their representatives lobbied both houses of Congress as well as a favorably disposed executive, and some were members of successive groups that devised a package of proposals for resolving the funding crisis.

Other groups representing organized labor (the AFL/CIO) and retired persons (the National Council of Senior Citizens, and less importantly the American Association of Retired Persons—AARP)[10] were more comfortable with a vision of larger, more active government. These groups tended to favor the resolution of the crisis through increased revenues that would allow the continuation of existing social security benefits. While these groups—like the elite coalition that they supported—lacked a unicultural voice, the AFL/CIO and the National Council projected clear egalitarian concern, consistent with their views on many other public issues, that an active public sector support the welfare of weak and vulnerable persons in the lower reaches of the socioeconomic hierarchy.

10. Some organizations with broad constituencies, such as AARP and also the Chamber of Commerce, were unable to adopt a position consistent with one of grid-group theory's cultures across the various issues relating to securing social security's funding.

Thus attentive elites were not only organized for political action on either side of the reduce-benefits/raise-revenues cultural divide but the organizations to which they belonged (e.g., factions of political parties and a range of interest groups) were mobilized for political action on this issue. The organization of significant segments of political elites, activists, and attentive publics reduces the level-of-analysis difficulties, as I discussed in Chapter 1, by providing persons sharing particular cultural identities with practical means for effecting their varying purposes. Different organizations are likely to provide incomplete (in terms of their coverage of cultural adherents) and imperfect (in the sense that not all members of an organization will be adherents of the same culture) representations of particular cultures. Yet in terms of societal public policy formulation, cultures often effect their purposes through the actions of particularly prominent individual adherents and the organizations whose activities they influence.

Appropriately worded surveys might improve the degree to which members of the general public could be categorized into one of grid-group theory's cultures, but existing data are not terribly helpful in this regard. In November 1982, for instance, while 49 percent of the public opposed tax increases, 75 percent rejected benefit reductions (Light 1995, 65).[11] Although these opinions provide little basis for estimating cultures, they alerted each side in the elite conflict over how to cope with OASI's funding crisis that large portions of public opinion were opposed to what they most wished to do.

Ronald Reagan's assumption of the presidency in early 1981 surely encouraged individualists to pursue their agenda of refashioning American political institutions by reducing the size and activity (apart from national defense) of the public sector. Nonetheless, the Reagan administration was initially hesitant to suggest proposals for resolving the social security funding crisis. Since individualists were strongly represented among national political elites, it was a foregone conclusion that the crisis would be resolved in part through benefit cuts. This being the case, the administration preferred to react to the suggestions of others in this regard rather than acquiring the onus themselves for initiating proposals that a large majority of the general public opposed. Further, the closer the social security system came to a crisis, the more leverage individualists thought they would have for making deep cuts. So they were in no hurry to move (Light 1995, 112).

11. Considerable overlap (i.e., persons loading themselves onto the indices of more than one culture) is fairly common among ordinary citizens (Coughlin and Lockhart 1998). But it virtually disappears among political activists and elites (Ellis and Thompson 1997).

Events initially appeared to be playing into the hands of the individualists. Early in 1981 Representative Pickle (D, Tex.), chairman of the Social Security Subcommittee of the House Ways and Means Committee, initiated what he saw as a responsible but relatively program-friendly proposal for resolving the situation through a combination of means. To meet his estimate of the short-term crisis, Pickle drew on general revenues (raised through less regressive taxation) and a variety of new accounting practices (e.g., interfund borrowing). He attacked the program's long-term financial problems through a combination of gradual future (beginning in 1990) increases in the retirement age to sixty-eight as well as reductions (by about 15 percent) in early retirement benefits. This proposal thus attempted to resolve the short-term crisis, attributable in large part to unforeseen short-term economic trends, by increased revenues so program beneficiaries would suffer no immediate unexpected loss of support. Then Pickle addressed the larger long-term problem through delayed and gradual reductions in benefits that reflected the increasing longevity of the American population. Since these long-term changes would not come on line for nearly a decade, persons would have time to adjust to these new more realistic provisions.

As a consequence of its general societal vision; however, the Reagan administration soon offered its own social security proposals rather than sticking with its initial strategy of reacting to initiatives proposed by others for solving the problems of the OASI. The overall character of the government had a much higher priority in the Reagan administration than its strategy toward social security, and administration budgetary requirements soon made certain demands on social security. David Stockman, director of the Office of Management and Budget, was attempting to reshape the federal government to the Reagan administration's preferences by raising defense expenditures, cutting taxes, and balancing the budget through cutting sharply everywhere else. By April 1981 Stockman concluded that nothing other than large immediate social security cuts would allow him to accomplish these objectives. Accordingly, he proposed within the administration sharp cuts in current early retirement benefits, elimination of the minimum benefit provisions, and delays in implementing COLAs. These cuts—with immediate effects on 60 million persons—would reduce federal expenses by $45 billion in the short term. Although their short-term effects were bound to upset a large portion of the public and the H-E elite social security coalition, the administration presented Stockman's recommendations to Congress in May 1981.

Reaction among interest groups representing the elderly and organized labor was swift and negative. Attentive publics reacted negatively as well. In April 1981 70 percent of the elderly approved of Reagan's activities as president. This support fell sharply and by August 1981 69 percent disapproved of Reagan's handling of social security. In spite of the obviously deleterious consequences to their own cause, individualists revived proposals for immediate benefit cuts on subsequent occasions over the next few months. In June, for instance, the administration was able to maneuver the elimination of the minimum benefit provisions through Congress. These provisions were eventually restored before any actual cuts in benefits occurred. But the Reagan administration's public opinion position suffered from portrayals of the potential consequences for approximately three million extremely poor elderly women affected by the elimination of the minimum benefit. Again in August, Stockman made another unsuccessful effort to attain a delay in implementing COLAs.

Proposals of immediate benefit cuts, for which beneficiaries could not reasonably be prepared, created a specter that was poorly accepted by the public. Changes in public opinion in turn emboldened the H-E social security coalition among national elites to resist administration efforts. Accordingly, President Reagan shifted strategy from a frontal assault on the program, driven by his general vision of the appropriate character of government, to an effort to achieve a compromise on social security in a setting offering more protection from the censure of public opinion. To this end President Reagan and House Speaker O'Neill, the informal leader of the H-E party to this struggle, collaborated in the formation of several informal or at least less high-profile groups whose purpose was to construct a compromise that institutions more in the limelight—the Congress and the presidency—could accept without taking full responsibility for the details.

Relative Reliance on Benefit Reductions as Opposed to Revenue Increases

While in 1980 social security still maintained a virtually unbroken record of growth across nearly a half-century, the election of 1980 signaled a shift of momentum between the ascendant individualists who had won the presidency and acquired greater influence—as registered by a Republican majority—in the Senate and the H-E coalition that had persisted since the Great Depression, but was—in the absence of similarly disruptive historical contingencies—now fading in preeminence. Although political party affiliation is, even among political elites, an imperfect index of culture, nonetheless, during the early 1980s and in both its general societal vision and the values underlying it, the Republican Party—which controlled the presidency and the Senate—was more thoroughly individualistic than the Democratic Party. Additionally, its economically conservative or individualistic faction was much more tenacious in its attack on social programs than its socially conservative faction was stalwart in their defense. Social policy represented the essence of the aspects of government that Ronald Reagan and many of his electoral coattails had come to Washington to crush. Across the early 1980s, the loose H-E coalition that supported social security found its primary base of operations in the Democratic Party and the House of Representatives over which the party retained control. Democratic representatives came from all three of grid-group theory's socially interactive cultures, but the "parliamentary" party was, nonetheless, distinctly less individualistic and more high-group than the Republicans. Thus the struggle over social security's financial crisis took place in a context in which individualists were resurgent and more influential among relevant political elites than the adherents of the high-group cultures.

The National Commission on Social Security Reform, the fourth such commission in three years (Light 1995, 154), was the first (appointed in September 1981) and most public of the groups tasked to work out a compromise agreement. While the National Commission's meetings were announced and open, they attracted less public scrutiny than the activities of Congress. The National Commission accomplished little until after the 1982 congressional election. While this election did not change the formal balance of power in either house of Congress, the increased popularity of Democratic candidates did suggest that the public was more favorably disposed to the H-E coalition's position on what had become the high-profile issue of social security reform. Thus the election further discouraged the individualistic forces that had already been bruised on social security issues during the preceding two years. Meeting in the immediate aftermath of the election (November 11–13, 1982), the National Commission was able to make some modest though important progress formulating significant aspects of the decision outcome. First, it reached agreement on the size of the OASI problem: $150–200 billion in the short term and 1.8 percent of payroll in the long term.[12] Second, while the National Commission did not officially sanction a compromise formula, these November sessions elicited

12. Using percent of payroll in the long term allowed both individualists and members of the H-E coalition to avoid speaking in terms of $1.5 trillion of tax increases or benefit cuts.

what became an informal guideline: roughly one-half of the required funds would come from increased revenues and the other half from benefit reductions. Media scrutiny hampered the National Commission's efforts at greater specification, so action on this issue moved to other forums.

Two subsequent groups were less formal than the National Commission. They sought to meet secretly and without public records. The first of these was a seventeen-member body formed in March 1982. This group also made little progress; the individualistic and HE members simply held irreconcilable positions. As member Paul Laxalt put it: "I rather think now, looking back, that this effort was dead in the water from the beginning. The philosophical differences were just too great to overcome" (Tate 1982, 968).

A second group, formed in January 1983, was smaller. It consisted of five members of the now defunct National Commission (Robert Ball, Barber Conable, Robert Dole, Alan Greenspan, and Daniel Patrick Moynihan) and four White House staffers (David Stockman, Chief of Staff James Baker III, Richard Darman, and Congressional Liaison Kenneth Duberstein). This group inherited and attempted to apply the November 1982 understandings of the National Commission. Its goal was to achieve a compromise proposal—acceptable to President Reagan and the Speaker of the House, Congressman O'Neill—that could be submitted at the outset of the new Congress on a take-it-or-leave-it basis and thus be in place in time to provide the necessary July 1983 OASI trust fund support.

This nine-member group reached an agreement on a package that derived a short-term infusion of $168 billion by relying predominantly on revenue increases. (See Table 7.) Their long-term package fell short of the 1.8 percent of payroll goal, totaling about 1.2 percent, and relied more thoroughly on benefit reductions. This pattern allowed persons to adjust to a new benefit structure over time and appears to have reduced adverse reactions among the general public. The group recommended that Congress either raise the retirement age or increase future OASI taxes to come up with the final 0.6 percent of payroll. This agreement was then attributed to the National Commission as a device for deflecting blame from Congress.

But Congress was left with the task of formulating provisions to add roughly 0.6 percent of payroll in the long term. The House, prompted by J. J. Pickle, voted to do this by gradually raising the future retirement age to sixty-seven (one-year steps in 2003 and 2027) and decreasing—by about 10 percent—early retirement benefits (Kato 1991, 105). These House decisions added benefit reductions to the total, producing a package in which

Table 7   Provisions of the January 1983 Recommendations of the National Commission on Social Security Reform

Proposal	Short-term (billions $)	Long term (% payroll)
Revenue increases		
Covering nonprofit and new federal employees	$20	.30
Prohibited withdrawal of state and local public employees	3	—
Tax acceleration	40	.02
Self-employment tax increase	18	.19
Lump-sum military wage credits	18	—
Benefit reductions		
Taxation of upper-income retirees' benefits	30	.60
Six-month COLA delays	40	.27
Increased benefits	(1)	(.17)
Total	$168	1.21

SOURCE: Light 1995, 180. The original score is National Commission on National Security Reform 1983.

benefit reductions predominated (55 percent) over revenue increases.[13] The Senate passed a contrasting bill, differing most importantly in the long term: raising the retirement age to sixty-six and cutting benefit levels beginning in the year 2000. A conference committee resolved most differences, including how to handle the long-term deficit, in favor of the House. President Reagan

13. Mathematical precision on this point remains hostage to categorization dilemmas. For instance, even bringing new workers into the system, while generally accepted as a revenue enhancement measure, would at some point during the period under consideration (1983–2025) entail benefit increases (i.e., more beneficiaries) as well. A more controversial issue is how to treat the taxation of upper-income retirees' benefits. This factor represents *both* a gain for revenues *and* a cut in benefits. Different categorization schemes will produce varying ratios of revenue increases to benefit reductions. But I think only strained interpretations will produce ratios at odds with my view of the latter predominating over the former. I calculate as follows.

First, I split the monies attributable to the taxation of upper-income retirees' benefits, counting half as increased revenues and half as benefit reductions. Then I add this latter amount to other benefit reductions and subtract benefit increases to get net benefit reductions: 0.30 (one-half of taxation of upper-income retirees' benefits) + 0.27 (COLA delays) + 0.58 (additional benefit reductions attributable to congressional initiative) − 0.17 (benefit increases) = 0.98. I calculate revenue increases as follows: 0.30 (one-half of taxation of upper-income retirees'

signed the bill on April 20, 1983, in time to avert a July 1983 shortfall. So in this aspect of the decision outcome, neither the individualistic faction nor the H-E coalition could impose its preferred policy design on the other. Each had to compromise its preferences significantly, but the ascendant individualists realized their preferences more fully than did the fading H-E coalition.

Explicitness of the Focus on Long-Term Financial Costs

As we shall see in subsequent cases, the political significance of specifying how program costs will be financed out into the future is a peculiarly American or, more precisely, individualistic concern. Clear delineation of how long-term revenue requirements will be met appears in none of the other cases in this study and likely represents an index of individualistic strength. Because of their hesitancy about the enterprise of public social provision, individualists are tenacious in directing attention to the uncertainties of long-term funding questions. The high-group cultures find these questions difficult to answer convincingly and try to find various ways of avoiding them. In the 1983 American instance, individualists wanted, not only to specify the sources of these additional revenues clearly, but also to pay for these revenue increases (necessary largely to fund existing benefits, not benefit increases) with benefit reductions.

When individualists are highly influential, adherents of other cultures must attend to their characteristic distaste for the long-term costs of public social programs. Consequently, in the current deliberations over social security's future, President Clinton and other relatively high-group defenders of social security have accepted what individualists claim is the program's traditional goal of assuring solvency an astounding seventy-five years into the future (Stevenson 1999). Few, if any, other and less-individualistic societies place much credence on requiring such remarkable foresight of public policy. Indeed, individualistic demands in this regard are likely better interpreted as efforts to hinder the formation of extensive public social programs than as confidence in careful public-sector planning.

---

benefits) + 0.30 (revenues from covering new persons) + 0.02 (tax acceleration) + 0.19 (self-employment tax increase) = 0.81. So benefit reductions represent 98/179 or 55%; while revenue increases amount to 81/179 or 45%. While the short-term column in Table 7 is weighted in favor of revenue increases, the amounts in this column are so much smaller that they have little impact on the long-term imbalance.

Cultural Mechanisms of Political Change

Individualists exercised remarkable influence on this agreement. Social security is the most popular of American social programs (Coughlin 1980), and it serves the largest beneficiary group, covering over 90 percent of the population. Further, the OASI aspects of social security are essentially scandal free, and the program's benefits are hardly extravagant in comparison to the cost of living. Moreover, as the public sector financial statistics presented earlier indicate (see Table 2), Americans are taxed less heavily than their counterparts in other advanced industrial societies. Additionally, in terms of future worker/beneficiary ratios and net pension liabilities (Table 6), the United States enjoys a favorable situation in comparison to the Federal Republic and Japan. So the 1983 decision on social security is likely the mildest of the four "pressured decision points" (Cook 1993, 6) considered in this study. Yet when OASI faced a funding crisis, individualists favoring program retrenchment had enough political strength to deflect the earlier trajectory of benefit growth sharply downward.

Thus the complete package required net benefit reductions of close to 1 percent of payroll (nearly $700 billion). Considering the trajectory that social security had followed from the mid-1940s, and particularly across the early 1970s, this result represented a sharp change in course. President Carter had made some modest benefit cuts in the late 1970s, but this was the first time that the program had suffered cuts in (largely future) benefits remotely approaching this magnitude. Against the program's historical experience, this decision represented a new trajectory and a substantial victory for individualists.[14]

This change in the trajectory of social security's development signals a return to the baseline of American political life: relative individualistic dominance. From the perspective of the early twenty-first century it looks as if the period during which high-group cultures experienced considerable success in realizing their preferences in a society in which individualism is frequently predominant, has come to an end. The Great Depression and the Second World War mobilized and emboldened the high-group cultures, sowed doubt among individualists, and fostered a coalition among adherents of all three cultures that created both a selectively focused welfare state (Skocpol 1987) and a large standing military. Yet the former in particular

---

14. For examples of increasing individualistic influence in social security's subsequent history, see Peterson 1996, Kingson and Schulz 1996, Passell 1996, DiLorenzo 1996, Pear 1997, and Heclo 1998.

fit poorly with the individualistic preferences that are so influential across the long haul in American political life (Devine 1972).

So while the dramatic mid-twentieth-century social dislocations created opportunities for the high-group cultures, more placid recent conditions have favored individualists. In the absence of recurrent historical contingencies as severe as the Depression, expensive social programs have overloaded a political system whose members may be willing to accept the benefits they provide but are sufficiently reluctant to levy the taxes required to fund their services that for a time government routinely ran large deficits (Free and Cantril 1967; Crozier, Huntington, and Watanuki 1975; Steinmo 1995). Accordingly, over the last two decades social programs have become increasingly vulnerable as individualistic pressure for balancing the federal budget through expenditure reduction has become more intense. While a few modest exceptions exist, the trajectory shift experienced by social security in 1983 has served as a bellwether for the general fortunes of American public social programs ever since.

THE SOVIET STRUGGLE OVER CONSUMER PRICE SUBSIDIES, 1987–1991

RELATIVE CULTURAL INFLUENCE AND INSTITUTIONAL CONSEQUENCES

In contrast to the preeminence of individualism in American political culture, Russian political culture—before, during, and after the Soviet period—has been dominated by hierarchy (Barghoorn 1952; White 1979; Hill 1985; Burant 1987; J. Hahn 1991).[1] Even in the near past, urban Russian Jewish émigrés, among the most cosmopolitan elements of the former Soviet population, were on average noticeably more hierarchical than Americans (Gitel-

---

1. My other three case studies focus on pension programs for the elderly, which are the single most expensive social programs in each of these societies. Further, I regard these programs as the central pillar of the welfare state in these societies. I think that consumer price subsidies, as opposed to pensions for the elderly, represent the counterpart for this pillar in the Soviet instance. If I am wrong about this, an examination of Soviet pensions for the elderly, which Gorbachev was expanding, would lead to similar conclusions about the relative influence of rival cultures. But the consumer price subsidies question was hotly contested and thus reveals far more about the cultural orientations of rival elite factions.

man 1977). According to Lapidus, Soviet citizens respected "order, discipline, paternalism and social conservatism. They highly value security and stability in social and political life and appear to assign relatively low importance to political and civil liberties" (1983, 189). But various historical contingencies have provided an idiosyncratic character to Russian hierarchy and shifting relations between it and other cultures. For instance, commentators have long remarked that the relatively closed or exclusive character of various Russian hierarchies produces large numbers of fatalists, particularly among society's lower ranks (Smith 1990; see also Inkeles 1988 and Inkeles and Bauer 1968).

Four distinct variations on the theme of hierarchy dominated Soviet politics in turn (Volkogonov 1998). The first of these was the bifocal EH-transforming-to-HE perspective of Lenin's revolutionary vanguard, which was preeminent from 1917 through roughly 1924. Stalin's subsequent rule, from roughly 1927 through 1953, represented a period of perverted (arbitrary and exclusive) tyrannical hierarchy. The years from 1955 through roughly 1982 mark the efforts of Khrushchev and Brezhnev to create a more routinized and inclusive Party-directed hierarchy free from the extreme personal indulgences of Stalin's period. During the 1970s, under Brezhnev, this effort lost its momentum, suffering increasing ossification and corruption. From 1985 through 1991 Gorbachev attempted to mix hierarchy with greater elements of individualism in both political and economic institutions.

Some Western Soviet analysts argue that Khrushchev and Brezhnev's more routinized and inclusive system of Party rule was based increasingly on an implicit "social contract" (Cook 1993; Lapidus 1983).[2] In effect, the Party applied its expertise toward providing a better life for the Soviet population. This better life had a progressively "consumerist" orientation, including concerns such as stable employment, better wages, more and better goods, and more inclusive and extensive social program benefits. In return, the Party demanded the unchallenged right to direct society. It expected interests such as labor to discipline themselves, thus helping to maintain an orderly work environment without strikes or other forms of disruption. But Brezhnev's favored practice of using central direction to mobilize great quantities of labor and other resources to the task of developing societal capacities, an approach that had worked effectively if extremely painfully during the first half-century of Soviet experience, produced increasingly dis-

---

2. See Hazard's related discussion of law under the "mature socialism" of Brezhnev (1982, 98).

couraging results amid the rapidly developing technology and shifting economic circumstances of the 1970s and 1980s (Nove 1986; Kaser 1982).

Gorbachev brought new ideas and great energy to the helm in 1985, seeking to invigorate both political and economic institutions through more explicit competition. He fostered a limited parliamentary democracy. Economically, he generated furious arguments by proposing the private ownership of productive property; the self-financing of enterprises; the linking of economic reward to performance, which would entail the firing of incompetent workers; and the reduction of price subsidies, which would increase the role of market forces in the setting of prices. While these suggestions acquired advocates among the limited audiences that were initially attentive, resistance grew as their practical consequences as well as the beliefs and values on which they were based became more widely and clearly recognized.

In striking contrast to the United States, Soviet national political and economic institutions exhibited an exceptionally centralized interaction pattern. Although the Communist Party comprised only a tiny fraction of the population, it held a virtual monopoly on political power. The Party, particularly through its Politburo, guided the activities of centrally directed and, in principle, closely coordinated government bureaucracies. Such ambitious social engineering efforts routinely proliferate inconvenient unforeseen consequences, however, and varying circumstances and interests at different locations within this dominant structure made policy execution and coordination more difficult than its high degree of centralization suggests.

Cultural preferences contributed importantly to the design of basic Soviet political-economic institutions. While scholars of Soviet politics differ in how they characterize the societal vision of early Soviet leaders (cf. Fainsod 1958, Tucker 1987, and Pipes 1994), there is widespread agreement that these leaders thought the appropriate means for constructing the good society from the ashes of the tsarist system were elite direction and close control of the general population. Thus we have a characteristic hierarchical view in which experts in various social matters—the Party—provide vision and direction for the rest of society. These experts proffer guidance in large measure by creating institutions designed to engender progress toward the vision—in this case the communist period of history. Ordinary humans, less capable of recognizing the goal or of independently coordinating their actions to achieve it, are then redeemed by the Party's efforts to integrate their lives—through force if necessary—into the activities of these institutions. The Soviets stand out among hierarchists primarily in their zeal to integrate virtually all aspects of life into their vision. Unfortunately, twentieth-century technology afforded them considerable capacity for furthering this totalitarian goal.

During the periods dominated by Lenin and Stalin, Soviet income maintenance programs and some social services fell into a familiar—from the tsars—abyss of relative neglect. Indeed, these aspects of social policy originally had no significant institutional presence above the republic level. The selective reversal of this marginalization of the Revolution's social policy agenda (Madison 1968, 80) began during the Khrushchev-Brezhnev years. But despite these changes in the 1960s and 1970s, the breadth and depth of Soviet income maintenance and social service programs, while much improved over the period dominated by Lenin and Stalin, remained "restrictive and niggardly" by the standards of Western Europe (McAuley 1979, 297; see also Dobson 1988, Davis 1988, and McAuley 1982). After the mid-1960s, however, Brezhnev's new social consumption spending began to be directed increasingly at need rather than work performance. This change developed less through altering the structure of income maintenance programs than through increasing reliance on employment, wages, and a type of social program, consumer price subsidies, that represents a hallmark of social systems with highly centralized and closely coordinated decision making (Denton 1981; Ofer and Vinokur 1988).

Esping-Andersen (1990) does not include the Soviet Union in his analysis because it obviously cannot represent a type of welfare capitalism. Nonetheless, Soviet experience can be related to Esping-Andersen's three models. In terms of policy outcomes the Soviet Union, surprisingly, most closely resembled the liberal welfare-state regime. Prior to the mid-1960s, the Soviet welfare state was quite small. Thereafter, the values underlying the attitudes of the Soviet leader toward social consumption increasingly resembled those which Esping-Andersen associates with corporatist welfare-state regimes. Accordingly, programs became more inclusive, and their benefits grew more extensive. This policy transition offers one index of the transformation of the Soviet leadership into a more conventional group of hierarchists. Additionally, various sorts of consumer subsidies grew even more sharply than income maintenance programs and social services, easing the material provision problems of large numbers of persons near the bottom of the socioeconomic hierarchy, including the vast majority of the elderly (Matthews 1986). Nonetheless, Soviet social policy outcomes continued to lag behind those of Western corporatist welfare-state regimes.

Comparing Soviet national account statistics with those of Western societies is generally fraught with hazards (Marer 1985; Aslund 1990); nonetheless, some basic comparisons are helpful. With a somewhat larger population than the United States (267 to 227 million in 1980), the Soviet Union had an economy that was about half the size of the American. In the early 1980s these characteristics produced Soviet GNP/capita figures roughly one-third those of the United States (Aslund 1990, 49; Marer 1985, 7).

Table 8 presents data at five-year intervals across the Soviet Union's last three decades that afford comparisons with the United States.[3] Additionally, according to Rowen and Wolf (1990), in the early 1980s the Soviet Union was spending a vastly higher proportion of its GNP (25 percent as opposed to 7 percent) on defense than was the United States. In essence, then, Soviet elites were guiding a society just beyond the third-world level that incongruously supported a large, relatively sophisticated and immensely expensive military-industrial complex. The high priority that these hierarchists placed on security and order severely limited the resources remaining for public social provision. Prior to the mid-1950s the leadership did not consider this to be much of a problem. Economic growth surged, and preeminent leaders did not place a high priority on social consumption.

Table 8 Soviet Economic and Social Policy Statistics

Year	Estimated GNP (in billions of rubles)[a]	Estimated GNP (as a percentage of the U.S. GNP)[b]	Social Consumption[c] (in billions of rubles)	(as a percentage of GNP)
1960	177.7	67	27.3	15.4
1965	242.4	63	41.9	17.3
1970	370.5	55	69.1	18.6
1975	475.8	56	95.0	20.0
1980	614.5	56	120.1	19.5
1985	778.3	53	141.6	18.2
1990	875.4	49	192.3	22.0

[a] Data are from Aslund 1990, 37, except for 1990 which is actually 1988 GDP from UN 1992, 2059.

[b] Data are from Shoup 1981, 385, and U.S. Dept. of Commerce (Statistical Abstract of the United States—various years).

[c] The Soviet "social consumption" category is roughly equivalent with total social program expenditures. Data are derived from McAuley 1982, 152, 155, and 1979, 324, and Aslund 1991b, 25. The ruble figure for 1980 is actually from 1979.

3. Estimates of Soviet GNP or GDP vary sharply; see Shoup 1981, 385. Nonetheless, I think that the trend in Table 8 is clear.

After the mid-1960s resource limitations on domestic material welfare became progressively more obvious and problematic. In the late 1950s Khrushchev could confidently predict that the Soviet Union would bury capitalism under a mountain of socialist products. By the mid-1970s it was becoming clear to a number of Soviet officials that it would not. So in spite of obvious determination to improve the material welfare of the Soviet population, Soviet leaders managed, across the last two decades of their society's existence, only to work *up* to the spending levels (as a proportion of GNP) of liberal welfare-state regimes. In spite of their aspirations to do better, their efforts were crippled by the inefficient economic institutions to which they were dedicated as well as the military options through which they supported their high-priority security and order concerns. These preferences were, in turn, characteristic of their hierarchical culture, and that culture, with its devotion to one right way (sanctioned by society's experts) of doing things, was highly resistant to recognizing these crippling effects.

Gorbachev aspired to furthering the transformation of Soviet social policy into a more thorough representation of the corporatist regime (Brown 1996, 102). But he needed first to accomplish more basic reforms: increasing the efficiency of the Soviet economy and constructing a more openly competitive political setting that would support controversial economic changes. The various partial changes in these directions that Gorbachev accomplished in the late 1980s, however, created a variety of new problems. Most important, success in moving to self-financed enterprises required the elimination of widespread consumer price subsidies on many basic goods. So Gorbachev's aspirations for economic and political reform created a direct clash with what had become an increasingly central element of the Soviet welfare state.

THE FATE OF SOVIET CONSUMER PRICE SUBSIDIES, 1987–1991

Nature of the Problem and Implications for Various Cultures

Central to Gorbachev's first wave of economic reform was the Law on State Enterprises, which was adopted by the Supreme Soviet in June 1987 (effective January 1, 1988). It drew on a broader effort to restructure the Soviet economy that included the Law on Individual Labor Activity (1986) and the Law on Cooperatives (1988). The Law on Individual Labor Activity altered previous assurances of employment in order to facilitate the shifting of workers from menial positions in agriculture and industry to what were hoped to be more productive positions in the service sector. The Law on State Enterprises focused particularly on creating self-financed production enterprises. That is, production units were to become self-supporting, which meant that they had to be able to control the number and capacities of their employees. Increasingly, enterprises were to derive their income from the direct purchases of other enterprises, which were attracted to their products rather than through massive state orders. While Soviet officials appear to have underestimated the potential for worker dislocation that these changes might produce (Cook 1993, 96), they nonetheless began constructing a society-wide system of job-placement services designed to link displaced workers with new employment opportunities. Further, Gorbachev initiated a meritocratic wage reform designed to fight "excessive egalitarianism" in the existing wage structure, promulgated a new system of third-party (i.e., neither enterprise nor government but still centrally directed) quality control (Gorbachev 1995, 223), and—through the Law on Cooperatives— authorized a limited privatization of various consumer services.

For these changes to succeed in generating economic benefits, enterprises needed to be able to adjust their prices with an eye toward both covering their costs and acquiring advantages over competitors. Yet a system of consumer price subsidies (price controls in a market setting) covering a range of commonly purchased goods stood in the way. These subsidies had to be removed (or at least sharply reduced in the short term in order for prices to reflect enterprise costs more adequately) if radical economic reform were to succeed. According to Gorbachev, for instance: "Radical reform of price formation is the most important component of economic restructuring. Without it a complete changeover to the new economic mechanism is impossible" (quoted in Cook 1993, 102; see also Gorbachev 1995, 229). Yet no general reduction—much less the complete elimination—of consumer price subsidies occurred until 1991.

While Gorbachev and other reformers thought that various market reforms (i.e., reforms of an individualistic character) were essential to improving Soviet economic performance and achieving related goals, they had as well considerable hesitancy about eliminating consumer price subsidies. The effects of the various economic legislative initiatives across 1986–88 were already distressing to the public. Reducing the virtual guarantee of employment within a small geographic area threatened to create pools of at least temporarily unemployed persons, a new and frightening phenomenon in the

Soviet Union. Limited privatization (largely of consumer service cooperatives) drove up the costs of crucial social services such as medical care, and
wage increases in enterprises further fueled inflation. Enterprises also used
their increased flexibility to avoid producing goods covered by consumer
price subsidies, frequently through modest changes that allowed them to
identify the products differently and thus to charge more for them. So the
Soviet economy was experiencing shortages of basic goods, inflation, and
the specter of unemployment simultaneously. Freeing prices would have
contributed to more inflation and, in the short term at any rate, more shortages triggered by panic buying. Gorbachev had the impression of a citizenry
in terror of the decline in living standards that they thought a free market—
"an unknown monster"—would bring (1995, 377). Like American individualists in the early 1980s, who grew hesitant about cutting next month's
social security benefits, Soviet economic reformers were reluctant to drop
consumer price subsidies and thereby dramatically increase the costs of
basic goods.

Even more important, the status of consumer price subsidies was the
lightning rod for the broader issue about the future character of Soviet economic institutions (indeed Soviet society generally). Suggestions of radical
reform elicited sharp resistance from a range of Soviet elites based on a
broad spectrum of concerns varying from personal self-interest and organizational integrity to more fundamental conceptions of the nature of constructive and moral social contributions. Many Soviet officials valued order
more than efficiency, believed in central political and economic control, and
resisted Gorbachev's efforts to achieve greater political openness and economic decentralization. Thus the last years of Soviet political life centered
around a conflict between persons for whom growing Soviet economic
problems represented an opportunity for rejuvenating the Soviet economy
and polity through introducing individualistic institutions (with which they
had little practical experience) and the supporters of traditional Soviet hierarchical institutions who recognized that their values and practical political
objectives were threatened by these prospective changes.

Options Considered and Their Association with Distinct Rationalities

No other conflict between culturally constrained rationalities of remotely
this prominence had occurred in the Soviet Union for a half-century.[4] So

4. This section draws particularly on Aslund 1991a, 1991b, and 1992; Brown 1996; Gorbachev 1995; and Cook 1993.

this episode is not typical of Soviet political life, and examining other conflict episodes across this half-century would reveal narrower issues among various tributaries of hierarchy. This anomalous episode arises in part from the distressing decline of Soviet economic fortunes in a changing world and as well from the somewhat surprising presence among prominent political officials of a small number of persons with significant individualistic faces to their bifocal cultural biases. These HI "bifocals" persisted in considering an unusual set of options for dealing with Soviet economic difficulties.

Yet movement toward radical economic change was piecemeal, and hesitancy about eliminating, or at least sharply reducing, existing consumer price subsidies so that prices better reflected production costs and market demand had more complex roots than merely self-interested pragmatism or sympathy for persons on limited incomes. The Soviet leadership, like the American leadership, was split by rival cultural conceptions of how the world worked, what was desirable, and how to achieve it. On one side of this conflict were the "radical economic reformers," whose cultural biases included a prominent face of individualistic views largely untainted by individualistic practice. The dominant figures in this faction varied a bit across time. Gorbachev, General Secretary of the Communist Party and later President of the Soviet Union, was the primary initiator. Eduard Shevardnadze, another Politburo member and foreign minister, was a major supporter, as were Alexsandr Yakovlev, Central Committee Secretary for International Policy, and Vadim Medvedev, Central Committee Secretary for Ideology, after they joined the Politburo. Prominent in this faction as well were leading academics, such as Tatyana Zaslavskaya, a sociologist, and a number of economists, including Abel Aganbegyan and Leonid Abalkin during the first wave of reform (1986–87) and Stanislav Shatalin and Nikolai Petrakov during the 1989–91 period.

This radical reform faction believed in and pushed—with varying pressure at different junctures—for the extensive replacement of existing economic institutions and subsequent heavy reliance on institutions associated with market individualism. Aganbegyan (1988, 67–81) asserts that the individualistic lodestar of economic efficiency was the central objective of the radical reformers. A survey of various voices in this faction suggests that economic efficiency was frequently an instrumental value (Aslund 1991a, 27–39). It was the means for achieving a better material life for the Soviet population and assuring the international status of the Soviet Union (Aslund 1991a, 28). At the outset of his leadership in 1985 Gorbachev appears to have been uncertain about the precise nature of the economic reforms he sought, but by the 1986–88 period in which his initial reforms were concentrated, the influence of academic economists had shifted his thinking in the direction of market economics similar to the path that the Hungarians had taken. As individualistic societal visions go, this one was both tentative and modest. No one in this faction would have felt comfortable with the America of Ronald Reagan's vision.[5]

Gorbachev's early rhetoric focused on problems so widely recognized by leading Soviet officials and academics that his criticisms and relatively vague suggestions for improvement, normally amounting to little more than slogans ("accelerating economic development"), were initially generally well received (Cook 1993, 89). But as the nature of the reforms that he sought became clearer across the 1986–87 period, resistance developed among the Soviet elite. The most fundamental opposition came from a neo-Stalinist group whose societal vision was realized in the great prewar development mobilizations. Yegor Ligachev, ironically brought into the Politburo by Gorbachev, was the most prominent spokesperson for this group. Ligachev adhered to a reform orientation similar to that which Andropov, who had been one of Gorbachev's mentors, had espoused in the early 1980s (Aslund 1991a, 55). Gorbachev and Andropov's common ground involved similar early recognition of economic problems. Ligachev, however, shared Andropov's sense of an appropriate solution, returning to the "discipline" of Stalin's era, that Gorbachev opposed. Among top leaders, Ligachev's closest allies in the latter half of the 1980s included fellow Politburo members Viktor Chebrikov, the chairman of the KGB, whose views were similar to Ligachev's, and—under the principle of politics making strange bedfellows—holdovers from the Brezhnev era, Vladimir Shcherbitski and Viktor Nikonov, Central Committee Secretary for Agriculture.

Ligachev fiercely opposed movement toward a market economy, perceiving Western mass culture and consumerism as evil and primitive (Aslund 1991a, 52–53).[6] His central values were discipline and order (Aslund 1991a, 55). Further, the "socialist morality" and "authority of honest and conscientious labor" that he upheld were clearly integral parts of the hierar-

---

5. For instance, the radical reformers showed a sympathy for the impoverished for whom work was impossible that was uncharacteristic of either liberal individualism or the socialist principle of distribution as practiced by previous Party leaders (Matthews 1989, 26–29; Gorbachev 1995, 383). Brown (1996, 102) argues that Gorbachev eventually came to see himself as a social democrat in the mode of the Federal Republic of Germany's social market economy.

6. According to Ligachev in 1986, for instance: "There . . . will be no talk of a market economy" (quoted in Aslund 1991a, 53). For him, markets created "injustice and inequality" (quoted in Brown 1996, 139).

chical socialist principle of distribution (i.e., to each according to his work) that developed under Lenin and Stalin. Ligachev's focus lay on the health of the social collective, which he perceived to be afflicted by a crisis that was more moral than economic.[7] Ordinary persons fit into Ligachev's worldview through disciplined contributions of their labor in accordance with an orderly central plan created by the Party's experts (Aslund 1991a, 56–57). While Ligachev did not oppose providing better incentives for improved performance of these contributions, he emphasized applying disciplinary measures for shortcomings. Ligachev did not share Gorbachev's vision of local managers, even professionally trained employees, making independent decisions and thereby contributing to a more efficient economy. Rather, in Ligachev's view the Soviet Union's economic difficulties were to be solved, not by emulating the permissive and perverted societies of the West, but by overcoming the ossification and corruption of the Brezhnev period and returning to the disciplined order that he perceived as having prevailed earlier in Soviet experience. The one aspect of Gorbachev's economic reforms with which Ligachev was sympathetic was basing increased income differentials on performance. Thus while Ligachev did not share the view of the recent Soviet past held by his fellow Politburo members Shcherbitski and Nikonov, he agreed with their opposition to any move toward a market economy at the expense of central direction.

In a fashion reminiscent of the struggle over social security in the United States just a few years earlier, neither of the factions among organized political leaders which defined the poles of elite cultural conflict (in this instance between a reform faction of HI or IH bifocals and another faction of more traditional—in Soviet terms—hierarchists) was in a position to make societally binding decisions on its own. Instead, the balance in the Soviet Union was initially held by a looser group located between them (Aslund 1991a, 66). In the Soviet instance this second hierarchical faction was composed largely of capable industrial managers who had achieved high Party positions and government offices. The most prominent figure in this group was Nikolai Ryzhkov, a member of the Politburo and Prime Minister of the Soviet Union. Other figures with similar views included Politburo members; Nikolai Slyunkov, the Central Committee Secretary for Economic Affairs until July 1990; Yuri Maslyukov, the chairman of Gosplan, the state central

---

7. Gorbachev agreed that there was much "laxity and irresponsibility in production and at all levels of management" (1995, 216), but his more individualistic conception of human nature led Gorbachev to attribute this situation more to inappropriate economic incentives than to widespread moral failure (1995, 217).

economic planning institution; and Lev Zaikov, the Central Committee Secretary for Military Affairs.

As I indicated in my discussion of factions among contemporary Japanese hierarchists in Chapter 3, grid-group theory cannot explain such intracultural divisions. They mark a limit on explanation in grid-group theory terms. So the group loosely organized around Ryzhkov is not really an analogue of the IH "wistful" individualists in the American instance. The Ryzhkov and Ligachev factions were both clearly hierarchists, and the differences in their institutional formation imperatives must be attributed to institutional factors rather than to differences in their cultures. As March and Olsen (1989) suggest, the disparities in their advanced education and the specifics of their professional careers are likely candidates in this regard.

Unlike the Gorbachev and Ligachev factions, the members of the group associated with Ryzhkov were technically trained (engineers for the most part), and most had had successful careers managing technical industrial activities. These extremely capable men were well aware of the Soviet Union's economic problems and, unlike Ligachev's group, generally favored experimenting with new approaches aimed at solving these difficulties. While members of the technical group were, as we shall see, as hierarchical as Ligachev's faction, the particular version of hierarchy to which they were loyal was based on technological and administrative expertise more than the political ideology that guided Ligachev's version. The policy position of this technical group varied a bit across time, but they frequently disagreed with the radical reformers in fundamental ways.

For instance, they had a great deal of faith in reforming central planning and direction processes. They not only viewed central planning as a capable institution, they perceived it as a moral one. By using this tool, the wisdom of society's most capable persons was applied to improving the social collective. Concomitantly, this group's enthusiasm for relying on markets to coordinate the economy was tepid. For them, markets were not only suspect in terms of their capacities, they were as well inherently associated with personal greed and corruption. While these men did not emphasize material over professional or moral incentives for improved performance, material incentives were acceptable to them so long as they were tied to social contributions, rather than the self-serving activities that they perceived as inherent in the market. Among the members of this group material provision was not perceived as an economic activity as that term would be understood in the West. Rather, it was essentially and appropriately a matter of expert planning and administration dedicated to the welfare of the social collective.

While Gorbachev viewed favorably the direction of Hungary's economic reforms (and subsequently those of the Federal Republic of Germany) as models and Ligachev was inclined toward the practices of the Soviet Union's own early industrial mobilization, the societal ideal of this middle group was provided by the German Democratic Republic's relatively (in contrast to the rest of Eastern Europe) effective innovations drawing on improved technical managerial competence. Unsurprisingly, the members of this group, who were dedicated to expert central direction, were also lukewarm about Gorbachev's democratization efforts.

Thus within the Politburo and in the relations of this body to other central Soviet institutions (e.g., Gosplan) cultural as well as cultural-institutional differences gave rise to sharply differing instrumental preferences about the institutions appropriate for realizing contrasting practical objectives (Brown 1996, 173–77). For instance, within the Politburo's dozen members only a third could be counted on to routinely support Gorbachev's interests in radical economic change and the democratization of political institutions. Roughly another third, while not always united behind Ligachev's program of disciplining incompetent or corrupt officials and alcoholic workers, could be counted on to resist many aspects of Gorbachev's reforms. Another third, the technocratic hierarchists, thus had to be won over by Gorbachev through compromises.

Across time Gorbachev and his allies found supporters particularly among economists and other (primarily Moscow-based) academics. Some of these persons transformed themselves into politicians across the late 1980s and early 1990s. Nonetheless, the resistance that Gorbachev faced among top Party and government officials had widespread sympathy throughout Soviet society (Cook 1993, 90–91). The radical reformers had cultural biases that were not common among the general population, who, with some reason, feared the economic disruption of transitioning to a market economy.[8] Additionally, enacting Gorbachev's proposed reforms would have created extensive dislocation among Party officials, government administrators, enterprise managers, many groups of industrial workers, officials of state agriculture, and others. For many persons in these categories

8. One factor contributing to Soviet perspectives in this regard was simple ignorance of conditions in the West. See Aslund 1991a, 28, 54. Additionally, Gorbachev suggests that having the black market as their primary firsthand experience with market activities contributed to their skepticism about the social merits of markets (1995, 216). Recent Russian experience with "every-man-for-himself" markets offers reinforcement of this perspective, although Brady's (1999) assessment of current conditions is more generous.

jobs would have been lost or become more demanding and relocation to less desirable regions would have been required. In short, the stability and security of the Brezhnev era would have been lost. So even those persons who were cognizant and supportive of markets as appropriate economic institutions had to weigh their abstract principles against the practical consequences that transitioning to a market economy held for their lives. Had Gorbachev succeeded in rapidly transforming Soviet central direction into a viable market economy, he would have done nothing less than work a miracle.

Gorbachev's struggles with consumer subsidies fall into two distinct phases. Although during the first, which lasted from the beginning of 1986 through the summer of 1987, he was somewhat vague concerning long-term economic objectives, its market orientation was clear enough to prompt strong reactions from persons with Ligachev's orientation. But during this period Gorbachev generally counted Ryzhkov's faction among his allies (1995, 230). Elite interaction during the second phase, covering the autumn of 1989 through the spring of 1991, was influenced less by persons of Ligachev's persuasion, as their voice was fading. Instead, as the market goals of the reformers were more clearly recognized, Ryzhkov's faction underscored its preference for a more restrictive economic transition that threatened less social disruption. Nikolai Petrakov, one of the leading market economists, once joked with Ryzhkov that for the latter's cautious faction the market had acquired a status similar to that which the communist period of history had held for earlier Soviet leaders in that its practical realization was forever receding into the future (Brown 1996, 149).

In order to gain support from Ryzhkov's faction during the first phase Gorbachev compromised some of his reform initiatives and introduced measures piecemeal rather than all at once. A crucial instance of half-measures involved the 1987 Law on State Enterprises. This legislation required managers to be self-financing (i.e., profitable); yet many consumer prices remained subsidized, thus placing producers and the economy generally in an increasingly untenable position across time. Incomplete packages of reform measures are hardly unusual in political life, but in this case they left the Soviet Union in a precarious position. Gorbachev accomplished enough (the Law on State Enterprises was the crucial step) to effectively cripple central planning and administration, but not enough (freeing consumer prices was an essential missing element) to make a market economy feasible (Brown 1996, 151–53). As a consequence, a variety of disturbing economic trends was set in motion, including shortages of goods, growing inflation, government deficits, and declines in productivity. In effect, immediate economic costs were being incurred without any prospect for promoting economic efficiency. Gorbachev appears to have despaired of achieving more thorough economic change through the existing political structure. So rather than continue to press his economic agenda against overwhelming odds, he shifted his emphasis from the summer of 1987 until the autumn of 1989 to the matter of political change (Brown 1996, 137; Aslund 1991a, 34), striving to create new political institutions that would be more sympathetic to his economic goals.

Gorbachev experienced varying degrees of success across the three elements of his strategy for altering Soviet political institutions. First, he wished to reduce the influence of the Communist Party and its previously preeminent institutions such as the Politburo and the Central Committee's Economic Department. Second, relative to the Party, he wanted to enhance the influence of governmental institutions, although their staffs were to be downsized (Brown 1996, 193–95, 198–202). These changes would leave the Soviet Union resembling Western democracies more closely with the government, rather than the Party, as the authoritative political institution. Third, Gorbachev wished to strengthen the presidency, then use its strength to overwhelm opposition to his economic agenda.

In politics as in other realms destruction is generally easier than creation. In part because of ethnic tension within the Soviet Union or empire, Gorbachev enjoyed broader support, especially among regional political elites, on his political agenda than he had experienced on economic transition. The Congress of People's Deputies was created in the form of a multiparty institution, and it in turn elected a new Supreme Soviet as a standing monitoring body. An independent presidency, which Gorbachev subsequently held, was designated as the crucial executive position.[9] A new Presidential Council was designed to serve the strengthened president, eclipsing the Politburo as a policymaking body and outranking the Council of Ministers.[10] The Communist Party could not dominate the parliament, and Gorbachev was gradually able to reduce its influence on the Council of Ministers. Thus, the stranglehold of the Party on Soviet politics was broken.

Building was more difficult. The presidency and the Presidential Council

9. This executive was elected by the Congress of People's Deputies rather than the citizenry. Brown (1996, 203) discusses the relative advantages and drawbacks of this method.

10. In reality the Council of Ministers, with far more staff, continued to be the primary policy-formulating unit. But the higher-ranking Presidential Council, for a time, routinely called for changes in ministerial proposals (Brown 1996, 209).

lacked the staff to create detailed legislation. Long-standing government institutions such as Gosplan that were skeptical about Gorbachev's economic proposals were generally better equipped in this regard.[11] Moreover, relations between members of the Presidential Council and government ministries were not clear. In the words of Council member Stanislav Shatalin: "May I ask, for instance, the minister of finance to do something, or do I have a right to tell him that he must do it?" (Aslund 1991b, 31). In short, Gorbachev's new institutions had difficulties gaining acceptance against the long-standing patterns of interaction among other government institutions. Additionally, while Gorbachev was able to reduce sharply the influence of persons whose views were similar to those of Andropov and Brezhnev, he did not eliminate bitter opposition entirely.[12] Most important, however, his conflict with what had previously been the middle ground of technically sophisticated advocates of central planning became more pronounced. Nikolai Ryzhkov, still prime minister and now a member of the Presidential Council; Yuri Maslyukov, chairman of Gosplan and also a member of the Council; other leading officials in a variety of ministries; and even some of the economists who had previously been associated with the radical reform group formed an opposition that perceived more potential in central planning than Gorbachev was willing to acknowledge.

Nonetheless, in the autumn of 1989 Gorbachev, perhaps having concluded that he had accomplished as much as he could in the political realm, directed his attention once again to economic reform. By now the consequences of the economic impasse created by his initial round of reforms were clearer. As a result of the incongruity between the expectations for enterprise managers (self-financing through profitability) created by the Law on State Enterprises and the pervasive system of consumer price subsidies, prices were rising less rapidly than wages and social program benefits. Shortages were thus common, and pressures for unraveling Gorbachev's early reforms were building. Hierarchical cultures believe in expert testimony, however. The Nineteenth Party Conference in the summer of 1988 adopted a resolution stating that "the country's slide toward economic and socio-political crisis has been halted" (Aslund 1991b, 31).

11. In fact, the State Commission on Economic Reform administered by Gosplan for the Council of Ministers became progressively more active in helping to block the reforms sought by the radical economists (Gorbachev 1995, 227).

12. With respect to radical economic reform, the Presidential Council was a surprisingly conservative body. Gorbachev appears to have given it this composition by following the custom of seeking consensus among various factions (Brown 1996, 201).

In October 1989 the recently created State Commission on Economic Reform issued a report by Leonid Abalkin which endorsed market coordination over central planning and explicitly favored letting prices float in order to allow the market to function effectively. Abalkin's plan did not press for private ownership of productive capital, nor did it offer a detailed persuasive schedule for the six-year transition to a market economy that it envisioned. Gorbachev lent his support to this plan, but it was opposed by a broad range of government officials who had more faith in central planning. Gosplan offered an alternative program focused primarily on stabilizing the existing deteriorating economic situation but also addressing the longer term. Prime Minister Ryzhkov supported an effort to bridge the differences between these two proposals in December. Ryzhkov's version (hereafter the Ryzhkov-Abalkin Program) was designed to hold more appeal for the radical reformers than the Gosplan proposal, but it postponed any movement toward market coordination and freeing retail prices for several years and increased central planning in the interim. Renewed efforts to stabilize prices through strengthened control measures were adopted as a result of Ryzhkov's program.

New proposals tried to break the stalemate over the long-term direction of the Soviet economy in the spring of 1990. Three young radical economists associated with the Reform Commission—Grigoriy Yavlinsky, Mikhail Zadornov, and Aleksey Mikhaylov—introduced a four-hundred-day (subsequently five-hundred-day) program for transition to private productive property and a market economy. This trio argued that partial reforms, such as those currently in place in the Soviet Union and envisioned for the future by the advocates of central planning, had been shown to be ineffective in several Eastern European societies and that what was needed was "shock therapy" along the lines of then current Polish practice. Surprisingly, this proposal garnered a good deal of support, including endorsements from Ryzhkov and Maslyukov. Nonetheless, it was rejected in April by a Presidential Council skeptical of radical economic proposals, returning attention to the December 1989 Ryzhkov-Abalkin Program for stabilization through recentralization, which had—in the interim—been accepted by the Congress of People's Deputies.

For a short while after the Presidential Council's rejection of the four-hundred-day proposal Gorbachev, now President Gorbachev,[13] continued to pursue the cause of radical reform. At the Twenty-Eighth Party Congress

13. He was elected by the Congress of People's Deputies on March 15, 1990.

in early July he further weakened the Party's position, effectively transfer-
ring the powers formerly held by the Politburo to the Presidential Council,[14]
and later that month he helped to set in motion the work of an extensive
group of radical economists under the direction of Stanislav Shatalin. This
group produced its report in late August, calling for some immediate stabilization measures, but more importantly providing the most detailed plan
to date for rapid transition to a system of market economic coordination
(Yavlinsky, Fedorov, and Shatalin et al. 1991, especially 38–41—hereafter
the Shatalin-Yavlinsky Program). The plans that were receiving close attention by top Soviet officials were thus shifting in the direction of radical
reform, and it was widely expected that Gorbachev would win approval of
the Shatalin-Yavlinsky Program in the Supreme Soviet in September 1990.
This body indeed granted Gorbachev the power to coordinate economic
policy on September 24. But presidential institutions (primarily limitations
on the number and knowledge of staff) appear to have been insufficient for
the task (Aslund 1991b, 31).

At this point in the struggle over economic reform there was broader
acceptance of the need for markets and increasing liberalism in foreign trade
than had previously existed, but numerous differences still distinguished the
Shatalin-Yavlinsky and Ryzhkov-Abalkin programs under consideration by
the Supreme Soviet (Aslund 1991b, 35–40; 1992, 113). Shatalin-Yavlinsky
proposed moving to market coordination for roughly three-quarters of retail sales in five hundred days and for sharp government budget cuts to
stabilize existing economic imbalances. It increased state revenues (important for economic stabilization) through selling state productive property
to private citizens. This proposal represented the clearest example of the
individualistic institutional design preferences of the radical economic reformers. Further, this program allowed the republics considerable autonomy. Indeed, the Shatalin-Yavlinsky Program merged aspects of economic
reform with nationalities/union questions in that, in a fashion similar to the
American Articles of Confederation, union tax revenues came through and
were dependent on the will of the republics (Gorbachev 1995, 372, 382,
384). Thus, this program was popular among republic officials seeking
greater autonomy from the Soviet Union and reviled by Party and government traditionalists anxious to preserve the union at all costs.

By comparison, the Ryzhkov-Abalkin Program focused more on immediate stabilization through centrally directed price increases (subsidy reduc-

14. Ligachev and others were simply retired.

tions) partially compensated for by pay increases with an eventual, relatively unspecified transition to markets. Additionally, this plan opposed private productive property. Moreover, it allowed republics only limited autonomy and thus, in sharp contrast to the Shatalin-Yavlinsky Program, was seen as helping to sustain the Soviet Union. Thus the Ryzhkov-Abalkin Program illustrated its relatively hierarchical (in comparison to Shatalin-Yavlinsky) core values and institutional design preferences by clinging more tenaciously to the political and economic institutions of highly centralized state expertise.

Each program had relative strengths and weaknesses, and Gorbachev asked Abel Aganbegyan to formulate a compromise from them (Brown 1996, 273–74; Gorbachev 1995, 383), but disliked the result, which he felt favored the Shatalin-Yavlinsky Program. In his view, while Aganbegyan's compromise removed the elements that prejudged the union issue, it still raised troubling concerns over transitioning to a market economy (Gorbachev 1995, 383). At this point Gorbachev shifted his own position sharply. He explains this shift, that others refer to as his "turn to the right" (Brown 1996, 269), as an effort to secure the union and buy time for achieving wider agreement on the long-term direction of economic reform (Gorbachev 1995, 376). He ceased to push for immediate economic reform and focused instead on stabilizing the existing economic situation through central direction. He also further transformed the government, having the Council of Ministers report to him rather than the—now displaced—prime minister (Brown 1996, 278). Moreover, the Presidential Council was abolished, and the Soviet government began to turn in a more authoritarian direction, operating increasingly on the basis of presidential decrees. Indeed, Gorbachev forged alliances with the KGB and other military-industrial complex leaders with whom he had not previously been close.

Relative Reliance on Benefit Reductions as Opposed to Revenue Increases

Staunch advocates of the relatively individualistic radical reform faction's program (Shatalin-Yavlinsky) were outnumbered in virtually all imaginable formulations of the relevant Soviet elite. Gorbachev was a regular supporter of this faction, and his support augmented its influence. But it was only by linking radical economic reform to other issues such as the nationalities/union question that it could garner meaningful support beyond the most cosmopolitan members of the Soviet elite. These included a relatively small number of prominent academics, exceptionally open-minded younger officials primarily in major urban centers such as Moscow and Leningrad, and a handful of top officials and their staffs. Thus as I discuss below, while Gorbachev might have decided to eliminate consumer price subsidies, putting that decision into practice and particularly using the decision as an effective device for transitioning quickly and successfully to a market economy were probably beyond his grasp.

So it is unsurprising that Gorbachev did not follow this path. Instead, in October 1990 he authorized a partial deregulation of wholesale prices. This had the primary consequence of reducing government income, since as these prices rose against retail prices (that were in many instances still depressed through consumer price subsidies), the state's turnover tax (derived from the difference between the two) was reduced. Then, in April 1991, in an effort to stabilize a Soviet economy drifting out of control (growing inflation and budget deficits along with sharply declining productivity), Gorbachev's reconstituted government finally did act with respect to retail prices. Prices were not freed, but consumer price subsidies were reduced, thus raising prices. This step was combined with wage and pension increases designed to offset most of the increased costs to consumers. This combination of reforms was met with widespread labor unrest because workers feared, and in many instances learned, that wage increases were inadequate to compensate for reduced consumer price subsidies. Strikes involving irate workers were generally resolved through further wage increases. Ironically, workers used the new conventions about political participation that Gorbachev had initiated to oppose some facets of his economic program.[15]

Consumer price subsidies thus declined in April 1991 (roughly six months before the fall of the Soviet Union), after lingering in uncertainty for four years. Yet this reduction was not—strictly speaking—aimed at cutting social consumption. Rather, this was an inadvertent consequence of efforts to achieve what was perceived as essential economic restructuring. Further, Soviet officials attempted to compensate for the losses in social consumption benefits that were the result of restructuring with increases in other social consumption programs. Groups that complained about the initial level of compensation invariably acquired better terms, although these activities generally involved various workers' associations rather than the elderly. Gorbachev and his colleagues were attempting to shield ordinary citizens from net reductions in social consumption benefits during a period of sharp

---

15. In spite of these problems, Gorbachev maintains that these price increases had positive economic consequences and moderated political discord (Gorbachev 1995, 389–90, 393–94).

political change. While the compensation offered in terms of better wages and pensions was not equivalent to the reductions in consumer price subsidies, it was designed to and likely did cover the vast majority of these losses. Further, widespread support existed among Soviet leaders for the extensive efforts that were made to compensate citizens by enhancing other forms of public social provision.

Explicitness of the Focus on Long-Term Financial Costs

Unlike their individualistic American counterparts, Soviet leaders in Gorbachev's faction were casual about working out the long-term funding implications of these social program increases. Both the wide-ranging policy alternatives whose introduction they were considering and the unfamiliar as well as shifting circumstances that they currently faced posed formidable issues requiring significant attention. Under these circumstances, even staunch individualists might have sacrificed close consideration of how the costs of the wage and pension increases would be covered. But as Brown's characterization of Gorbachev as a German-style social democrat suggests (1996, 102; also see note 5), Soviet radical economic reformers were individualistic in comparison with the rest of the Soviet elite, but in comparison to the American individualistic faction in the 1983 struggle over social security, their HI or perhaps occasionally IH bifocal cultural biases represented a much more tepid and certainly less experienced commitment to individualism.

Cultural Mechanisms of Political Change (or Lack of It)

Soviet attention focused on the fate of consumer price subsidies as a signal about alternative paths of future economic and societal organization. Subsidies were integral to the Soviet command economy and anathema for a market economy. While subsidies were reduced in April 1991, they were not eliminated, and the road to a market economy was not taken. From October 1990 on, it was clear that the political momentum behind radical economic reform was fading. Gorbachev hesitated and then backed off just as he had acquired the political capacity to realize his reform legislation. Western economists (Aslund 1991b, 40; 1992) are critical of his late conversion to gradualism, arguing that only a radical change could have rescued the Soviet Union's deteriorating economy. Gorbachev now appears to accept that going slowly was a mistake (Brown 1996, 269). Brown argues that

Gorbachev's hesitancy at this point was tactical rather than a sign of a shift in his purposes and political loyalties (Brown 1996, 313). As the preeminent responsible official Gorbachev was less insulated from a range of practical considerations than Western economists.

From Western perspectives of individualistic practice, this failure to shift from a seriously troubled economic system to a market economy seems strange. The Soviet Union faced vastly more severe economic difficulties than any of the other three societies examined in this study, so taking dramatic steps toward a system of economic organization that was performing better in other societies appears from this perspective to represent a sensible course of action. But as Eckstein (1988) argues, persons shift from one systematic set of beliefs and values to another with great difficulty, even if shifting facilitates personal interests and organizational activities, much less threatens them (see also Brown 1996, 17). As I demonstrated in Chapter 2, Gorbachev did not develop his individualistic beliefs and values quickly. They are obvious aspects of his culture from his youth. However, Gorbachev was but one, albeit a powerful, actor on the Soviet stage, and he was unusual among Soviet leaders. Yet in Chapter 4, I showed how shifting coalitions among cultures can contribute to political change without shifts in personal cultural orientations. Numerous aspects of the shifting global economic environment of the late 1970s and 1980s posed severe new problems for conventional Soviet hierarchical economic practices. These new circumstances offered opportunities for a rival individualistic culture to introduce alternative practices that might improve economic performance in these altered conditions. So why was the resulting transition effort so ineffectual?

Several problems stood in the path of realizing this individualistic opportunity, and the inability of Gorbachev and others to introduce a market economy is likely overdetermined. Nonetheless, examining various factors offers insight as to why this decision process worked out as it did. First, the problems were severe. Daunting economic difficulties were intertwined with intractable nationalities issues, creating a formidable challenge.

Second, the Communist Party had been so effective at eliminating opposition to its hierarchical culture that the low-grid cultures were extremely weak. The grip of a narrow range of hierarchical perspectives on Soviet life (e.g., those of the Ligachev and Ryzhkov factions) was thus firm. Gorbachev's group of radical economic reformers was small, and its struggle with various factions of hierarchy was so lopsided that it would have been remarkable if it had produced great change. For instance, garnering sufficient support for eliminating consumer price subsidies among political elites was distinct from and insufficient for persuading large numbers of government officials, enterprise managers, and workers to live by new rules that at least initially were unfamiliar and foreboding. Gorbachev's *Memoirs* (1995) have numerous references to disparities between what he preferred and what was feasible. In explaining the slow pace of economic reform, Brown (1996) emphasizes this gulf between the economic preferences of the relatively modest numbers of radical reformers gathered around Gorbachev and the preferences for traditional Soviet institutions common within the government, Party, economic enterprises, defense forces, KGB, and general population (150, 209, 269, 273). He points out that previous general secretaries with more conventional ambitions had experienced difficulties gaining adequate cooperation from various bureaucracies (132). Brown argues that Gorbachev's greater success in foreign as opposed to domestic policy derived from his ability to execute decisions in the former realm more effectively (130–31).

Third, the radical economic reform faction confronted, not only the resistance of others, but its own hesitancy. According to his economic adviser Stanislav Shatalin: "I understand that even [Gorbachev and Ryzhkov], who started *perestroika,* are not able—if you wish, do not have the biological facilities—to change their philosophy instantly, to move from the existing way of thinking to the new realities. Like everyone else, they have been fed for decades with the ideas of a strict plan and a technocratic approach to the solution of economic questions" (quoted in Aslund 1991a, 30). Although Gorbachev held individualistic (as well as hierarchical) beliefs and values, most of his life was spent in thoroughly hierarchical institutions. His limited experience made taking a risky leap to a market economy appear intimidating (see Gorbachev 1995, 324). Even the most enthusiastic of Soviet advocates of market institutions in the late 1980s had, at best, limited experience with them.[16] Gorbachev's own explanation for going slowly, for instance, focuses less on the resistance of thousands of "little Ligachevs" than on uncertainty and concern about the short-term economic consequences of shifting to a market economy on the population's welfare—an issue long-

16. For instance, even Abel Aganbegyan, long one of the leading advocates for radical reform and among the Soviet Union's most preeminent economists, argued late in the struggle over consumer price subsidies for the reform of retail prices *after* the stabilization of the market, surely a non sequitur (Aslund 1992, 98).

recognized as being of considerable importance to him.[17] He was, in other words, concerned to avoid as much as possible of the dire economic consequences that have afflicted Russians during the last few years.

Fourth, the uncertainty of the radical reformers was frequently unpersuasive against the most principled arguments of their opponents. Some resistance to radical economic reform arose from narrowly self-interested concerns for personal convenience or organizational integrity. A market economy would have displaced many persons from positions of relative privilege and disrupted many organizational routines. But some of the opposition arguments were based on hierarchical values that also formed a portion of Gorbachev's bifocal cultural bias. For the persons expressing these views, societal stability and security were more important than innovation (liberty) and efficiency (Aslund 1991a, 27–61; Berliner 1983; Gorbachev 1995, 374). Moreover, many agreed with Ryzhkov that markets elicited a perverted self-interested ("black-market") orientation that contrasted shamefully with the faithful administration of a production plan that they viewed as a valuable social contribution. So while increased capacities for innovation and efficiency were of interest to some highly placed, sophisticated hierarchists (e.g., Prime Minister Ryzhkov), their higher priorities of societal stability and security as well as in fostering moral social contributions led them to favor improving the central control mechanisms of the hierarchical institutional formation imperative rather than adopting a market economy.

Ryzhkov is immensely capable; he retains prominence in contemporary Russia and would thrive across a range of institutional environments. Yet his deepest moral commitments led him to prefer administrative social contributions to what he perceived as self-serving market activities (Aslund 1992, 110). Little about contemporary Russian society suggests that his wariness in this regard was foolish. In the absence of cultural prerequisites such as beliefs in fair competition, relaxing hierarchical restraints released fearsome passions on a highly tilted field of competition. Ryzhkov's ally, Gosplan chairman Yuri Maslyukov, held similar views, being "deeply convinced that the state can in no way rely on the automatic functioning of the spontaneous market" (quoted in Aslund 1992, 110).

17. This concern was shared and expressed by several of Gorbachev's colleagues who were fearful that freeing prices would end the "achievement of socialism" in terms of widespread availability of economic necessities. Additionally, as hierarchical leaders, these men felt a shared responsibility to provide a societal entitlement in the form of a stable economic environment (Cook 1993, 139–40, 147; Brown 1996, 140).

Overall, then, the hierarchical Communist Party's success in nearly eliminating rivals left the Soviet Union with alternative cultures insufficiently developed to foster successful adaptation to new circumstances. The relatively individualistic radical economic reform faction was simply too small, unsure of itself, and unpersuasive in the face of principled hierarchical arguments to foster the transition to an economic system that likely offered better long-term prospects. Implementing the relatively individualistic policy preferences of the radical economic reform group would have altered the trajectory of Soviet society generally. Consequently, the reformers' proposals became the central elements of a society-consuming political controversy. But these proposals were not adopted. While the Soviet government shifted emphasis among its social consumption programs in the spring of 1991, relying more heavily on wages and pensions and less thoroughly on consumer price subsidies, changing various societal trajectories was forestalled until after the demise of the union itself later that year.

SEVEN

GERMAN RELUCTANCE TO SHIFT THE TRAJECTORY OF PENSIONS, 1989

RELATIVE CULTURAL INFLUENCE AND INSTITUTIONAL CONSEQUENCES

Huntington (1981, 42–44, 113) offers a general characterization of European political cultures that can be applied to Germany fairly well. According to him, until the eighteenth century major European societies were thoroughly dominated by hierarchical structure similar to that of the ancien régime in France. Thereafter, this culture lost some of its preeminence in these societies as versions of individualistic (classical liberal) culture gained influence with varying speed and in different degrees across the continent. Late in the nineteenth and across much of the twentieth century, varieties of socialist (egalitarian) culture also acquired considerable influence in this region as well.

In the German-speaking part of Europe feudal hierarchy relinquished its hold slowly and in piecemeal fashion, retarding the development of a free and equal citizenry and the associated open exchange of ideas. Accordingly, the most obvious aspect of individualism that developed in late-nineteenth-century Germany was its entrepreneurial dimension, although the state retained impressive public industrial activities until the twentieth century (Dahrendorf 1967, 37–40). Moreover, private industry in Germany drew on a concentrated banking system, and sectors developed from the outset in the form of a few large, frequently loosely associated firms that were generally state-friendly (Dahrendorf 1967, 37–40; Hall 1986). So from the beginning of industrialization, corporatist collaboration characterized state-entrepreneurial relations. The state was never reduced to night-watchman status, and its relations with industry were frequently positive and cooperative.

Socialist organization followed industrialization and prompted Bismarck to initiate the programs associated with the modern welfare state (see Carl Jantke as quoted in Dahrendorf 1967, 41–42). Yet while the leaders of this corporatist structure evinced concern for the welfare of the working class, they were firmly opposed to "the development of the subject into the citizen with all the rights of this social character." Workers were instead to be "treated like children of the patriarchal family" (63, 64). Bismarck's concern with the welfare of the working class arose at least in part as a consequence of the latter's potential for social disruption if it became sufficiently disenchanted. According to Katzenstein, the depression conditions of the 1870s convinced Bismarck "that liberal capitalism was causing a social disintegration that required positive state action" (1987, 171). As Max Weber put it: "It is not the purpose of our work in social policy to make the world happy, but to unite socially a nation split apart by modern economic development for the hard struggles of the future" (quoted in Dahrendorf 1967, 41).

This approach reveals the hierarchical hallmark of structuring society from above so that all segments contribute to the guiding experts' vision of the good of the whole.[1] As Dahrendorf states: "Not even industrialization managed, in Germany, to upset a traditional outlook in which the whole is placed above its parts, the state above the citizen, or a rigidly controlled order above the lively diversity of the market, the state above society. Wherever one would hope for the word 'rational,' the other one, 'national,' appears instead as an argument for policy decisions" (1967, 42).

---

1. "The whole matter centres in the question, Is it the duty of the State, or is it not, to provide for its helpless citizens? I maintain that it is its duty, that it is the duty not only of the 'Christian State,' but of every State" (Bismarck speaking before the Reichstag, March 15, 1884, in support of the Accident Insurance Bill; quoted in Dawson 1973, 118). See also Dawson 1973, 110, for the kaiser's similar views and related expressions from Bismarck (34–35, 110, 119).

In short, the predominant German culture through the First World War was hierarchy.[2] A central feature of this culture involves deference to authorities generally and the state in particular. As Dahrendorf relates: "Many institutions of German society have been and are still set up in such a way as to imply that somebody or some group of people is 'the most objective authority in the world,' and is therefore capable of finding ultimate solutions for all issues and conflicts. In this manner conflict is not regulated but 'solved' " (1967, 137). This perspective, which grants certainty to some (i.e., truth is "manifest" to particular elites), grows out of a fear that socially destructive conflict may arise from contending views and contrasts sharply with the skepticism of liberal democracy. Again, Dahrendorf clarifies: "We (liberal democrats) have spoken of the fundamental uncertainty of human existence with respect to justice or truth. This assumption not only provides a basis for the theory of government by conflict, the meaning of the experimental approach in science may also be derived from it. If truth cannot be known, or if at least we cannot know whether what we know is true, then we have to find ways and means to avoid dogmatizing the false" (159). Accordingly, in liberal democracy the citizens are granted sufficient competence (e.g., common sense) to be largely the masters of their own fates. As Dahrendorf has it: "Common sense is not in itself a source of truth or of certainty. It means little more than the ability to represent a self-interest, enlightened by the recognition of useful rules of the game. In Germany, not only is it frequently doubted that every man has an ability of this kind, but a political system that is supposed to work by the market competition of such crude talents is ridiculed" (162).

Some of the most tumultuous events of the twentieth century altered the pattern of hierarchical dominance that I have portrayed. Liberal democratic institutions were imposed by the victors in the aftermath of the First World War, and for a time individualism and egalitarianism were both more (and socially conservative hierarchy correspondingly less) influential than they had been previously. But this situation was short lived. Difficult circum-

2. According to grid-group theory, culture arises from experience, so we should not be surprised to find hierarchy dominating German cultural biases until recently. The means of forging the German state in the 1860s assured that Germany and its encircling neighbors would all feel insecure. In Chapters 4 and 5 we saw that a sense of societal insecurity produced more hierarchical attitudes and institutions even in the highly individualistic United States. We should expect, and—at least until recently—we find, hierarchy as the dominant German culture. It is difficult to imagine a German version of Hobbes (the product of an island society) allowing individuals unilaterally to relinquish their obligations to the sovereign if the latter's actions endanger their lives.

stances overwhelmed the Weimar Republic in a little over a decade. Hierarchical forces of both the right and the left contributed to liberalism's demise. Indeed, the economic, political, and social chaos of the Weimar years left egalitarianism and individualism in weaker positions across much of the late 1930s and early 1940s than either had suffered during the late nineteenth century. However, while Nazi hierarchists clearly dominated the narrow individualistic culture that by this time provided a substantial portion of Germany's industrial entrepreneurial skills, they also relied on this culture for realizing renewed prosperity and military production.

The societal influence of the egalitarians suffered even more severely. While the Social Democratic Party of Germany (SPD) was the leading partner in the first Weimar coalition government, the party's leaders perceived themselves to be forced by circumstance to cooperate closely with the military and other conservative hierarchical groups.[3] Egalitarianism was further undercut during the Weimar years by SPD defections to the more radical communists and other leftist splinter groups. During the subsequent Nazi period (1933–45) the SPD lost ground among workers to a romantic version of hierarchical radicalism. The institutions of this bizarre hierarchy initially restored German prosperity and order and then brought war, total defeat, and national dismemberment.

This war's consequences were sufficiently severe, for both Germany and its former adversaries, to once again revise patterns of relations among German cultures (Berg-Schlosser, and Rytkewski 1993; Gaffney and Kolinsky 1991; Hoffman-Lange 1991; Roberts 1984). These changes were prompted by the victorious allies and fostered more assiduously than their related efforts following the First World War. A group of predominantly individualistic German elites met with Western constitutional experts and devised the Basic Law of 1949 in the form of a parliamentary democracy, and the three Western allies merged their occupation zones, forming the Federal Republic of Germany. Under the early leadership of Konrad Adenauer and Ludwig Erhard, in particular, the Federal Republic became a parliamentary democracy with a relatively independent (social) market economy spurred by infusions of resources from the Marshall Plan.

So, as I suggested in Chapter 4, an externally prompted and supported effort inverted the relationship between the two cultures forming the longstanding dominant coalition. Thus, rather than a rapid reorientation of ex-

---

3. This orientation has a long history. See Ferdinand Lasalle's 1862 view on this matter as quoted in Dahrendorf 1967, 188–89.

isting cultures, there was instead a rapid reversal of relative influence between individualism and hierarchy in the dominant coalition. Additionally, the conditions fostered by the victorious allies provided considerable scope for realizing individualistic ambitions and more limited avenues for achieving hierarchical aspirations. These circumstances encouraged West Germans with bifocal (particularly IH—e.g., Konrad Adenauer—or HI) cultural biases to apply their individualism more extensively in public life. Moreover, youngsters who have grown up under these new social institutions have been relatively effectively socialized to them (Baker, Dalton, and Hildebrandt 1981; Pulzer 1989; Rohrschneider 1994; Grendstad 1999).

Egalitarians have also taken advantage of these new circumstances, evinced willingness to cooperate with hierarchists and individualists, and raised their profile in the Federal Republic more persistently than in previous German states. From 1969 to 1982 the SPD governed through coalitions, first with the Christian Democratic Union (CDU), then with the (classically liberal) Free Democratic Party (FDP). So egalitarians are now well integrated into the Federal Republic. In the 1980s, political issues in the Federal Republic reflected a series of coalitions with I-H (CDU), individualistic (FDP), and E-H (SPD) elements.[4] Corporatist issues elicited a loose H-E coalition involving the SPD and portions of the CDU. Market issues attracted a loose I-H coalition bringing together the FDP and other portions of the CDU. Civil-political rights issues prompted a loose I-E coalition between the FDP and the SPD (Padgett 1989, 125).

Institutional interaction in the Federal Republic reveals a distinct mixture of concentration and decentralization. While the market and quasipublic spheres of society vary across sectors, relatively high degrees of centralization, characterized by peak associations of sectoral interests, are typical (Katzenstein 1987, 169; Dyson 1989, 149). Decentralization is more characteristic of formal political structures. Following the Second World War, the Western allies imposed Basic Law provisions that weakened various security institutions and decentralized control over institutions particularly prominent as agents of socialization (e.g., the schools and the mass media). The Basic Law thus created a federal system whose states have significant powers.

Yet the Federal Republic's formally decentralized political institutions op-

4. The Greens, even at the parliamentary level, which is less "pure" than many of their grassroots supporters would prefer, represent a purer, more authentic version of egalitarianism and were, until the late 1990s, far less prone to compromise.

erate in ways that achieve a surprising degree of coordination (Katzenstein 1987, 169). National and state-level governments generally cooperate well and often complement one another by managing distinct aspects of multifaceted policies. Moreover, with one exception, all the central governments of the Federal Republic have required coalitions.[5] Further, while conflict between the CDU and SPD has been bitter on specific issues at particular times, cooperation has as well frequently been possible between government and opposition (Padgett 1989, 125). Katzenstein refers to this party system as centripetally competitive (1987). Coordination with nonconstitutional institutions (e.g., the Bundesbank and the two established churches) has also generally been smooth.

Overall, German social programs have displayed remarkable continuity across multiple societal upheavals and regime changes. According to Mangen: "Apart from the unemployment fund, which was first introduced in the 1920s, the features of German social insurance are essentially those instituted by Bismarck one hundred years ago" (1989, 172). While access to the social policy formulation process was once narrow (Adenauer's changes to medical-care insurance and particularly pensions in the mid-1950s), it has grown increasingly inclusive as the major political parties have become more cooperative. Policy outcomes still allow regional variations in some substantive areas (e.g., medical-care insurance). But the national government sets substantive standards and procedural guidelines that create social rights for societal contributors and limit regional disparities. Further, the national government foots increasing portions of the bill for various social programs. Nonetheless, in contrast to the programs of the British welfare state, German social programs are still remarkably decentralized and differentiated in their actual operation. For instance, pensions for former industrial workers are administered by the state governments in which the workers live (Mangen 1989, 171), and the Federal Republic has distinct retirement pension programs for blue-collar workers, white-collar workers, farmers, professionals, civil servants, and even miners (Liebfried 1978, 65). Across these various programs the so-called "equivalence principle" produces sharply varying benefits reflecting the income differentials that characterized persons during their working lives (Zapf 1986).

Esping-Andersen's (1990, 27–28) characterization of the corporatist wel-

---

5. The exception is the 1957–61 CDU government, which retained its coalition with the FDP in any case.

fare-state regime finds thorough realization in the Federal Republic. In the terms of its early preeminent officials (e.g., Konrad Adenauer and Ludwig Erhard) the Federal Republic represents a "social market society." This is an entirely fitting combination for the H-I, shifting to I-H, coalition that dominated the Federal Republic in its early years. Leaders of this coalition viewed numerous features of the market as essential for the generation of wealth and extensive public social programs as required for blunting the sharp edges of markets for employees as well as for building a cohesive social collective (Katzenstein 1987, 187; Dyson 1989, 148, 155; Mangen 1989, 169). The resulting social market relied more heavily on close relations between banking and industry as well as various peak associations than the markets favored by Thatcher and Reagan (Dyson 1989, 149–50). Leading German market advocates have been unabashed in their predilections for order, stability, and predictability (Dyson 1989, 161, 165), and they constructed what Abelshauser (1984, 287) calls "societal corporatist" institutions that provided these qualities along with high levels of productivity.

In the last couple of decades a gradual transition in the influence of rival cultures in German society is finally beginning to affect even social programs. Conradt (1980; 1978, 49) and others (Dalton 1989, 100–104; Baker, Dalton, and Hildebrandt 1981; Pulzer 1989) have shown that the Federal Republic's postwar population cohorts are progressively less hierarchical in their orientation than those who grew up prior to the Second World War. Grendstad (1999) offers an interpretation of this change in terms of grid-group theory's cultures. His data suggest a startling transformation in the cultural composition of the Federal Republic's (the former West Germany) population; the low-grid cultures constitute a majority.[6] (See Table 9.) Grendstad's scales are relatively new and thus have undergone limited testing, but he appears to have captured the cultural composition that others (Inglehart 1977; Banfield 1958) have associated with various societies (i.e., high levels of egalitarian influence in the Netherlands and the Scandinavian countries as well as exceptional levels of fatalism among the populations of Ireland and the Mediterranean countries), and this lends credibility to his more surprising results in the case of Germany. So, it is reasonable to imagine that support for generous social program benefits has declined in the Federal Republic over the last couple of decades.

6. Dahrendorf (1967, 441–42) offers a similar although largely impressionistic interpretation.

Table 9   Varying Strength of Rival Cultures in Societal Populations (in percentages of representative samples)

	Year of survey	Hierarchy	Egalitarianism	Individualism	Fatalism
Norway	1982	25	36	18	21
	1990	23	45	17	15
Denmark	1981	29	37	16	19
	1990	18	53	17	12
Sweden	1981	34	36	11	19
	1990	37	39	12	12
Iceland	1984	45	38	7	11
	1990	39	45	6	10
Great Britain	1981	30	23	15	32
	1990	23	21	18	38
Ireland	1981	34	18	12	36
	1990	18	21	21	40
The Netherlands	1981	27	37	16	20
	1990	28	47	11	14
Belgium	1981	25	19	16	40
	1990	22	24	18	36
West Germany	1981	16	33	28	23
	1990	15	34	29	22
France	1981	12	16	26	46
	1990	12	15	27	46
Spain	1981	16	22	28	35
	1990	8	9	29	54
Italy	1981	10	15	29	46
	1990	8	19	36	37
Total	1981	24	27	20	30
	1990	18	26	23	33

SOURCE: Grenstad 1999, 473.

THE 1989 DECISION ON GERMAN PENSIONS

Nature of the Problem and Implications for Various Cultures

Four principal elements interacted to create the Federal Republic's "crisis of pensions" (Mangen 1989, 184) in the late 1980s. One involved the cumulative effects of the gradual change in the relative prominence of rival cultures in German society that I introduced in the previous section. Hierarchy and its firm support of the historically paternalistic German welfare state have suffered from the growth of egalitarianism and individualism across the development of the Federal Republic. Increased liberal individualistic influence has undercut support for the existing comprehensive and generous social programs; whereas the development of egalitarianism has sparked demands for significant program design changes that provide citizens with more equal results. Three specific historical contingencies have interacted with these shifting predispositions.

First, recognition developed in the mid-1970s that the Federal Republic had, even by the standards of other advanced industrial societies, an exceptionally low birthrate (1.3 per woman—Mangen 1989, 184). By the mid-1990s the Federal Republic had already acquired a worker/pensioner ratio lower (1.65) than that which is projected for the United States when the bulk of the baby boomers begin to receive social security pensions after 2020 (Collier 1995, 251 n. 9; see also Haanes-Olsen 1989, 15; Kristof 1996, E5; Zeitzer 1983, 54; and Davis 1995, 45). Further, current projections indicate that this ratio will continue to fall in the Federal Republic. This will put severe strains on at least one generation of workers in the future (Cowell 1997a). Thus while the Federal Republic's immediate situation was not as severe in any respect as the Soviet Union's, in terms of short-run and long-term worker/beneficiary ratios as well as net pension liabilities the Federal Republic confronted more difficult circumstances than the United States.

Second, again since the mid-1970s, rates of productivity increase and economic performance generally in the Federal Republic have slowed from the pace of the previous two decades (Dyson 1989; Cohen 1997). Yet wages, including unusually expensive fringe benefits, are high, and German exporters, once widely envied, have found themselves increasingly beset by competitors in global markets. As profits have grown less rapidly, German employers have become more guarded in their support of comprehensive and generous social programs for their employees (Andrews 1996). Even more startling, unemployment, essentially unknown from the late 1950s through the mid-1970s (a period during which the Federal Republic imported ever larger numbers of "guest workers"), has been a regular problem for the last two decades and has grown particularly with reunification.[7] Among the societies considered in this study, the Federal Republic has been the most prone to attempt to deal with unemployment problems by encouraging early retirement (Esping-Andersen 1996, 18–20; Gruber and Wise 1999, 5–7). This practice has, in turn, exacerbated pension costs. Overall,

---

7. Persistent unemployment is especially problematic among a portion of younger workers, who do not appear sufficiently motivated to acquire the skills necessary for steady employment in the contemporary economy (Haanes-Olsen 1989, 15; Kalberg 1992; Münch 1992).

these new economic circumstances have increased the Federal Republic's social program expenses, particularly for public assistance and unemployment insurance programs, which have the least support among individualists (Coughlin 1980).

Finally, the 1989 reunification with the former German Democratic Republic (GDR) has placed extensive burdens on the Federal Republic's public finances and its social programs (Cowell 1997b). Indeed, the design of the Federal Republic's social policy ensures that these strains will be particularly troublesome. The Federal Republic relies more extensively on (contributory) social insurance than many other welfare states, and while public assistance became more user friendly across the 1960s and 1970s, in a strict technical sense the vast bulk of the monies expended through the Federal Republic's social programs go to social contributors, not simply citizens. Accordingly, the extension of the Federal Republic's social program benefits to citizens of the former GDR has been, not only costly, but has as well violated the tradition of no benefits without prior contributions. This is a specter that is likely to turn individualists, already skeptical about the virtues of public social provision, into active critics of these programs.

Across the late 1970s and early 1980s, a number of relatively modest steps were taken in an effort to cope with the early signs of the problems discussed above. As Mangen (1989, 175; see also Puidak 1987) shows, these steps raised certain revenues and reduced some program benefits, but they were insufficient, given the problems facing the Federal Republic, to relieve the growing strains on its public social programs and particularly its pensions for the elderly. Consistent with Huntington's suggestions (1981, 42–44, 113), the resulting controversy over changing pension policy offers a fine example of competition among grid-group theory's three rival socially interactive cultures. Influential German hierarchists have been slow to come to grips with the implications of historical contingencies that have made their social policy tradition less viable and, as we shall see, have pressed on with proposals for generous differentiated pensions. Liberal individualists, in contrast, have been quick to recognize features of Germany's changing social environment that make the support of these pensions more difficult and have taken advantage of this opportunity to argue strenuously for trimming the extensiveness of current pensions in a manner designed to prompt beneficiaries to greater self-reliance. Even egalitarians have recognized some need for budgetary restraint, but they have been far more concerned to take advantage of the scrutiny focused on public pensions in order to reformulate them in a more redistributive fashion that supports the less well off more thoroughly.

Options Considered and Their Association with Distinct Rationalities

Clear relations between these three cultural orientations and the Federal Republic's major political parties are well known. But while cultures and institutions are mutually reinforcing, two sorts of factors produce discrepancies. First, a variety of incentives (e.g., long-standing personal associations and other loyalties) prevent institutions from becoming culturally pure. There are members of the CDU who have more in common with the members of the FDP than with many members of their own party.[8] Similarly, in the United States we once spoke of (relatively unusual) liberal Republicans and (not so unusual) conservative Democrats, and the Republicans have recently had an economically conservative individualistic faction (George W. Bush et al.) and a socially conservative hierarchical faction (Pat Buchanan et al.). So particularly among organizations that strive to appeal to broad swaths of the public, cultural purity is neither expected nor desired.[9] Second, even political institutions that are relatively pure representations of a culture (e.g., the individualistic FDP) are often not in a position to support their ideal preferences through their actions. For instance, during the years of the Federal Republic, the FDP has essentially had the choice of realizing a portion of its ideals through junior partnership in a coalition government or refusing to compromise its ideals and having no practical influence on policy whatsoever.

In spite of these two caveats, Germany offers the clearest example (of the four that I consider in this study) of interaction among three rival, organized, culturally constrained, elite rationalities. The FDP and the Greens are both small disciplined parties that represent relatively pure examples of individualism and egalitarianism, respectively. The FDP has been a regular junior coalition partner of both the CDU and the SPD. By accepting such a

8. For instance, Kurt Biedenkopf, a prominent member of the CDU parliamentary delegation, argued that the CDU's pension proposals underestimated the severity of the Federal Republic's demographic trends and economic problems. Biedenkopf was more inclined toward the FDP's pension proposals than toward those of his own party's leadership ("Feines Ergebnis," 1988, 22).

9. Kirchheimer (1966, 184–92) calls political parties with this character "catch-all" parties and uses the CDU as one of his primary examples.

position, it routinely compromises its members' policy ideals, but there is little doubt that the FDP is more thoroughly individualistic than the other three major parties. Accordingly, the FDP has close relations with representatives of German business, including such peak associations as the Federal Union of German Employer Associations (BDA).

As their slogan—"work differently, distribute differently, live differently, and help differently"—suggests, many Greens aspire to the egalitarian ideal as I characterized it in Chapter 1. Intraparty tension arises from differences between grassroots "Fundis" (fundamentalists) and more pragmatic "Realos" (realists), the latter more prominent among the party's Bundestag representatives. Generally, the Greens want German society to shift away from its environmentally destructive industrial practices and its vision of more as better. For them, as for Schumacher (1973), "small is beautiful." Since becoming the junior partners in an SPD-led coalition government (1998), governing has fostered Green pragmatism, but the Green Party of the 1980s was more idealistically egalitarian.

Since the 1960s, both the CDU and the SPD have been examples of what Kirchheimer (1966, 184–92) calls catch-all parties that strive to appeal to a broad range of voters. So in contrast to the cultural purity of the FDP and the Greens, these parties are cultural coalitions, although both have relatively disciplined parliamentary delegations. The CDU represents a coalition of individualism and hierarchy (IH). Yet as Padgett (1989, 125) suggests, corporatist issues involving public social provision bring out the CDU's hierarchical face and—since the early 1970s—foster high-group cooperation on concerns shared by the CDU and prominent segments of the SPD. In contrast, the market issues involved in monetary policy bring out the coalition's individualistic face and align it more with the FDP.[10] The CDU inherited from its predecessors, the Catholic center parties of the Imperial and Weimar periods, an orientation toward social policy strongly influenced by the Roman Catholic Church (Mangen 1989, 177). The Church viewed the secular state as something of a rival, but nonetheless sought to imbue it with social obligations concerning public welfare.

Alone among contemporary German political parties, the SPD has a continuous history that extends deep into the Imperial period. Through 1958, it was a classic example of an egalitarian party preoccupied with the con-

10. We encountered a related phenomenon in Chapter 4 involving American individualists supporting some different values in sequential alignments with egalitarians (the Revolutionary coalition) and hierarchists (the Federalist coalition).

cerns of industrial workers. Controversial efforts, begun in the late 1950s, to expand the party's electoral appeal eventually succeeded. Accordingly, the party shared in governing for over a decade from the late 1960s through the early 1980s (initially in a "grand coalition" with the CDU and subsequently as the major partner in a coalition with the FDP). In the process, the party's character as a high-group (E-H) coalition became more evident—particularly during the period of Helmut Schmidt's chancellorship— and the party retained this character throughout the 1980s.

Against the war-ravaged social context of the late 1940s, the Federal Republic's first chancellor, Konrad Adenauer (CDU), supported social programs for reasons similar to Bismarck's. Comprehensive generous social programs were appropriate for a Christian political party, and they were also thought to be essential to the provision of societal amity and order that were in turn crucial for the resurgence of economic prosperity (Katzenstein 1987, 187; Dyson 1989, 155). In the mid-1950s Adenauer updated both the Federal Republic's pensions and its medical-care insurance (Safran 1967). The pensions that arose from Adenauer's struggles in the 1950s afforded no benefits to noncontributors and thus offered a social policy schema of limited offensiveness to individualists. These pensions were closely linked to prior earnings and indexed to prevailing wage rates so, as productivity gains and inflation raised wages, the elderly shared in the increases. Overall, the social insurance benefits that the Federal Republic provided after Adenauer's program expansion efforts were comprehensive and generous, ranking the Federal Republic's social policy provisions at or near the top of the then extant welfare states.

By contrast, in the mid-1980s some members of Helmut Kohl's CDU expressed growing interest in a "subsidiary principle" for pensions (Mangen 1989, 176–77). This principle was similar to but less extreme than the "three-legged stool" idea of the individualists in the 1983 American social security instance. By this principle public social programs would help persons to cope with the social hazards that confronted them, particularly aging, but persons would be expected to rely more extensively on their own private savings.[11] The CDU was also urged to trim existing pensions by its liberal (individualistic) coalition partner, the FDP, and some parliamentary and other prominent members of the CDU held views that were virtually

11. The third leg of the American "stool" of retirement supports, a system of private pensions, is less applicable in the case of the Federal Republic, where these pensions are far less common than in the United States (Mangen 1989, 184; see also Davis 1995, 55).

indistinguishable from the individualism of the FDP on this issue (e.g., Kurt Biedenkopf—see note 8). But this orientation toward pensions did not dominate the CDU. A sense of social responsibility, particularly for families (i.e., the party as a secular church), remained common among CDU members. But within both the CDU and its coalition with the FDP there was increasing conflict over the appropriate character of pensions and social policy generally. The problems facing public pensions had grown more acute, and the orientations of some CDU members had become less hierarchical ("Feines Ergebnis," 1988, 22).

Among political parties, the individualistic FDP provided the impetus across the 1980s for social program retrenchment. It sought to prompt greater individual initiative and responsibility. Its spokespersons argued that reduced reliance on public social provision would facilitate a more efficient and thus prosperous economy. The FDP favored reducing pensions and other public social programs to more modest levels, encouraging persons to supplement these benefits through private means, and reorganizing social services in more competitive ways offering greater efficiency (Mangen 1989, 179).

At least through Willi Brandt's chancellorship the SPD remained a stalwart supporter of comprehensive generous national social programs similar in broad outline to those that Bismarck had initiated.[12] More recently, however, the SPD split into two factions. The dominant faction—once led by the party's former chancellor, Helmut Schmidt—adopted a progressive compromising approach prompted by concern for maintaining both economic prosperity in an increasingly competitive global economy and the breadth of the party's electoral appeal. The minority faction supported, not only generous pensions and other social policy benefits for workers more ardently, but also evinced growing skepticism about Bismarck's traditional means of delivering workers' benefits through large-scale, relatively impersonal, central-state programs. This faction preferred to transform Bismarck's system into numerous local "grassroots" citizens' associations that would plan, organize, and deliver social program benefits (Mangen 1989, 178).

Members of the mainstream SPD faction generally stood by the loose,

---

12. This affinity between the SPD and Bismarck on social policy is not surprising. Bismarck saw himself as engaged in state socialism (Dawson 1973, 28, 34–35, 119), and he and socialists such as Gustav Schmoller held some similar views on social programs (Katzenstein 1987, 171).

informal, high-group (HE) coalition that has been the basis for the welfare state in Germany and elsewhere across this century. As it had in previous rounds of social policy conflicts, this faction preferred pensions with greater redistributive effects, but it has not pressed hard for major changes since the Willi Brandt years. Instead, this faction, particularly through the 1986 report of the party's Social Policy Commission, focused on program changes aimed at modest economies and reducing various specific benefit discrepancies and inequalities.

Since the mid-1970s the high-group (E-H) coalition that forms the SPD has shared representation of egalitarian views with the more thoroughly egalitarian Greens. Along with the SPD, the Greens express a preference for pensions and other social programs that are more thoroughly redistributive. But the Greens emphasize particularly matters of gender equality as opposed to the class divisions that have historically been the primary focus of the SPD. The Greens also prefer local participatory means of social program planning, organization, and delivery in contrast to the central-state bureaucracies that the SPD has long supported. Additionally, the Greens advocate social program benefits on the basis of citizenship rather than contribution (labor-market participation) to society.

Across the 1980s, then, the pension policies of the Federal Republic's political parties clearly reflected the contrasting preferences for distinctive institutional designs that we associated with rival cultures in Chapter 3. The hierarchical face of the CDU's I-H coalition that dominates on social policy retained its preferences for extensive but highly stratified pensions. Recent historical contingencies had, however, prompted the CDU to make some modest cuts in the benefits of these comprehensive and generous programs. Those in the party's individualistic faction reacted to these historical contingencies by calling for more retrenchment, advocating leaner pensions similar to those proposed by other individualists in the FDP. The FDP straightforwardly called for sharply reduced standard pension benefits, and thus for greater personal initiative and responsibility, in order to increase the German economy's competitiveness. The traditional faction of the E-H coalition that has historically provided the basis for a governing or governing-capable SPD acknowledged the need for some pension retrenchment. But it argued for increasing the pensions of persons with low wage-histories and financing these improvements through reductions in the replacement rates of relatively well off pensioners, creating a more redistributive benefit structure. This faction also stood by the provision of benefits through relatively centralized state bureaucracies. The minority faction of the SPD and the Greens favored more redistributive programs and wanted to shift program control into the hands of local boards dominated by ordinary citizens.

Pension policy preferences of the major parties (i.e., the CDU, the FDP, and the SPD-Greens) thus reflect hierarchical, individualistic, and egalitarian institutional design preferences, respectively, with a clarity that is exceptional even for the Federal Republic. As Heine (1989, 146) suggests, the roughly contemporaneous struggle over reformulating healthcare policy provides less clear-cut, culturally constrained party preferences. In the healthcare policy instance, the governing parties (CDU and FDP) were both torn by conflicting considerations. For the FDP, a strong abstract preference for a leaner state conflicted with the deleterious consequences for profits that trimming public medical-care program benefits would mean for some firms in the healthcare industry. The CDU was concerned to maintain its preeminence in expert and prudent public management, which, in this instance, was challenged by various healthcare provider organizations on issues such as the use of generic prescriptions. In contrast, pensions, which are delivered by the state itself and go to individual citizens, create fewer cross-pressures and thus lend themselves to purer realizations of culturally constrained positions.

Actual policy in the mid-1980s reflected the CDU position.[13] The Greens and the minority faction of the SPD had little influence on policy. Further, while FDP views received growing press coverage, particularly as important business interests began to advocate similar positions, German politicians—like their American and Soviet counterparts—were extraordinarily reluctant to make substantial cuts, particularly in the near term, in benefits that their citizens had become conditioned to expect. In the American and German instances the explanation for this hesitancy is often couched in terms of fears of electoral retribution, and this may be an adequate explanation for individualists. However, the Soviet hesitancy in this regard suggests that hierarchists may perceive such cuts as an abrogation of their duties to society's weak and vulnerable members. In any case, the process of achieving sufficient policy change to secure the Federal Republic's public pensions in a less economically prosperous era, further burdened by a falling worker/beneficiary ratio, advanced only hesitantly and partially across the mid-1980s.

---

13. This position is not so very different from that advocated by Helmut Schmidt's (SPD-FDP) government in the late 1970s and early 1980s.

A crisis atmosphere in social program funding—prompted more by immediate problems with medical-care insurance than by pensions—developed in 1987. The FDP advocated a flat-rate minimum public pension that persons could supplement through private means. The FDP recommended that favorable terms for private supplementation be made available for persons who had contributed to public pension funds for lengthy periods. As expected, some members of the CDU joined the call for such a scheme, but the party did not, as a whole, endorse this approach. The SPD—supported by organized labor's peak organization, the German Trade-Union Association (DGB)—reacted to calls for sharp retrenchment by advocating the retention of much of the existing system of benefits, but changing the basis for employer contributions from a percentage of payroll (in effect, a tax on positions) to a tax on employee turnover. Additionally, the SPD favored assuring a minimum pension to all in order to upgrade pensions among workers with low wage-histories. In this crisis atmosphere the Greens advocated a more generous basic pension than that favored by the FDP. The Greens intended that this pension be available to all citizens. Employers' contributions to this basic pension would be based roughly on the environmental destructiveness of their economic activities. The Greens also supported a mandatory system of supplementary private pensions, a scheme similar to that currently practiced in Sweden. So as they entered this "pressured decision point" (Cook 1993, 6), the FDP, SPD, and the Greens continued to advocate program renovation preferences indicative of their individualistic, E-H, and egalitarian institutional design ideals.

Discussions over pension policy were furthered as well by the 1987 report of a public commission. Several of its suggestions were familiar from the 1983 American social security episode. These proposals included further reducing indexation, more thoroughly subsidizing pensions through the general revenues of the federal government, and reversing the increasingly popular trend toward early retirement (Mangen 1989, 185; "Ende der Stange," 1988). This commission also offered suggestions for ways to achieve greater equality in the pensions of men and women by taking into consideration child-rearing activities and care for the elderly and disabled (Puidak 1987).

Pension reform picked up momentum in the autumn of 1988 when the leading player, the CDU, weighed in with its own proposals. These initiatives were introduced through Norbert Blüm, the CDU's minister of employment (Bundesminister für Arbeit and Sozialordnung 1988). Blüm's (and thus the CDU's overall) explicit strategy was to formulate revised provisions

that would sustain the pension system through 2010 and be capable of garnering a near consensus, not only between the governing parties (CDU and
FDP), but with the SPD as well. Thus pension reform was designed to represent German politics near its centripetal apex, although the range of agreement Blüm achieved was narrower than that which he sought. The Greens
maintained their support for a relatively sharp reformulation of pension
policy and remained outside the group supporting Blüm's proposals, and
they were joined by some in the SPD. The SPD leadership resisted Blüm's
proposals for raising the retirement age (to be discussed below). More significantly, some members of the governing parties opposed aspects of
Blüm's approach. Generally, intragovernment opposition was based on perceptions that Blüm's proposals were inadequate for solving the long-term
problems posed for pensions by prevailing demographic and economic
trends ("Feines Ergebnis," 1988, 22). In contrast to the situation in the
United States five years earlier, however, no person occupying a position
of political responsibility suggested eliminating pensions or sharply cutting
publicly mandated supports for the elderly in the near term.

Unsurprisingly, given the continuity of pension policy history across four
regimes (including the Federal Republic), Blüm did not recommend altering
the fundamental structure of pension programs. His recommendations continued to clearly reflect aspects of the hierarchical institutional formation
imperative that the CDU had long applied to pension issues. Pension benefits retained both their close relationship to prior earnings and their linkages
to changes in the standard of living. So German pensions sustained, in broad
outline, their differentiating character, thus assuring that pensioners would
retain their relative socioeconomic status. But Blüm's proposals did include
some innovations reflecting a liberalizing trend. Efforts were made to reduce
differentials between men and women arising from matters such as the treatment of child rearing, personal employment histories, care for the elderly
and disabled, and retirement age. The CDU adapted some of these proposals from Green initiatives partially in the hope that certain innovations
would help to spur employment and/or the birthrate and thus gradually ease
the difficult economic and demographic circumstances that pension policy
currently faced.

While the SPD in particular fought hard on certain matters, the CDU's
strategy of compromising in order to achieve consensus worked fairly well.
Public pronouncements to the effect that since pensions represented a vital
matter for everyone, there ought to be widespread support for pension policy, fostered an environment of cooperation and compromise. In contrast to

the press coverage of the 1983 social security "crisis" in the United States, the revision of German pension policy passed virtually without comment.[14] Nonetheless, some of the new provisions would have been extremely controversial in the United States.

Relative Reliance on Benefit Reductions as Opposed to Revenue Increases

In 1989 the CDU leadership remained true to its tradition on this public social provision issue by presenting a largely hierarchical face. Thus while rival cultures preferred conflicting institutional designs, the high-group cultures were heavily represented, and their shared preference for retaining extensive public pensions carried the day. The FDP's parliamentary delegation was tiny in comparison to that of either the CDU or the SPD, and its influence was limited largely to the somewhat deferred issue of raising the retirement age. Indeed, conflict between the CDU's hierarchical differentiating approach and the SPD-Green's egalitarian redistributive concerns was nearly as prominent as the issues dividing the concerns of the high-group cultures for retaining generous pensions from the FDP's individualistic interest in program retrenchment.

Thus the German pension law of December 1989 (effective January 1, 1992) grew out of relatively broad high-group agreement involving significant elements of the governing parties and the SPD, leaving only some segments of the FDP and associated business interests as well as the Greens voicing serious disagreement. The most important aspects of this compromise legislation are as follows (Frerich and Frey 1993, 255–56; Heine 1989; Bundesminister für Arbeit and Sozialordnung 1988). First, in order to generally maintain and indeed in some instances enhance monthly support levels, program revenues were increased. These increases included both the contributions of persons covered by various pension programs as well as the contributions of the federal government from general tax revenues. The use of general tax revenues as a funding source would have been highly controversial in the United States, where however mistaken the claim may

---

14. Actual legislation was passed in November and December of 1989 and went into effect January 1, 1992. These were tumultuous times in the Federal Republic. The Berlin Wall came down in December 1989 and the Soviet Union came apart in the autumn of 1991. *Der Spiegel*, which had covered a range of domestic policy issues in 1988 and early 1989, became increasingly focused on the Federal Republic's relations with the East (activities in the former German Democratic Republic, refugees from a variety of locations in Eastern Europe, and the Soviet Union/Russia) in late 1989 and late 1991.

be, one of the supports for social security over the years has been the argument that recipients are paying for their benefits. Indeed, even in Imperial Germany individualists succeeded in opposing Bismarck's preference for a contribution to pension funds from the central government (Katzenstein 1987, 171). Certainly since the 1980s, however, specified funding of pensions from the general tax revenues of the central government has been relatively uncontroversial in the Federal Republic. Across the 1980s, use of general revenues had risen rapidly, as had the contribution rates for program participants ("Feines Ergebnis," 1988, 23).[15] The 1992 law envisioned that across the foreseeable future a substantial and growing proportion of the funds needed to pay pensions would come from this source.

Second, a series of benefit reductions was introduced. Most important, beginning in 2001 the retirement age for full-scale pensions was to be gradually raised to sixty-five for most persons. This step reversed in the German instance a well-established recent trend among corporate welfare-state regimes involving a willingness to grant pensions to progressively younger persons as a means of coping with rising levels of long-term unemployment among younger workers (Haanes-Olsen 1989, 16–17; Esping-Andersen 1996, 18–20; Gruber and Wise 1999, 5–7). This reversal was the price of FDP cooperation and also the major source of SPD dissatisfaction with the pension agreement (Heine 1989, 197). German retirement age increases were to come first for men with limited years of contributions, then move to men with more years of contributions (2006), and finally be applied to women (2012). The retirement age for workers with certain disabilities would remain at sixty. Since many workers in their late fifties acquired disability pensions that carried them into retirement, it was not clear how effective raising the retirement age would be in reducing total pension expenses, although it would shift some expenses from retirement to disability pensions (Börsch-Supan and Schnabel 1999). The 1989 decision also revised the formulas through which pensions are calculated with an eye, not only to increasing incentives for retiring after sixty-five, but encouraging more lengthy records of contributions generally. Additionally, in the future pensions would be calculated on the basis of retirees' former net (i.e., after tax), rather than gross, incomes.

Third, a variety of measures, holding more modest consequences for pro-

---

15. Indeed this trend has recently been expanded. The 1997 agreement on taxes and pensions authorizes the Federal Republic to pay the contributions of some individual workers who interrupt their employment—e.g., women who leave the workplace for a few years to take care of small children (German Information Center 1997, 1).

gram finances than those discussed in the previous two paragraphs, were introduced as means for achieving greater equality of treatment among various categories of persons (men and women; workers, students, and persons in military service; and persons with exceptionally low wage-histories) or assuring greater procedural fairness. For example, the number of years credited for child care was increased, and the period of a child's development across which these years could be applied was expanded. Related changes were allowed for the care of elderly and disabled family members. Additionally, a standard minimum pension, entailing considerable redistribution, was established for persons with extremely low incomes but at least twenty-five years of contributions.

As the need to frequently revise various national pension programs attests, estimating the precise consequences of various program changes a number of years down the road is notoriously difficult. The package of changes the Germans introduced in 1989 was extremely complex and required modification fairly quickly. Nonetheless, reasonable expectations for this package can be characterized as follows. The benefit reductions entailed by various retirement age increases outweighed other provisions providing more extensive benefits (e.g., counting more years devoted to the care of various family members as contributory years). So the 1989 package produced net benefit reductions. However, at least across the period on which both the CDU and the SPD focused the bulk of their attention (1989–2010), these benefit reductions would—barring future changes—have turned out to be less extensive than the package's revenue increases, required largely to fund preexisting benefit levels ("Feines Ergebnis," 1988, 23; Frerich and Frey 1993, 259–60). This edge of revenue increases over benefit reductions was an artifact of juxtaposing the informal 2010 horizon and the staged introduction of retirement age increases. This artifact, in turn, signified the reluctance of the high-group, CDU and SPD leaders to recognize the implications of certain features of reality (i.e., a declining worker/beneficiary ratio and the poor fit between longer life spans and lower retirement ages) that pose difficulties for their pension policy preferences. Essentially, high-group leaders stalled on new arrangements that would be more adequate across a longer term in the hopes that circumstances more encouraging for their favored institutions would turn up in the interim.

Explicitness of the Focus on Long-Term Financial Costs

Overall, this legislation was inadequate to the task of sustaining the Federal Republic's pension system financially across a span of time remotely similar to the seventy-five-year horizon American individualists now ask of social security (Stevenson 1999). Additional revenue increases have already been required to sustain current benefit levels into the near future (German Information Center 1997, 1), and the schedule of retirement age increases has been advanced (Börsch-Supan and Schnabel 1999, 148). It seems likely that, at some juncture in the not-so-distant future, even more significant benefit reductions will have to be introduced (Cohen 1999). The 1989 changes may point in a sufficiently new direction to indicate important elements of a long-term solution (e.g., more revenues from general taxation in conjunction with reductions in benefits through increasingly demanding age requirements). But in the face of demographic and financial prospects more dire in both the short- and long-term than those facing the United States in 1983, German public officials chose in 1989 to rely on increased revenues more heavily than reduced benefits to cope with the difficulties pensions posed in the near future. In contrast to their individualistic American counterparts, dominant German H-E elites focused their attention on a less-distant time horizon and did not high-profile revenue increase / benefit reduction ratios. Longer time horizons and ratio calculations would have highlighted the poor fit between features of their preferred policy solution and the demographic and economic circumstances confronting it. Further, this approach had broad—though not universal support—within the CDU and the SPD. Only the extremes of individualism (primarily within the FDP and some business associations) and egalitarianism (primarily the Greens) voiced sharp disagreement. It is clear that a substantial majority of German political elites regarded the financial security of the elderly as an extremely high priority. Moreover, they were predisposed to use the traditional hierarchical mechanism of increased support from large central-state bureaucracies to secure this objective.

Unsurprisingly, this legislation not only fell short of solving the long-term difficulties of German pensioners, it also failed to silence opposition from groups whose concerns had been insufficiently addressed. German business interests in particular perceived in this legislation a wake-up call. The BDA has since redoubled its efforts to draw attention to what, with some justification, it perceives as a crisis in policy (Collier 1995).

Cultural Mechanisms of Political Change

Contrasting the 1989 German decision on pensions with the United States decision of 1983 is instructive. The two societies faced similar, though not identical, situations concerning their pensions for the elderly. As Table 6 shows, the Federal Republic faced a lower worker/beneficiary ratio in both the short- and long-term. Further, its pension program finances produced a proportionately larger net liability. Moreover, in the years prior to its "pension crisis" the Federal Republic had conditioned German workers to expect an increasingly lenient early retirement policy. It seems reasonable to conclude that the Federal Republic confronted a more dire situation.

Additionally, a similar range of opinion existed among American and German political actors, but egalitarians and hierarchists were much more thoroughly represented among relevant German political elites; whereas individualistic influence was much more extensive among their American counterparts. In the late 1980s, questions of pension policy in the Federal Republic still brought to prominence the CDU's corporatist or hierarchical face, which was reinforced with related values and sympathies among the SPD (E-H). In the United States powerful individualists struggled with a weaker H-E coalition.

American and German political elites applied similar solution elements involving a variety of revenue increases and a mixture of benefit increases and reductions that produced net benefit reductions. But they employed these elements in different proportions. Within the distinctive time horizons on which they focused, United States individualists succeeded in deflecting a previous trajectory of program growth downward more sharply than their German counterparts. Indeed, the focus of the German high-group leaders on a time-horizon roughly half as long (from 1989 to 2010) as that employed by the American decision makers (from 1983–2025) reflected their collective unwillingness to allow changing circumstances to disrupt their policy preferences. In the United States individualists actively sought a longer time-horizon in order to dramatize what they perceived as the socially destructive consequences of the existing social security program's size and expense.

Among the prevailing German high-group leaders, a generous societal (public) commitment to economic security for the elderly—long-term yet vulnerable contributors to the social collective—clearly had an extremely high priority. This was true even in the face of approaching historical contingencies, to which the FDP and business groups drew attention, that made such a commitment challenging, even foolhardy. Moreover, the preferred means for achieving this characteristic high-group (and particularly hierarchical) objective involved increased support from central-state bureaucracies. Yet in the United States influential individualists were more concerned with reducing the activity level of the central government and thereby stimulating individual initiative. It is clear that American individualists took advantage of similarly shifting circumstances to produce more political change than their German counterparts, depressing the trajectory of social policy growth far more sharply than German high-group leaders, because the pre-existing situation was more unsatisfactory from the standpoint of their culturally constrained institutional preferences. In contrast, the dominant German high-group leaders resisted a similar of change in policy trajectory because it threatened existing programs consistent with their culturally constrained institutional preferences.

EIGHT

HALF-MEASURES ON JAPANESE PUBLIC PENSIONS, 1985

`

RELATIVE CULTURAL INFLUENCE AND INSTITUTIONAL CONSEQUENCES

Of the four societies that I examine in this study, Japan is likely the most thoroughly high-group (Richardson 1974; Tsurumi 1970; van Wolferen 1990; Lipset 1996). According to Ishida: "The individual is submerged in a group-oriented society; minority opinions contrary to established group desire are disregarded by a tradition which values group harmony. This process produces a tendency toward national conformism which in turn leads to discrimination against the minority" (1983, 13). Japan has supported no extensive individualism. There has been and remains much interest in economic development. But this goal has generally been furthered through means that in the United States would be unfavorably characterized by individualists as government "intervention" in the private sector.[1] While Japa-

1. Such perceptions are not unknown in Japan, and they may sometimes arise from Smithian individualistic orientations. They also frequently reflect "sour grapes" attitudes among corporate executives who have lost public favor to other firms or industries (Johnson 1982).

nese business enterprises fail as well as succeed on the basis of their market experience (Turner 1989, 302–3), major Japanese corporations have had much closer relations than their counterparts in the United States with public bureaucracies striving—with varying success during different periods—to further national economic development (Johnson 1982).

Additionally, like Rohrschneider's (1994) portrayal of eastern members of the united Berlin parliament, Japanese conceptions of democracy differ from the negative liberty / personal rights against government orientation characteristic of individualism. As Turner shows, Japanese views of democracy include avoiding hierarchical tyranny. But when stated positively Japanese conceptions of democracy entail the characteristically egalitarian vision of inclusive participation in the decisions that affect one's life (1989, 305–9). So neither the capitalistic nor the democratic aspects of contemporary Japan provide evidence for the strength of individualism. While Japanese individualists exist, Japan is a society dominated by the adherents of high-group cultures.

More controversial is the relative influence between the high-group cultures. Egalitarians influence certain aspects of Japanese society. The various opposition parties are predominately egalitarian (advocating as they do varieties of socialism). Further, some aspects of public policy (e.g., primary and secondary education) have followed egalitarian (socialist) practices (Cummings 1980; Kristof 1997). Moreover, some analysts remark on the relative absence of social classes. Income, for instance, is more evenly distributed among the Japanese than it is among the citizens of most Western European societies and the United States (McKean 1989), and Steven (1983) reports little class consciousness.

But what is modest is class conflict and the consciousness that such conflict helps to foster within Western societies, not social differentiation. Japan is a highly stratified society (Ishida 1983; Tsurumi 1970). The structure of families, industries, the labor market, and the character of the public policy process all demonstrate this stratification (Pempel 1982, 14, 22, 30). The relative absence of conflict in the face of such—largely hierarchically based—stratification indicates the relative weakness of the low-grid cultures, egalitarianism included. Class conflict is relatively absent *because* Japan is such a thoroughly hierarchical society. Persons generally accept their niches in the series of nested hierarchies (e.g., family, company, nation) that form Japanese society (Verba et al. 1987, 23).

The economic difficulties that afflicted Japan across the 1990s illustrate how limited support for Smithian market economics is in that country.

Contact with Western powers in the mid-nineteenth century reinforced the predominance of hierarchy by creating a long-term security crisis. The Japanese witnessed China's subjugation and dismemberment by technologically superior Western powers and feared that they might suffer a similar fate. The threat of domination by Western powers divided the Japanese leaders of the day and eventually produced the 1868 Meiji Restoration with its central objective of national economic and military development. Each side to the dispute that resulted in the Restoration revered the basic hierarchical values of national security and integrity. Traditionally, Japanese elites had realized these values by turning inward, virtually ignoring the outside world and controlling the flow of persons and information into their islands. Feudal armaments had worked fairly well to deter previous foreign military threats, and aversion to foreign contacts had preserved Japanese beliefs and values from external pollution. But a number of mid-nineteenth-century Japanese elites thought that this strategy was insufficient for securing Japan from Western imperialism. Instead, they argued that the preservation of Japanese sovereignty required emulation of the economic and military practices of the Western powers. For elites favoring the traditional approach, massive emulation of the West meant the destruction of Japanese integrity, but Restoration elites won this dispute, and a mobilization designed to secure Japan from foreign imperialism became *the* central political objective.[2]

This revolution from above signified the ascendance of modernizing elements of a military hierarchy, in conjunction with commercial interests, over more tradition-bound, agriculturally oriented hierarchists (Dower 1975, 158). While this was a coalition of "sword and yen," the commercial elements remained dependent on the hierarchical *samurai*, largely displaced former warriors (Dower 1975, 168, 189). In the name of the emperor, a government comprised largely of aristocratic civilian and military bureaucrats launched the nation on an extensive technological, economic, and mili-

---

2. As was the case with the distinction between Ligachev's "party" and Ryzhkov's "technological" Soviet hierarchical factions that we encountered in Chapter 6, grid-group theory's cultures cannot explain the differences in institutional preferences of these two Restoration-era hierarchical factions. Intracultural differences such as these are likely the result of distinctive institutional experiences, which prompt adherents of a common culture to turn to different specific means to realize closely related values. In the Restoration instance, persons with rural institutional niches were more likely to seek national integrity through isolation; whereas persons whose institutional niches had brought them into contact with Western emissaries were more likely to opt for security through emulation. I apply this view below in distinguishing between traditional and conventional Japanese hierarchists in the contemporary period.

tary mobilization. As "late developers," the Japanese had numerous models on which to draw. They emulated aspects of German, French, British, and American practice, carefully choosing the approaches to particular aspects of public policy and industry that seemed best suited to Japanese beliefs and values (Powell and Anesaki 1990, 27). So while the institutions that the Restoration elites built were often sharply different from their traditional Japanese counterparts, these new institutions were examples of what Eckstein calls "pattern-maintaining change" (1988, 793–94). That is, through the Restoration, hierarchists sought to build new institutions designed to preserve their enduring, high-priority values in changing social circumstances.

This mobilization effort continued under varying auspices from the early 1870s through the first four decades of the twentieth century. It achieved remarkable successes such as the Japanese victory in the Russo-Japanese War in 1906. But as the mobilization confronted the major historical contingencies in the twentieth century, it also experienced difficulties. As Johnson (1982, 310–11) shows, central-state bureaucrats tried different strategies for fostering what they saw as desirable development under varying circumstances. Further, as the military, which was responsible only to the emperor, became increasingly prominent in the central leadership during the 1930s, the mobilization was deflected in a direction that eventually brought humiliating defeat.

Throughout the prewar development period (1868–1941), hierarchy was virtually pervasive, characterizing nearly all social institutions. As Pempel relates, the 1889 Meiji constitution was aimed at achieving "national cohesion and centralized authority," producing a "strong central government" that could "act purposefully and with minimal opposition" (1989, 19). The emperor was sovereign, not the people, and the central bureaucracy was responsible to him, not the Diet. The lower or elected house of the Diet had little prospect of influencing policy. Further, the male franchise that developed after 1889 was sharply limited by socioeconomic criteria until 1925, and women could not vote at all until after the Second World War. Some opposition parties were illegal at times. A portion of an 1889 speech by Prime Minister Kuroda sums up the situation: "It goes without saying that the citizens have nothing to say either for or against the Constitution" (Pempel 1989, 20).[3]

3. Pempel also points out that "the prewar Japanese political system contained within itself the potential to become more democratic, and indeed did so" (1989, 20). But this was less a result of the purposes of leading political figures than an unintended consequence, similar to

In the aftermath of the Second World War, Japan experienced vast changes, particularly in the public sphere (Krauss and Ishida 1989, 327–36). The American Occupation (1945–52) initially demilitarized Japan and imposed the formal institutions of democracy, among them a constitution stressing personal rights such as citizen (as opposed to imperial) sovereignty, a bicameral parliament in which both houses are elected through universal suffrage, a cabinet arising largely from and responsible to the parliament, and elected local and judicial officials. Originally, the Occupation sought considerable economic reorganization as well, but the conflict in Korea led Occupation officials to place a higher priority on economic recovery than on reorganization.

The Occupation had less effect on the private sphere of Japanese life. Japanese families remain predominantly hierarchical (Shinkawa and Pempel 1996). And while Japanese primary and secondary education have been remarkably egalitarian for much of the postwar period, this is beginning to change, and private universities operate on increasingly hierarchical principles—in addition to the inherent criterion of intellectual ability (Beauchamp 1989). The labor market is stratified both vertically and horizontally with most private-sector worker organization taking an intracompany form. While the prewar *zaibatsu*, vertically integrated industrial conglomerates, were technically destroyed by the Occupation, looser versions of these interlocking directorates (*zaikai*) have appeared and dominate the postwar economy (Fukushima 1989). Criteria of family background, gender, age, and—on the rare occasions when it arises—ethnicity create a vertical social context for persons in which they relate routinely to social superiors and subordinates and less commonly to relative equals (Ishida 1983; Verba et al. 1987, 23).

Postwar Japanese have thus lived in two conflicting social milieus. As family members, workers, and in private life generally, their social world has been vertically organized. In contrast, as citizens, they have been supported by an array of legal rights that afford all persons similar formal protection (Pempel 1989, 22). Naturally, these disparate social milieus interact and influence each other (Smith 1997). For instance, in spite of formal legal protection against discrimination on the basis of gender or ethnicity, the preferences of the hierarchical private sphere result in habitual discrimina-

---

the Soviets learning that contemporary office equipment (e.g., personal computers, the internet and copying and fax machines) reduce hierarchical leaders' capacities for controlling information.

tion on these grounds. As one union official—apparently without intended irony—put it: "We are all equal union members and equal as workers—all of us—from the president all the way down to the part-time women" (Turner 1989, 317). Yet in spite of the pervasive hierarchy of the private sphere, some forms of tyrannical intervention in persons' lives that both private and public prewar authorities routinely practiced are now illegal and relatively rare (Turner 1989, 305).[4]

In the postwar period economic development has been valued as a means of achieving a broader range of objectives, including domestic prosperity and international status and influence—likely the only means to these latter ends, since military power was precluded by Occupation-imposed demilitarization (Pempel 1982). The ground rules for development decisions also changed. External imposition of democratic institutions created more players who were formally eligible to engage in the processes by which important political-economic decisions were reached. Different decision-making processes characterize distinctive policy areas in postwar Japan (Krauss 1989). Crucial economic development decisions have generally been dominated by a modestly more inclusive version of the process such decisions followed during much of the prewar period. Initiative still lies primarily with central-state executives, particularly top officials in the Ministry of Finance and Ministry of International Trade and Industry (MITI). In formulating initiatives ministry officials typically work closely with high-ranking officers—frequently their former ministry colleagues—of major corporations. Once policy initiatives have been developed, ministry officials must persuade prominent members of parliament (e.g., generally leaders of various Liberal Democratic Party—LDP—factions) to enact their proposals.

Prior to the Second World War, the development of social programs in Japan fit into the overall process of economic mobilization as particularly clear-cut reactions to threats that central political elites perceived in various historical contingencies (Shinkawa and Pempel 1996; Collick 1988). So, for instance, the Health Insurance Law of 1922 was narrowly focused on wage workers in the large firms that were most central to economic development. Japan's continental Asian war in the late 1930s, along with the prospect of a broader Pacific war, superimposed worries about military preparations on the constant concern with industrial harmony. Accordingly, a new Ministry of Health and Welfare was created in 1938. In the same year Japanese politi-

---

4. For a chilling example of the sort of intervention that private-sector authorities still consider within their grasp, see Fukushima 1989, 265.

cal executives broadened the existing system of medical-care insurance for employees. Additionally, in 1941 the Employee Pension System (EPS) was adopted. As Shinkawa and Pempel (1996) show, these program development steps were aimed as much at military readiness as at mitigating the problems of vulnerable citizens. The focus of the expanded national health insurance was the physical condition of male industrial workers of draftable age, among whom tuberculosis and other communicable diseases were widespread. The new pension system would not pay benefits for twenty years, but it initiated worker contributions, thus increasing state revenues, just prior to the expansion of the war.

Calder (1988, 361–75) contends that the social policy initiatives of postwar Japan have also been responses to crises. But the nature of the crises and the parties who have perceived threats have varied from the prewar period. Postwar social policy development is not the result of powerful national executives responding to various external security problems. External security has generally been perceived as less of a problem. Additionally, neither the Ministry of Health and Welfare nor the Ministry of Labor—the likely executive sources of social program initiatives—is a powerful institution (Pempel 1982, 139). More important, among the most powerful national executives, those in the Ministry of Finance and MITI, social policy growth has generally been perceived as conflicting with economic development. Accordingly, they have been skeptical about expanding social programs (Noguchi 1987).

Ministry of Finance and MITI officials epitomize the "traditional" Japanese hierarchists I introduced in Chapter 3. Their institutional niches have fostered a "late developer" preoccupation with economic development; and as hierarchists, they prefer to make societal decisions according to their own and related expertise rather than to allow ordinary citizens or their parliamentary representatives to make them. Concerning social policy, for instance, traditional Japanese hierarchists fear that the general public is apt to be ignorant of important factors bearing on the development of social programs as well as egoistic and thus willing to press parliamentary representatives for benefits that hindsight will reveal as destructively generous. In contrast, private employers are, from this perspective, keenly aware of the market value of their employees as well as of the various economic consequences for their firms of varying levels of employee fringe benefits. Accordingly, traditionally hierarchical Japanese managers, both public and corporate, prefer to keep as high a proportion of material resources as possible in the hierarchically arrayed private domain where these resources may be more effectively employed for national economic development. So through the 1950s, across which these central-state executives were extremely influential, Japanese social programs remained modest, deflecting few resources from the continuing national developmental effort (Noguchi 1986, 175). Social policy focused narrowly on pensions for the elderly and medical-care insurance for a limited range of workers and made little use of need-based public assistance (Bronfenbrenner and Yasuba 1987, 130–35).

From around 1960 through the early 1970s, elected officials responded more thoroughly to the dissatisfaction of many ordinary citizens, who felt left out of Japan's rapidly improving economic circumstances, by expanding Japanese social programs. Indeed, for a time the "crises" that drove social policy development were LDP leaders' anxieties over maintaining their party's dominant electoral position, and many LDP Diet representatives provide good examples of the "conventional" Japanese hierarchists I also introduced in Chapter 3. Their institutional niches prompt greater interest (i.e., than among traditional Japanese hierarchists) in the concerns of ordinary citizens. They consider responding to these concerns as conducive to societal order generally and important for maintaining the enlightened (i.e., in contrast to the opposition parties) societal leadership the LDP offers. Thus, like socially conservative hierarchists in Germany, they have supported the social program expansion favored by large portions of the citizenry. Accordingly, another medical-care program was developed in 1959; this one serving persons who were not employees. Further, a National Pension System (NPS) was initiated in 1961, covering the bulk of the population not already under the umbrella of the EPS or one of the various pension funds for public-sector workers. Pension levels remained modest by European standards until the upgrading of 1973, which also indexed benefits to prices and wages (Fisher 1973; Collick 1988; Aldrich 1982, 5). Child allowances were introduced in 1973, the year the LDP's national economic plan called for a "vigorous welfare society" (Pempel 1982, 142). Another legislative initiative revised the Occupation unemployment program significantly in 1976, making job-search assistance a more prominent component and focusing attention on older workers displaced by technological innovation or the early retirement practices applied by many firms.

Yet as public social provision costs rose and economic difficulties (e.g., the "oil shocks" of the 1970s) as well as demographic concerns appeared, various central-state executives succeeded in recapturing predominance on social policy initiatives across the late 1970s. Shifting the locus of social program initiatives from LDP leaders to executive officials has meant that development efforts have frequently been replaced with retrenchment measures.

In his 1990 typology of corporatist, liberal, and social-democratic welfare-state regimes Esping-Andersen does not explicitly consider Japan. He subsequently addresses where Japan fits in this typology (1997), arguing that attempts at definitive categorization are premature but concluding that Japan likely represents a hybrid of his corporate and liberal models. In contrast, I contend that the Japanese welfare state is the result of interplay between traditional and conventional hierarchists. While the former, like individualists, prefer modest state expenditures, they share with conventional hierarchists a preference for applying state expertise to various economic issues. Thus in contrast to individualists, traditional Japanese hierarchists favor a state that takes an active role in societal direction. Additionally, an industrial policy that strives to provide (frequently multigenerational) households with sufficient gainful employment, rather than extensive income-maintenance programs, is their social policy of choice.[5] Whereas individualists and conventional hierarchists differ on both value priorities and preferred institutional designs, traditional and conventional hierarchists share value priorities, but they employ different institutions to realize these values. Some of the institutional preferences of both of these hierarchical factions are distinct as well from the institutional designs favored by individualists.

Such intracultural differences in institutional preferences cannot be explained by grid-group theory's cultures. Rather, like the differences between the Ligachev ("party") and Ryzhkov ("technological") factions of Soviet hierarchy that we encountered in Chapter 6, they are the result of different institutional experiences. As the index of their common support for an expert and socially interventionist state suggests, both of these contemporary Japanese factions are clearly hierarchical. Yet the institutional missions of central-state executives responsible for development prompt different institutional preferences (i.e., an active industrial policy) for the problems which public social programs are aimed at ameliorating than the options (e.g., income-maintenance and social service programs) favored—on the basis of

---

5. As Hashimoto shows, traditional Japanese hierarchical conceptions of adequacy focus on realizing a group-based conception of security, providing an elderly parent enough to be able to contribute to and thus share an adult child's household. In contrast, low-grid conceptions of adequacy are more likely to emphasize a capacity for personal autonomy (1996, 183–86).

their distinctive institutional dilemmas—by the elected representatives of the dominant political party (i.e., LDP).

Traditional Japanese hierarchists thus contribute to producing a truncated version of the corporatist welfare-state regime in which the—often egalitarian—influence of labor is relatively weak: "corporatism without labor" (Pempel and Tsunekawa 1979; but see as well Shalev 1990). Labor's influence in Japan is segmented both horizontally (by the predominance of company unions) and vertically (by the sharply varying status of workers in the same field who are employed by companies enjoying different degrees of favor from the state). Traditional Japanese hierarchists have taken advantage of these circumstances, thus retarding development of the income-maintenance and social-service forms of public social provision characteristically favored by conventional Japanese hierarchists as well as egalitarians among Japanese labor associations and opposition political parties.

Accordingly, Japan devotes less of its GDP to its public sector than any other major advanced industrial society. (See Table 5.) Further, this has been the case throughout the postwar era, including the period in the late 1970s and early 1980s that marked the heyday of the welfare state in Japanese society. Except for a period around 1980, Japan's public sector has spent roughly ten percent of GDP less than the United States, which with its Lockean heritage might be expected to be the ultimate small-state society. Table 10 compares Japan's "national effort," or the proportion of GDP represented by public social policy expenditures, with those of the Federal Republic of Germany, a representative corporatist welfare state, and the United States, the obvious liberal welfare state. Japan's national effort appears modest in these data; only in the 1980s did Japan work its way up near the U.S. level of spending.

THE 1985 CONSOLIDATION OF PENSIONS FOR THE ELDERLY

Nature of the Problem and Implications for Various Cultures

In spite of skeptical attitudes shared by many central-state and corporate executives, LDP parliamentary leaders had, by 1973, created the basis for a Japanese welfare state similar to Esping-Andersen's corporate welfare-state regime. Japan's public retirement programs were not as "mature" as those of Germany or the United States, so they were serving a smaller portion of

Table 10   National Effort: Public Social Policy Expenditures as a Percentage of GDP[a]

	1960	1965	1970	1975	1981	1986	1991
Germany	20.4	22.4	23.5	32.6	31.5	29.1	29.5
Japan	8.0	9.4	9.3	14.2	17.3	18.0	18.6
United States	10.9	12.3	15.7	20.8	20.7	21.9	24.5

[a] Most data are from OECD 1985. Data for 1986 and 1991 are from OECD 1995. I have supplemented OECD 1995 with data from the OECD's annual Economic Surveys series of specific societies. See OECD 1996, 1993, and 1992.

its citizenry, and through the mid-1970s Japanese pensioners received lower replacement rates than those designated for future beneficiaries during the early 1970s (Fisher 1973, 27–28; Campbell 1992, 340),[6] so Japanese social policy expenditures remained lower than those of European corporate welfare states. Nevertheless, against a background of over two decades of record-shattering economic development and prodded by electoral competition, the LDP-dominated Diet altered its vision of a desirable future to include a generous welfare state.

Yet historical contingencies of the mid-1970s threatened this vision. Japan's problems of access to raw materials leave it more vulnerable than many other advanced industrial societies, so the "oil shocks" of the 1970s hit the Japanese particularly hard. Moreover, after the mid-1970s the remarkably successful coordination between MITI bureaucrats and major corporate executives that Johnson (1982 and 1990) describes deteriorated in quality and produced less impressive results in global markets (Callon 1995). Further, by the late 1970s there was growing recognition that Japan would experience a sharp decline in its worker/beneficiary ratio early in the twenty-first century. Growing numbers of pensioners receiving increasingly generous pensions was a vision that fit less well with an economically troubled future than with the developmental successes of the recent past.

For traditional hierarchists among Japanese central-state executives, these contingencies offered an important opportunity. Postwar national executives have seen their role as guiding macroeconomic affairs to achieve a form of development that affords prosperity for the vast majority of house-

6. In terms of private-sector supports, Japanese households save more than their American counterparts (Bronfenbrenner and Yasuba 1987, 100; Rose and Shiratori 1986). But the levels of protection provided by private (as opposed to public or public-mandated) pensions and life insurance are modest by American standards (Davis 1995, 54–56). Japanese citizens acquire little more protection against life's vicissitudes from these latter sources than citizens in the Federal Republic of Germany (Noguchi 1986; Rein 1982).

holds willing to work hard. Thus the state, while expert and socially interventionist, is also appropriately small and low-budget, freeing as much in
the way of societal material resources as possible for corporate executives
to use in achieving economic development. The upgrading of social programs that reached a peak during the early 1970s, in conjunction with less
encouraging economic and prospective demographic trends, created the
specter of future public sector obligations inconsistent with the traditional
hierarchical view about the appropriate role and size of the state. Whereas
the rapid economic growth from the late 1940s through the early 1970s had
distracted attention from this inconsistency, the difficulties which confronted—or at least were visible to—Japanese public executives during the
late 1970s highlighted it. For many Japanese central-state executives, reversing the social policy trajectory of the 1960s and 1970s became an increasingly urgent imperative. Only such a move, many thought, would save
Japan from the "English disease" (i.e., an economy eviscerated by excessive
public social provision prompted by competition for the votes of an egoistic
and myopic public) and their society's ensuing downward economic spiral.

In contrast, even in the late 1970s Japanese egalitarians clung to the hope
of a more generous future for ordinary persons inspired by existing legislative promises. Their spokespersons pointed out that public officials had long
enjoyed generous pension programs, and after many years of prosperity it
was high time to expand ordinary citizens' benefits. Similarly, Campbell
reports that, among the citizenry generally, the problem with pensions was
that benefits were too low (1992, 316). The leaders of various Japanese
labor associations were the primary advocates for this view (Verba et al.
1987, chap. 4), and they sought to upgrade the public social policy benefits
of private-sector workers—those near the bottom of the socioeconomic lad-
der in particular. They were joined in this effort by most of the generally
egalitarian opposition parties.

Options Considered and Their Association with Distinct Rationalities

One consequence of "corporatism without labor" (Pempel and Tsunekawa
1979) is that specific Japanese central-state executives succeeded in shaping
public discussion of pension issues largely in terms of their hierarchical perspective and thus narrowed the range of policy options seriously considered
across the early 1980s.[7] But momentum for program retrenchment devel-

---

7. This section draws heavily on Campbell 1992, chap. 10. I am also grateful to Professor
Campbell for opportunities to clarify various points through several private communications.

oped slowly. The Ministry of Health and Welfare's Social Security Long-Term Planning Discussion Group (hereafter, Social Security Discussion Group) led the transition from the welfare state emphasis of the early 1970s to a policy stance that ministry bureaucrats found more appropriate for the less supportive circumstances appearing later in the decade (Campbell 1992, 318–21). Advocates of this program consolidation orientation required several years to produce a coordinated approach to a myriad specific political and technical issues among relevant bureaucracies. There was as well the problem of how to appeal to the LDP parliamentary leaders for whom incremental benefit increases had become a popular way to curry favor with the voting public. The Social Security Discussion Group could not do better in the late 1970s than raise awareness of its vision of a forthcoming crisis and the consequent necessity for cutting future, rather than current, benefits (Campbell 1992, 322).

As a result of these problems, the Social Security Discussion Group's first policy proposal for effecting a transition from social program expansion to retrenchment in the late 1970s ended up reflecting this objective poorly. The Group's proposal had three elements. First, it recommended incremental increases in the dependents and survivors' benefits associated with the EPS.[8] This was an attempt to respond positively to widespread public perceptions of pension inadequacies. Second, in an effort to achieve program consolidation, the Social Security Discussion Group proposed that housewives would have to choose between their husbands' dependents benefits through the EPS and their personal benefits acquired through their enrollment in the NPS. Third, the ministry wanted to reduce pension costs by raising, across a period of twenty years, the eligibility age for EPS pensions from sixty to sixty-five. This third element represented a "lightning rod" as a consequence of a retirement practice common among Japanese firms by which employees are retired from career positions at fifty-five. Some employees are then re-hired, normally in reduced positions and at reduced salaries, on a year-by-year basis for a few years. The lump-sum retirement benefits that many firms have traditionally awarded retirees are sufficient to cover only a limited span of years. So raising the eligibility age for public retirement pensions to sixty-five was likely more controversial in Japan than it would have been in most other advanced industrial societies (Murdo 1993, 4; Kii 1991; Fisher 1973).[9]

8. As a public issue, this became an effort to increase what were publicized as "widows' pensions," a technique that has been successful in other societies (Skocpol 1992).

9. In contrast to the situations in many other advanced industrial societies, Japanese labor associations have been trying to legislate a *higher* retirement age in an effort to stop employers from forcing employees to retire at fifty-five (Murdo 1990, 10).

In an unusual assertion of dissent from bureaucratic initiatives, both the labor and business representatives on the Employee Pension Division of the Social Insurance Deliberation Council, to which these proposals had to be presented, rejected raising the age of eligibility for EPS pensions. The experienced welfare minister, Hashimoto Ryutaro, initially appeared to consider the whole proposal moribund. But an unexpectedly poor LDP showing in the October 1979 parliamentary election led the party to resurrect the increase in survivors' benefits (e.g., the "widows' pensions") under the EPS. The finance ministry, in turn, refused to accept these increased expenses without offsetting reductions. So the savings from increasing the age at which persons became eligible for EPS pensions were needed, and these two elements of the originally tripartite proposal were approved by the cabinet and became an official government legislative proposal.

Resistance from the largely egalitarian opposition political parties and labor union associations arose immediately. These groups took advantage of this opportunity to publicize the government's insensitivity to the plight of private-sector retirees and particularly to highlight the inequalities between the pension systems available to private-sector employees and the more generous pensions for which public bureaucrats had long become eligible at age fifty-five. These opposition groups made good use of what was called the "officials-people differential" in the press (Campbell 1992, 325–26).[10] Thus the government, in an unusual and humiliating move, dropped raising the age of eligibility for EPS benefits from its prospective legislation. So 1980 ended up as a year of pension enhancement, through the increases in "widows' pensions," rather than pension retrenchment.

After briefly licking their wounds Ministry of Health and Welfare officials regrouped and, using the next Fiscal Review (in 1985) as a deadline, worked to build a broader coalition for their preferred objective: a consolidated basic pension. Their lengthy and ultimately successful struggle was spearheaded by Yamaguchi Shinichiro, who became director of the ministry's Pension Bureau in August 1981. Yamaguchi was a particularly capable administrator who had extensive experience designing pensions and related social programs (Campbell 1992, 329–30). He also embodied both the traditional and conventional Japanese hierarchical perspectives.

As a traditional hierarchist, Yamaguchi believed that exceptional societal

10. A 1979 government initiative raised the retirement age—across a period of twenty years—for all public sector retirement funds from fifty-five to sixty (Campbell 1992, 325; Collick 1988, 225).

elites (both central-state and corporate bureaucrats) had an obligation to provide sufficient quantities of appropriate types of paid employment that ordinary persons could use to sustain themselves in the process of contributing to society. Additionally, against a background of less promising economic conditions and deteriorating demographics, he thought that the future pension obligations created by the LDP-dominated Diet needed to be reduced. But as a conventional hierarchist and prominent bureaucratic "guardian" of Japanese public pensions, Yamaguchi was familiar with both the strengths as well as the weaknesses of European social programs, and he was more intrigued with the potential for pension adequacy to contribute to social harmony than were Ministry of Finance officials. So he carved out a position between the egalitarian opposition parties and the most zealous of the small-state advocates among public bureaucrats and associated interests. He then cultivated progressively broader support for his position among political elites and various attentive publics.

Yamaguchi's task in overcoming various opposition parties and the labor associations was eased by the distinctive, even conflicting, concerns and priorities of various socialist groups. For instance, in the aftermath of the 1980 conflict over disparities between the pensions of public bureaucrats and those available to most workers in the private sector, the pension enhancement goals of labor associations representing the private sector and some opposition parties were focused on acquiring parity with the benefits that public workers enjoyed. A goal of particular importance for these groups was facilitating passage through the hiatus between a mandatory retirement at fifty-five, which was still fairly common in the private sector, and the onset of EPS pensions at age sixty.

In contrast, the most important constituency of the major opposition party, the Japan Socialist Party (JSP), was composed of public employees, and the party focused primarily on shielding the pension programs of these constituents from the retrenchment that its leaders anticipated was about to occur in public pensions for private-sector workers.[11] This lack of unity among groups with generally egalitarian objectives, in combination with the

---

11. The Second Temporary Commission on Administrative Reform (Rinchō), which advocated reducing government expenses, took the lead in revamping the pension systems of public employees during the early 1980s. Its action was prompted by a crisis in the funding of the railroad workers' pension system. While the original dates for achieving particular goals were subsequently moved back, legislation initiated by the commission that amalgamated the various pension programs serving public employees with the larger systems serving private-sector employees and other citizens was adopted by the cabinet in April 1983 (Campbell 1992, 335).

fact that their policy preferences fit uncomfortably with economic conditions affording only modest growth and a rapidly deteriorating demographic situation, contributed to egalitarians having little influence on the direction of Japanese pension policy changes in the early 1980s.

Yamaguchi was not sympathetic to the pension enhancement or maintenance proposals of the egalitarian left, yet he also distinguished his preferred design from varying proposals of small-state zealots among Japanese public executives and business associations. The Ministry of Finance, for instance, wanted to tax pensions, thus offsetting the increased drain on public coffers that future benefits represented by augmenting general revenues. Like their German counterparts, some business associations advocated an extremely modest basic pension that could be supplemented by corporate and individual efforts. Still others were interested in reviving earlier proposals by the Social Insurance Deliberation Council for dropping the social insurance (contributory) aspect of pensions and funding them instead through a new general tax created specifically for this purpose. Exchanging pensions funded through significant beneficiary contributions for pensions funded exclusively through general taxation would likely have made pensions, like public assistance, more politically vulnerable across the future. Yamaguchi, and the Ministry of Health and Welfare generally, successfully resisted these suggestions and created a progressively broader coalition behind their own proposal.

Yamaguchi worked out the details of the Pension Bureau's proposal in part through a series of bureau colloquia in which the discussion was unusually open (Campbell 1992, 330). The bureau's resulting reform proposal reflected basic objectives similar to those of the Ministry of Welfare's 1980 offering, but the bureau designed different and broader specific measures to address these goals. First, concerning the adequacy of pensions, the bureau addressed what it perceived as the last serious transfer-payment inadequacy. This involved upgrading the benefits awarded to working-aged adults who suffered from various disabilities. These improvements were not expensive in comparison to benefits for the elderly, and they were supported by small but well-organized interest groups. Moreover, including this expansion of benefits in the overall package frustrated opponents in their efforts to portray the proposal as an instance of social program retrenchment.

Second, the bureau acted on a concern that it had held for over two decades, program rationalization or consolidation, by proposing a new, eventually universal, compulsory Basic Pension.[12] Persons would become eligible

12. This pension is compulsory between the ages of twenty and sixty, but there is no enforcement mechanism, and there are numerous noncontributors (Murdo 1993, 7).

for the Basic Pension at age sixty-five, and forty years of contributions were required for full benefits, although reduced benefits would be available after twenty-five years of contributions. Essentially, the bureau was broadening the scope of the NPS by bringing into it participants in the EPS. While the eventual goal of the basic pension was universal coverage, the Pension Bureau proposed postponing the inclusion of the public employee pension funds in the 1985 legislation in order to avoid a confrontation with the unions representing these workers. The Basic Pension was to be financed by contributions from future beneficiaries and general tax revenues in a two-to-one ratio. Persons enrolled in the EPS (and eventually those served by various public-sector pension funds as well) would receive supplementary benefits beyond the Basic Pension as a consequence of additional employer and employee contributions. Firms meeting relevant size criteria would continue to be encouraged through tax policy to contract their second-tier pensions out of the EPS by providing their employees better benefits (Ostrom 1997, 5–7). As before, these "contracted-out" second-tier pensions would have to meet certain publicly mandated criteria, but questions about their precise character would lie largely in the hands of private employers.

This consolidation involved considerable pension retrenchment and public sector savings. In about 70 percent of Japanese households, wives participated in the NPS and were eligible for separate benefits as dependents though their husbands' participation in the EPS. The consolidation ended this double coverage. Yet the specific amalgamation rules proposed by the Pension Bureau also exacerbated benefit inequities between couples and single persons as well as between employed and self-employed persons, favoring the former in each case.

Third, and more generally in order to reduce pension costs, the Bureau proposed revising the formulas governing replacement rates so that more years of contributions were required (e.g., forty as opposed to thirty-two previously under the EPS and twenty-five under the NPS) to achieve the maximum pension. Further, while the Basic Pension was to be indexed annually to prices and at five-year intervals to wages, the replacement rate for full pensions was stabilized at 68 percent of average earnings. This reduced the replacement rates that had previously been anticipated for the future but not actually practiced among contemporary beneficiaries (Campbell 1992, 340–41). Additionally, the age at which women became eligible for EPS benefits was to be increased gradually from fifty-five to sixty, but in contrast to the 1980 reform proposal, no effort was made to increase the age of EPS eligibility to sixty-five. Finally, like the 1983 instance of the American social security program, the pensions of current beneficiaries were to be unaffected by these changes. Rather, the changes in the formulas were to be applied only to those who had not yet begun to receive benefits.

I have portrayed the Pension Bureau's proposal as the product of a bifocal cultural-institutional perspective. That is, Yamaguchi's orientation combined elements of both the traditional and conventional contemporary Japanese hierarchical perspectives, each the product of both cultural and institutional influences. By working with others who shared portions of his orientation he was able to shape an institutional design that fit this perspective. While this design represented a particular hierarchical perspective, it clearly embodied a hierarchical, rather than an egalitarian or individualistic, institutional design. The Pension Bureau proposal sought to provide limited, orderly (i.e., no double coverage for spouses) security to all citizens under the state's social policy safety net. Yet it retained a schema of second-tier coverage that was, not only sharply differentiating, but differentiating on the basis of employer status rather than employee skill. This schema was too differentiating and its benefits too meager for ordinary beneficiaries who lacked second-tier augmentation to be the product of an egalitarian institutional design. Further, the Pension Bureau rejected proposals such as extremely limited public support (i.e., similar to one leg of the American "three-legged stool" of retirement support) and resting pensions entirely on general taxation rather than a significant element of beneficiary contribution—thus increasing their political vulnerability—that individualists might find appealing.

Yamaguchi worked to create a consensus on this proposal within the Ministry of Health and Welfare generally. Once this was acquired, he sought to bring other relevant groups on board as well. These included additional social policy experts elsewhere in the government, universities and business; and attentive audiences among elected political elites and the general public. The Pension Bureau publicized events that supported its proposal effectively. These included the unexpected development of the near-term bankruptcy of the railroad workers pension fund. Although this was a public-employees pension fund, and thus not immediately within the scope of Yamaguchi's proposal, the plight of this fund highlighted the long-term problems facing Japanese pensions.

Yamaguchi's support from Rinchō (The Second Temporary Commission on Administrative Reform) and other interested elites was facilitated by his adroit use of a survey that the Pension Bureau made of one thousand social policy elites (including university professors, journalists, business and labor leaders, Diet members, and executive officials) in 1982. The bureau included with the mailed questionnaire a lengthy document explaining and supporting its own pension reform proposal. Further, the wording of the questions and the response alternatives offered were designed to yield support for the bureau's proposal (Campbell 1992, 331–32). The survey's results indeed did support the bureau's proposal, and the bureau highlighted these results through publications aimed at various elite and mass publics. The bureau's success in these coalition-building efforts was such that no serious challenge was mounted to its proposal, which was adopted by the cabinet and later passed with little resistance by the Diet on April 24, 1985.

Relative Reliance on Benefit Reductions as Opposed to Revenue Increases

Yamaguchi's adroit use of various contingencies (i.e., deteriorating economic circumstances and unfavorable demographic trends) thus enabled the triumph of an institutional design moderately sympathetic to what I have called the traditional faction of Japanese hierarchy. Victory over poorly represented and weakly organized egalitarians in the opposition parties and various labor associations was, typically, fairly easy under these circumstances. Yamaguchi's ability to deflect the recent enthusiasm for social program development among conventional Japanese hierarchists, particularly LDP Diet representatives, was more impressive. In this regard, Yamaguchi's traditional hierarchical sympathies were reinforced by powerful allies in the Ministry of Finance and Rinchō. He also made clever use of contingencies, such as the financial collapse of the railroad workers pension fund, through the elite survey which he initiated in support of the Pension Bureau proposal. These tactics appear to have been essential for bringing leaders of various LDP Diet factions to accept the Pension Bureau's initiative.

Japanese officials included modest benefit increases, primarily for disabled working-aged adults, in their 1985 pension revision. Overall, however, the 1985 package leaned toward benefit reductions. These included eliminating the dual participation of married women in NPS and EPS and changes to the formulas for calculating pensions that reduced future replacement rates, increased the years of contributions required for maximum pensions, and raised women's EPS retirement age. The pension reductions employed by Japanese officials altered the expectations of future beneficiaries rather than the experiences of current recipients.

While the 1985 Japanese decision reduced future public pension benefit obligations, it did nothing to create the additional public resources necessary for funding even the consolidated pension benefits that remained

(Campbell 1992, 347–48). So, while Pension Bureau executives relied more heavily on benefit reductions than revenue increases, they did so by ignoring the pressing need for the latter. As Campbell (1992, 350) suggests, the failure to develop new resources for funding existing pension obligations marked the 1985 Japanese package as politically unrealistic. Even considering the reductions that this package made in future pension levels, the rates required—in the absence of immediate action to upgrade pension premiums—were calculated at around 25 percent of contributors' wages at their high point in the early twenty-first century. Yet the political will to develop the more extensive reserves necessary to pay for future program benefits was lacking in 1985 and even beyond.[13]

Explicitness of the Focus on Long-Term Financial Costs

Juxtaposing the willingness of dominant Japanese hierarchical officials to face squarely the long-term financial obligations of the pensions they supported with the willingness of their German and American counterparts is instructive. Like the dominant hierarchical German elites in 1989, Japanese central-state executives and, less significantly, LDP parliamentarians were reluctant to face the public revenue demands that their preferred pensions for the elderly generated. German hierarchists focused on an artificially short time-horizon to delay dealing with the long-term financial ramifications of the pension benefits they preferred. Individualists, in the FDP and various business associations, were quick to point out that the German solution of 1989 was unrealistic in this regard, but the high-group leaders of both the CDU and the SPD remained largely unmoved. Acting from similar motivations, hierarchical Japanese public officials focused on one face of their problem by reducing future program benefits. Yet while they were aware that, barring immediate measures to increase revenues, the future tax rates required by even the remaining benefits were not politically viable, they did not act to increase program revenues.

These Japanese and German orientations represent a sharp contrast with the perspectives of dominant individualists in the United States. The American focus, like that of the FDP and its business allies in the Federal Republic, was on the public revenues necessary to pay for future benefits. They chose

13. Indeed, even when eligibility ages and premiums were increased in 1994, these changes came in response to unexpectedly dire demographic projections and still left payroll tax rates for the first couple of decades of the twenty-first century at nearly 30 percent (Ostrom 1997, 3–4).

a lengthy time-horizon as a means for underscoring the immensity of these revenue requirements. In this way they hoped to make social security's financial costs appear overwhelming and to shift the program's trajectory of development sharply downward, eventually diminishing both the program and what they perceived as the socially deleterious expectations for public entitlements that it fostered.

This disparity in strategy distinguishes the pension preferences of the high-group cultures on one hand from individualists on the other when pensions for the elderly confront difficult financial circumstances. Hierarchists and particularly egalitarians, who are favorably disposed toward generous pensions (albeit egalitarians prefer more redistributive pensions), react by stressing the importance of the needs that pensions help to support and trying in various ways to sidestep the problems for public finance that these pensions pose. In 1985, Japanese egalitarians, free from the constraints of governing, focused on upgrading pension adequacy. A loose coalition of governing hierarchical factions was spearheaded by bifocal (traditional/conventional) Pension Bureau executives who were acutely aware of the need for both reducing future pension obligations and increasing inadequate current revenues. This coalition adopted a half-measure that essentially ignored this latter concern. In contrast, individualists, desirous of program retrenchment, strive to attract attention to the huge revenue increases frequently required for funding benefits, not sweep them under the rug. Indeed, the explicitness of the 1983 United States negotiations about the relationship of benefit reductions to revenue increases, an explicitness not found in the other cases of this study, is likely a hallmark of significant individualistic influence.

Cultural-Institutional Mechanisms of Political Change

Culture alone is not sufficient for characterizing significant orientations of political elites toward the appropriate character of pension policy in Japan. It is not, of course, the case that intracultural differences on the specifics of institutional design are absent among the political elites of the other societies. Yet these differences are more significant in Japan. Whereas a focus on hierarchical, egalitarian, and individualistic perspectives captures the essential diversity of the program options considered in the Federal Republic's deliberations in 1989, it is not possible to portray adequately the Japanese struggle over pensions, either in 1985 or particularly across the years leading up to that "pressured decision point" (Cook 1993, 6), by relying only on culture. Two related factors appear to be responsible for this cross-societal difference. First, the dominance of hierarchy in Japan, at least in this particular instance, is extensive. No clearly individualistic perspective appears, and egalitarian preferences have relatively weak support among political elites. Second, as we witnessed in the Soviet instance, it seems likely that, when one culture is preeminent in a society, institutionally prompted divisions among the adherents of that culture become more prominent. All of grid-group theory's cultures offer partial and thus in some respects inadequate explanations of how the world works, what humans are really like, and related matters. So particularly when one culture enjoys thorough societal domination, some of its adherents are apt to have experiences at odds with its preeminent interpretation. These experiences may not prompt persons to adopt a new culture, but persistent discrepancies of (institutionally based) experience among the adherents of a single dominant culture may well prompt preferences for different policy responses.

For instance, shifting historical contingencies provided different factions of Japanese hierarchy with, arguably, more appropriate insights and, certainly, political advantages at different times. From the mid-1940s through the late 1950s when Japan was recovering from the destruction and disruption of the Second World War, traditionally hierarchical central-state executives dominated Japanese political life. They held a development-above-all-else perspective that left little room for expensive social programs. For them, an active industrial policy that provided employment which households could use to support themselves was a sufficient social policy. Peculiarities of Japan's experience as a late developer fostered cultural-institutional preferences for limiting the size and expense (though not the expertise or societal involvement) of the public sector in order to maximize the societal resources remaining in the private sector where they could be optimally employed in furthering economic development.

By the late 1950s, Japan had made remarkable economic progress, and across the ensuing decade the LDP parliamentary majority responded to more prosperous conditions and also electoral competition from the JSP and other opposition parties with a cautious program of social policy development. By the early 1970s, after another fifteen years of exceptional economic growth and electoral competition, a number of increasingly conventionally hierarchical LDP leaders had developed institutional design preferences with respect to social policy that are difficult to distinguish from those advanced by the hierarchical partners in Western European social democratic coalitions. In fact, these conventional Japanese hierarchists relaxed their late-developer perspectives so thoroughly that they declared 1973 the first year of the welfare society era and further expanded social programs.

After the mid-1970s Japanese economic development faltered, and a sharp decline was predicted for the worker/beneficiary ratio early in the twenty-first century. These new circumstances emboldened traditional Japanese hierarchists and fostered uncertainty among the ranks of their conventional counterparts. The former thus moved to reassert their long-standing preferences for a less expensive public sector, initiating wide-ranging social program retrenchment (i.e., in public medical-care programs as well as pensions). In the case of pensions for the elderly, the initiating Pension Bureau elites were not as zealous as their counterparts in the Ministry of Finance. But the pensions for which they were responsible would confront sharply deteriorating demographic circumstances at the century's end. So they saw themselves as compelled to act to reduce their program's long-term unfunded liabilities, although they could not bring themselves to face the increased revenues required for the pensions that remained.

Thus across roughly four decades of postwar Japanese political life public pensions—and social policy generally—have followed a shifting trajectory. Program development was initially tightly constrained. Then programs expanded rapidly in the 1960s and early 1970s. And as daunting economic and demographic difficulties loomed in the mid-1970s, systematic program retrenchment followed. This erratic path arises from interaction between shifting social circumstances and competing factions of hierarchical elites in different public institutions. Difficult circumstances have facilitated traditional hierarchists, primarily central-state executives, in their efforts to limit public expenditures in the service of fostering private-sector economic growth. Prosperous times have aided conventional hierarchists, primarily in the popularly elected Diet, to share economic benefits broadly through social program expansion.

CONCLUSIONS

This study began with a practical political question and a hypothesis offering a general answer. The question was why societies reacted differently to the problems afflicting public social provision for the elderly in the 1980s. My hypothesis was that cultural conceptions of what is appropriate provided the key to explaining how societies responded to 1980s pressures on public protection for the elderly. In this chapter I assess the two processes underlying my hypothesis on cultural influence and then examine its implications for protecting the elderly.

GRID-GROUP THEORY'S CULTURES AS EXPLANATORY VARIABLES: PURPOSES

In this section I consider the capacity of the rival constrained beliefs and values of grid-group theory's three socially interactive cultures to predict and explain distinctive institutional design preferences. Rival ways of life attend to and interpret the same or similar social phenomena in distinctive ways. Thus they reach different conclusions about the nature and the functioning of the social world. Even when different cultures share a sense of alarm about a particular situation, they frequently advocate different remedies, for they disagree about what fundamental moral objectives humans should strive for, given the character of this world, and what courses of action (i.e., institutional formation and development) are appropriate for realizing these goals. With rare exceptions, conventional rational choice theory focuses almost exclusively on this last, instrumental issue, covering the others through assumptions about an intersubjective reality and economic-man purposes.

Disparate Ontologies

The ascendant culture among the American political elites who constructed the 1983 solution to social security's financial difficulties was individualism. These individualists perceived a social environment rife with opportunities and humans capable of mastering their own fates. In such a world, and among such persons, social programs are not only unnecessary but socially destructive. They burden otherwise self-reliant persons with taxes that jeopardize their ability to make their own way. Moreover, active social policies are harbingers for the general growth of government and a way of life dependent on it that is ill-suited to fostering the innovation and initiative of which unique individuals are capable, thus slowing the pace of social progress.

In contrast, a significant portion of the German CDU, including the bulk of the party's leadership, perceived a more complex and daunting social environment, complete with various social hazards. Moreover, they perceived most persons as requiring help—through state guidance and support—from societal elites in order to cope successfully with this environment. In such a world, and among such persons, social programs represent crucial tools. They effectively bolster the limited capacities of ordinary persons with the superior capabilities of societal leaders, providing guidance on how it is appropriate to live and support for dealing with inevitable social hazards. Social programs augment the capacities of persons with varying but ordinary abilities to serve the social collective in their distinctive ways, thus confirming the collective as an organic caring social entity.

Egalitarians employ a third ontology, conceiving of fragile environmental conditions. In their view, all—relatively equal—humans need to cooperate in helping one another simply to survive.

Hierarchists among the Japanese, the Soviet, and even the American (where they are less numerous and influential) political elites have similar orientations about the composition and operation of the world. Similarly, individualists in Japan, the Soviet Union, and Germany exhibit ontological perspectives related to those of their American counterparts, although individualists do not have as extensive influence in these other societies, appearing in noticeable numbers among national political elites only in the Federal Republic. In terms of social policy, the crucial ontological difference in perspective between these two cultures involves juxtaposing the severity of the hazards posed by the social environment and the coping capacities of ordinary persons. Individualists perceive humans as capable of making their own way in a bountiful environment; whereas hierarchists see pitfalls in the environment and think that ordinary persons need guidance and support.

American analysts often interpret interpersonal differences in assessing this crucial relation between environmental demands and human capacities as a reflection of the contrasting (economic-man) self-interest of persons in various socioeconomic classes, e.g., the wealthy visualizing sufficient personal capacities while the poor perceive daunting external hazards. This interpretation ignores the support that hierarchical elites in other societies extend to social programs. Moreover, as Hochschild (1981) shows, perspectives similar to those that I have referred to as individualistic, hierarchical, and egalitarian all occur across the American socioeconomic spectrum. Adherents of these rival cultures employ their disparate beliefs about what the world is composed of and how it operates to construct distinctive selves who pursue different values and interests. So these ontologies lay the basis for adherence to different moral principles which further the development of rival cultural identities.

Rival Culturally Constrained Value Clusters

Given their ontological presuppositions, individualists strive to realize values such as liberty, personal economic success, economic efficiency, and—through them—societal economic growth. These values shape the cultural identity of "economic men"—capable hedonistic egoists (Lockhart and Wildavsky 1998). Liberty in the negative Lockean sense of freedom from external constraint can be optimized only if the same procedures are applied to all (Hayek 1976), so individualistic institutions operate through what Fishkin (1983) calls procedural fairness, which optimizes as well the principle of merit and thus various aspects of economic efficiency. While economic development may be realized by various means (e.g., societal economic growth through the Japanese development state—Johnson 1982), individualists believe that realization of liberty, personal economic success, and economic efficiency are best furthered by reducing the size and activity of coercive stultifying government institutions so that the capacities for innovation and initiative of individuals will be constructively fostered through competitive market circumstances. Accordingly, since 1983 American individualists have used their growing societal influence to progressively reverse the trajectory of relatively rapid social program growth that had characterized the preceding half-century.

From the contrasting ontological perspective of hierarchists, true liberty is recognized, not in terms of the absence of external constraints, but in the appropriateness of persons' actions. Action is most likely to be appropriate if it is guided by expertise, and appropriateness is measured in terms of contributions to social order and harmony. These values produce a motivational basis that contrasts with the egoistic hedonism of individualism; hierarchists foster collective and dutiful cultural identities (Lockhart and Wildavsky 1998). They pervasively infuse societal institutions with the expertise of the most capable, stratifying society harmoniously in the process, and order society by central design, striving to attain widespread recognition of persons' varying obligations to the social collective. These values are consistent with their ontological presuppositions of a complex social environment with many subtle pitfalls and humans of widely varying practical and moral capacities. Accordingly, in 1989 the leadership of the German CDU wanted to increase financial support for time-honored German pensions. As Zapf (1986, 129) indicates, these pensions—and German social programs generally—are model institutions for combining the goals of education and social control. These programs were designed by the central state's experts. They inform ordinary citizens of the nature of their most important obligations to the social collective (e.g., their duty to work in socially productive ways). Moreover, they reward long-term performance of these duties with comprehensive and generous support in the face of various social hazards. Thus these pensions contribute to an orderly society with a minimum number of "strays" among ordinary persons who, relying on their own resources, might lack the foresight and discipline to behave properly.

Once again, egalitarians adopt yet a third value cluster centered on achieving greater equality of interpersonal respect and material condition. These values counter what egalitarians perceive as the pernicious effects of hierarchical and individualistic penchants for social stratification.

Hierarchists in Japan, the Soviet Union, and their less influential counterparts in the United States hold values similar to those exhibited by these German political elites. Likewise, individualists in Germany and their more marginalized colleagues in the Soviet Union and Japan share values with their far more influential counterparts in the United States. The critical differences between the value clusters of these rival cultures with respect to social policy involve the following contrast. Seeing themselves as experts in social organization, hierarchical elites feel responsible for devising central institutional means that will help ordinary persons cope with various social hazards. Facilitating this coping requires educating these persons to constructive habits and monitoring their disciplined adherence to appropriate patterns of behavior. In contrast, since individualists perceive humans as generally capable of doing well through self-regulation, they perceive little need for the social programs that hierarchists develop. Further, they see the social consequences of encouraging unique individuals to master their own fates by exercising liberty through various initiatives and innovations as more salutary than those that derive from the heavy hand of a paternalistic state.

Culturally Specific Preferences for Distinctive Institutional Designs

Since they hold different ontological beliefs and commit themselves to rival value priorities that are compatible with those beliefs, individualists and hierarchists hold preferences for distinctive institutional designs as means for realizing these values in their social lives. For German hierarchists, nothing could be more natural than to construct central-state institutions and to rely on them for achieving important political objectives such as sustaining the material needs of elderly social contributors. Yet while hierarchists agree that ordinary persons require guidance and assistance from the most capable and morally sound to make their way successfully in the world, they do not always turn to the same mix of institutions for achieving this goal. For instance, Soviet hierarchists added consumer price subsidies to the pensions and related social programs employed by their German and American counterparts. Through subsidies, Party experts could guide ordinary persons in wise consumption. In the Party's view, markets could not achieve this objective, for no one was in control. Party elites perceived markets as catering to greed and preying on the weak. So they purposely constructed alternative economic institutions that would, as they perceived the matter, serve the nutritional needs of society's vulnerable. Additionally, the members of the traditional faction of Japanese hierarchy prefer to rely more heavily on an extremely active industrial policy to create a prosperity so robust that ordinary persons, often members of multigenerational households, need less help from income-maintenance and social-service programs than other hierarchists generally perceive necessary.

In the United States influential adherents of individualism had different institutional formation imperatives. While some wanted to eliminate social security altogether, most were willing to settle for retrenchment that left the program as one of three roughly coequal sources of retirement support: personal savings, private pensions, and social security. At this level, social security taxes would not constrain employers as severely, nor would the program provide a similarly bright beacon for the growth of government. Moreover, average citizens would have to rely more heavily on their own ample talents, and a variety of useful initiatives and innovations would arise as millions of capable persons turned their unique capacities toward coping with this challenge. Similarly, German individualists in the FDP have encouraged significant retrenchment in central-state social programs. They too prefer a shift in emphasis toward personal responsibility whereby capable individuals would contribute more extensively to their own private retirement resources and to societal prosperity.

Egalitarians want institutions to realize various conceptions of equality of condition and respect. Thus both workers' associations in Japan in 1985 and the German SPD in 1989 strove to increase the redistributive character of public pensions. Additionally, the German Greens advocated grassroots collectives as means for administering social programs because these collectives avoided the stratification central-state programs necessarily entailed.

Summary

In the case studies of Chapters 5 through 8, I have shown that organized groups of elites, identified on grounds distinct from the decisions examined in this study as hierarchical, individualistic, or egalitarian, routinely perceived various "pressured decision points" (Cook 1993, 6–7) through lenses consistent with those that the theory predicts for their cultures (e.g., that individualists will perceive in the financial difficulties of public pension programs for the elderly opportunities for program retrenchment). Further, I have shown that these rival elite factions supported different purposes and proposed distinctive solutions to the problems of public social program support for the elderly that are also consistent with those that the theory predicts for their cultures. In short, these elite factions realized contrasting, culturally constrained rationalities through which disparate ontologies foster rival value clusters that in turn prompt efforts to construct distinctive institutional designs. I regard the delineation and limited empirical substantiation of this purposive process as the major contribution of this study. The Federal Republic offers the broadest instance of illustrating these rival, culturally constrained rationalities in action, since all three cultures are clearly represented through the leading political parties. The United States and the Soviet Union support a more limited range, since in neither society does an egalitarian position clearly distinguish itself on the issues considered in this study. Similarly, a clearly individualistic perspective does not appear in the Japanese instance, which is, however, complicated by the presence of two influential hierarchical factions, which prefer to apply different policy mixtures to public social provision concerns. I return to this aspect of the Japanese instance at several points below.

RELATIVE CULTURAL INFLUENCE AS A CAUSAL VARIABLE: DECISION OUTCOMES

I examine as well a causal process whereby variations in the relative influence of rival cultures among relevant political elites across societies shape social policy decision outcomes differently. The four societies on which I focus in this study offer considerable variation on the major independent variable in this process. By the early 1980s, the Soviet Union represented a society in which cultural alternatives to a narrow range of hierarchical factions had been driven nearly to extinction among the political elite. Only a small minority of bifocal HI or, in some instances perhaps, IH "radical economic reformers" arrayed themselves against the various tributaries of the hierarchical mainstream on the future of consumer price subsidies. All three of grid-group theory's socially interactive cultures maintained an obvious, well-organized presence among the Federal Republic's political elite, but the 1989 decision on pensions was dominated by a loose, informal, high-group coalition between preeminent hierarchical and subordinate egalitarian forces which overwhelmed most individualistic resistance. In Japan, hierarchical central-state bureaucrats dominated the 1985 decision on pension consolidation. In 1983 American individualists were ascendant over a fading hierarchical-egalitarian coalition on the future of social security and the arc of the societal trajectory generally.

In my analysis of the decisions concerning public support for the elderly, I focused on two related features indicative of relative cultural influence. First, I examined the relative use of revenue increases as opposed to benefit reductions in resolving the financial difficulties afflicting certain public social programs benefiting the elderly. The Soviet, German, and American decisions offer considerable, though not optimal, consistency with grid-group theory's predictions that when high-group cultures are dominant, they will rely more thoroughly on revenue increases, whereas when individualists are preeminent, they will prefer to use benefit reductions more extensively. Most members of the Soviet political elite (including most radical economic reformers) found easy agreement in upgrading wages, pensions, and other social consumption benefits to offset the consequences of raising consumer prices, thus relying more heavily on revenue increases than on benefit reductions.[1] Additionally, certainly within the informal time horizon of 2010 employed by the dominant high-group cultures in the Federal Republic, revenue increases outweighed benefit reductions. But the case of American social security, the clearest of these three instances and the one in which individualists were particularly influential, was resolved by relying more heavily on benefit reductions. So while these three instances fit with the direction of grid-group theory's predictions, the Soviet and German cases involve bothersome definitional issues. Further, the Japanese instance, in which hierarchists were clearly dominant, deviates from this pattern. Japanese political elites cut future program benefits sharply but failed to increase the revenue stream in order to sustain the remaining benefits. Thus they left

1. Yet even this seemingly confirming instance may be viewed differently. If the Soviet decision to reduce consumer price subsidies is construed as an integral part of the social policy decision, then the Soviet instance relies more heavily on benefit reductions than revenue increases. Across these four cases, I have taken a consistent alternative view. A variety of developments—some intended, others the unforeseen and/or unwanted consequences of actions taken for other purposes—create gaps between the resources required for existing, expected, and generally statutory levels of social policy protection and the resources available. Political elites then react to these shortfalls through some mixture of accepting reductions in future program benefits and increasing program revenues. The decision on consumer price subsidies, made for reasons independent of their social consumption role, created a gap of this sort similar to those arising in the other societies included in this study. Soviet elites responded to this shortfall by trying to fill it with increases in a variety of public social consumption benefits.

a situation which in the early twenty-first century will require extremely high and politically impractical tax levels to pay for the remaining benefits. So using grid-group theory to predict relative reliance on revenue increases as opposed to benefit reductions produces this clearly nonconfirming instance.

Second, I have examined how straightforwardly societies confronted the long-term costs of public support for the elderly. Grid-group theory's capacities in this regard are better. All four of these societies offer clear support for the theory's prediction that the adherents of the high-group cultures seek to avoid facing the difficulties these costs pose for their preferred pension designs, whereas individualists insist on resolving such difficulties as a means of opposing programs inconsistent with their values. None of the three societies in which hierarchical or high-group elites dominated the social policy decisions in question gets high marks on confronting the long-term costs of public social program protection for the elderly. Soviet officials engaged in virtually no such effort, eventually resorting to handing out increased benefits in response to citizen agitation. In the Federal Republic high-group leaders in both the CDU and the SPD applied an artificial and unrealistically short-term time horizon as a delaying tactic in the hopes that conditions more supportive of the generous pensions that they preferred would develop in the interim. Japanese central-state executives effectively ignored the additional resources required to fund the program liabilities that remained after their 1985 pension consolidation efforts. In contrast, in the American instance individualists assured a clear focus on long-terms costs by insisting that they "paid for" through roughly equivalent amounts of benefit reductions and revenue increases.

With respect to the United States, the Soviet Union, and the Federal Republic, then, the relative influence of grid-group theory's cultures does a reasonable, though sometimes imperfect, job of predicting and explaining the various decision outcome characteristics on which I have relied as dependent variables. I view this finding as a significant contribution of this study. In a series of "pressured decision points" (Cook 1993, 6), with numerous common elements, predominant Soviet and German hierarchists made decisions that differed sharply from those made by their ascendant individualistic counterparts in the United States. This occurred in spite of the greater severity of the Soviet and German public social provision predicaments, which—had a single (economic-man) rationality been at work in these cases—might well have argued for the Soviets and Germans being more cautious about revenue increases or concerned about long-term program costs than their American counterparts. It is clear that the distinctive, culturally constrained institutional preferences of rival elites, predominant in different societies, contributed to contrasting decision outcomes in these instances.

Predicting and explaining the 1985 Japanese decision on pension policy is more challenging. The eventual decision to reduce benefits but ignore the remaining need for revenue increases can—as indicated in the previous paragraph—be seen as another hierarchical device for avoiding coming to grips with pension costs, similar generically to the German use of an artificially short time horizon in 1989. Yet by ignoring the revenue side of the issue, the traditional Japanese hierarchical faction ended up relying on benefit reductions exclusively, and this runs counter to the actions of hierarchists in the other three societies. While traditional and conventional Japanese hierarchists adhere to similar value clusters and share broad institutional preferences (e.g., for an expert and societally interventionist state), peculiarities of their institutional niches foster differences with respect to the specific institutional mixtures they prefer for realizing similar purposes. Within a social context in which multigenerational households are common, traditional Japanese hierarchists prefer to rely on an active industrial policy to bring about general prosperity and less thoroughly on public programs. Particularly during the 1970s, conventional Japanese hierarchists favored more extensive reliance on these latter programs, a preference that is generally typical of hierarchists in other societies. Both of these factions of contemporary Japanese hierarchists are clearly applying perspectives rooted in cultural *and* professional institutional experience. While this is undoubtedly true of political elites in other societies as well, the implications for social policy decisions are much more significant in the Japanese instance. Thus we must consider how additional independent variables such as institutional position complement culture in explaining policy preferences.

Methodological Concerns Revisited

In the course of explaining social policy differences between Sweden and Japan, Verba et al. argue that "the (Japanese) government's values and ideology make all—or most of—the difference" (1987, 270). This study supports a related position, relying on rival cultures with contrasting beliefs and value priorities to explain the adoption of distinctive institutional designs. In all four of the cases that I have examined, social policy decisions are broadly consistent with the beliefs, values, and institutional preferences of the culture or cultures represented most prominently among the elites making the decisions. But we need to recognize some limitations on culture as an explanatory variable and consider the contributions of additional variables.

Limitations on Culture

First, I consider limitations internal to the formulation of grid-group theory that I have employed in this study. While three socially interactive, global cultures are less constraining than the single, economic-man motivational basis conventionally employed by rational choice theorists, they are insufficient for fully characterizing a number of persons. Even with my introduction of bifocal cultural biases in Chapter 2, the resulting cultural categories do not adequately reflect the world's complexity. For instance, when surveys of the general population afford respondents the opportunity to do so, they load themselves onto multiple cultural biases (Coughlin and Lockhart 1998). While the artificiality of survey instruments likely contributes to this tendency, it is also the case that all of grid-group theory's cultures have some degree of face validity. Most persons, for instance, probably consider humans both unequal and equal in different respects, so they may respond favorably to hierarchical and individualistic or egalitarian conceptions of human nature.

Specifying context and increasing experience both engender clearer adherence to particular cultural perspectives. For instance, a person may perceive humans as both unequal and equal, but think that they are unequal in their capacities while regarding them as equal in holding certain basic rights such as freedom from incarceration and torture for their political beliefs. Such a person may then generally favor governance by experts but think that even experts are appropriately constrained by constitutional limits, thus developing a bifocal HI cultural bias. Further, as persons become actively involved in particular political issues—e.g., environmental policy, they generally come to view the controversies of this issue area from the perspective of a particular culture (Ellis and Thompson 1997).

This latter tendency arises at least in part because, as persons become political activists or elites, they increasingly have to act on their beliefs and values. This requirement characteristically forces them to choose the institutional designs of one culture over those of another. For instance, in terms of perspective I am sympathetic to individualistic claims that candidates for various academic positions should be chosen on the basis of their professional qualifications as construed fairly narrowly, what Fishkin (1983) calls "procedural fairness." But I also recognize the appropriateness of what Fishkin calls "equality of life chances," and since various persons have had vastly different opportunities for developing academic qualifications, I am sympathetic as well to egalitarian pleas for extending preferential treatment to candidates whose records are encouraging—though perhaps not strictly competitive—in spite of extremely limited prior opportunities. Yet if, as a public official, I acted to shape the societal institutions through which academic positions are allocated, the resulting institutions would either extend preferential treatment or not. Acting routinely—through perhaps not invariably—requires choosing the instruments of one culture over those of another.[2] Thus while perceptions may be continuous (i.e., in the sense of coexisting individualistic and egalitarian sympathies), actions generally fall into discrete cultural categories.

In spite of action's capacity for overcoming the shallowness of a limited number of cultural identities and ambivalence among them, I think that future and improved schemata used for distinguishing rival rationalities should strive for greater sophistication than the current formulation of grid-group theory offers. This will likely involve systematically admitting additional variables (e.g., institutional experience) as shapers of perspectives and preferences. However, such efforts are apt to incur losses as well as garner gains. As the number of cultural-institutional categories multiplies, the parsimony and power of the theory declines. But creating combined cultural-institutional indices is probably preferable to a strategy of improving purely cultural indices by, for instance, making more refined qualitative distinctions (e.g., strong versus weak adherence to a particular culture). While distinguishing strong and weak adherence has clear benefits with respect to ascertaining persons' motivation, it may not improve capacities for predicting outcomes. Across most of the 1980s, for instance, the more fervently German FDP parliamentarians believed in and stuck to individualistic preferences with respect to pensions, the less influence they had on the actual character of public policy. Further, such refinements are not apt to overcome

2. Nonetheless, different means of preferential treatment may be more or less irritating to individualists. For instance, assuring admission of the top ten percent of the graduates of all a state's high schools (including those with predominantly or exclusively minority student populations) to the state's universities (even though the top ten percent at one school has vastly higher SAT scores than the top ten percent at another school) appears in the current period to be less grating on individualistic sensibilities than granting individual students preferential treatment based either on their ethnicity or on individual histories of disadvantaged opportunities.

the problems we encountered in the Japanese instance, so political culturalists must draw on additional variables.

Additional Explanatory Variables

First, greater attention might usefully be focused on how varying historical
contingencies affect the specific character and relative influence of rival cultures in societies. By the early 1970s, for instance, fifteen years of unprecedented economic development had enlarged the conventional faction of
Japanese hierarchy and emboldened it to set aside concerns associated with
the late-developer perspective that had so preoccupied Japanese hierarchists
across the previous century and to construct a Japanese welfare society.
Further, the American decision on social security in 1983 signaled the declining position of HI statists who owed their unusual degree of influence
from the 1930s through the early 1970s to the historical contingencies of
the Great Depression and the Second World War (Uchitelle 1997). Ironically, as soon as Prime Minister Tanaka declared the beginning of the "welfare era" in Japan (Bronfenbrenner and Yasuba 1987, 132) and President
Nixon announced that he had become a Keynesian (Silk 1972, 14), new
historical contingencies began to cut away at the bases for their respective
positions.[3]

Second, we need to add more systematic consideration of various institutional factors. One such factor involves the varying organizational effectiveness of different groups of organized elites. I have used fairly crude indices:
the relative prominence of high-profile cultural adherents and the numerical
size of rival cultural factions. But greater sophistication would likely help.
For instance, both the American Republicans and the German CDU represent IH coalitions of economic and social conservatives. As Padgett (1989,
125) relates, through the 1980s the CDU's hierarchical, socially conservative faction dominated on social policy issues. It remains unclear in the 1989
pension decision why the CDU's individualistic, economically conservative

---

3. Relatedly, the progressive development of global economic competition in combination
with Germany's deteriorating demographic situation led Helmut Kohl's governing coalition to
recommend sharp social policy cuts in 1996. Nonetheless, the specific cuts in social—primarily
medical-care—program benefits that Kohl recommended in April 1996 reduced what would
likely be considered remarkably luxurious program design features (e.g., lengthy spa vacations)
in any of the other three societies examined in this study. See Cowell 1996, 4, as well as
German Information Center 1996—October 4, 3; October 11, 5; October 18, 1; October 25,
4. Moreover, some of these retrenchment proposals, which were initially strongly supported
by the individualistic representatives of employers' associations, were subsequently withdrawn
as a consequence of labor (egalitarian) resistance. See Andrews 1996.

faction accepted this dominance. Acceptance might arise as a consequence of a log-rolling arrangement. But it might also be that the CDU's individualistic faction was simply less effectively organized, at least on this issue.

Relatedly, in the instance of the American Republicans, social program retrenchment was a central concern for the individualistic, economically conservative faction; whereas in the early 1980s, the hierarchical, socially conservative faction focused on "moral" issues (e.g., advocating prayer in the public schools and fighting abortion rights).[4] The CDU is certainly no less Christian than the Republican Party, but its hierarchical faction focused the major public policy outlet for its social conservatism on secular social programs rather than religiously related moral issues. It seems likely that the relative influence of rival cultures in the two societal contexts, organizational differences, and interaction between these two variables contribute to these differences.

Another institutional factor that ought to be examined more carefully in future culture-centered analyses of decisions is the influence of varying adult institutional experiences on the institutional preferences of political actors. The intracultural split between traditional and conventional contemporary Japanese hierarchists offers a particularly clear example of how different institutions can divide common or at least highly similar cultural beliefs and values into distinctive institutional preferences. Traditional and conventional Japanese hierarchists share sufficient beliefs and values to agree on the broad outlines of the appropriate character of the Japanese state: an expert state that plays an active role in guiding society. Thus as we saw in Chapter 3, the Japanese state may be financially small in terms of the proportion of GDP it consumes, but as a result of its active role in guiding society, it is far less restrained than the individualists' ideal, night-watchman state. Yet these two factions of contemporary Japanese hierarchy, owing to their distinctive institutional locations, tend to favor different social policy institutions. Largely Diet-based, conventional hierarchists have displayed preferences for substantial income-maintenance and social-service programs similar to hierarchists in Western Europe. Yet central-state bureaucratic, traditional hierarchists have been more reluctant about these programs, preferring to rely more heavily on the salutary effects of an ambitious industrial policy on a population in which multigenerational households are common.

This instance is the most significant, but not the only, example that we

4. Patrick Buchanan subsequently raised socioeconomic issues as a spokesperson for this faction, but these matters remained less central to the faction's concerns than moral issues.

have encountered in this study of distinct institutional environments dividing a single cultural predisposition on institutional design into multiple related forms. The disparity in the institutional preferences displayed by Ligachev's and Ryzhkov's hierarchical factions in the Soviet struggle over consumer price subsidies and the division between isolationists and Western-emulators in the Meiji Restoration provide additional examples. It is, of course, also the case that not all German egalitarians favor exactly the same institutional design innovations at a particular juncture or that the SPD leadership favors exactly the same institutional designs across time. Institutional position—and other variables including personality idiosyncrasies (Downs 1967)—regularly influence institutional preferences, particularly the institutional maintenance imperatives on which many institutional studies focus (March and Olsen 1989). Yet among American, Soviet, and German organized political elites and within the context of "pressured decision points" (Cook 1993, 6), grid-group theory's cultures perform pretty well in terms of characterizing distinctive, constrained, institutional design preferences and even social policy decisions. But the Japanese case demonstrates that explaining a broader sample of cases requires that institutional variables supplement cultural explanations. However, interaction between culture and institutions can make distinguishing their specific contributions difficult.

Symbiotic Interaction and Control

Perhaps the most daunting problems for using cultural and institutional variables in a complementary fashion are posed by the symbiotic relationship between culture and (institutional) social structure (Elkins and Simeon 1979). For instance, Japanese labor has been organized in a highly fragmented way that gives it far less political influence than its German counterpart. So it would be reasonable to argue that Japan's relative ease in achieving program retrenchment in 1985 stems from this institutional characteristic. Further, this institutional form might be argued to foster hierarchical attitudes among Japanese workers (Rohrschneider 1994). So institutions cultivate and maintain certain cultural predispositions. Yet it is important to investigate why German and Japanese labor are organized differently. German labor has been organized largely by relatively egalitarian socialists locked in a lengthy struggle with an H-I political-economic coalition. It has sought solidarity both within and across industries and produced powerful peak associations. In contrast, Japanese labor has been organized largely by hierarchical corporate representatives. Company unions are the norm, and peak organizations while present are weak. That Japanese workers initially accepted and continue to acquiesce in this situation surely reveals greater support for hierarchy among them than has existed among their German counterparts. So cultures foster and support distinctive institutional forms, and—with this symbiosis—it is difficult to separate clearly cultural and institutional influences.

I have tried to combat this problem in two ways. First, I have routinely examined "pressured decision points" (Cook 1993, 6), instances which have at least portended significant political change. In some of these instances, it seems difficult to argue that the sources for this change lie in the varying socialization effects of existing adult political institutions (e.g., Gorbachev's long-standing interest in decentralized economic institutions and market incentives). Second, I have started with what I take to be the broader variable (i.e., culture), traced out its influence, and only when the results are unsatisfactory turned to factors specific to particular institutions. I do not intend by this strategy, which is roughly the opposite of Johnson's (1982), to characterize institutional variables as residual. There is a vibrant field of institutional analysis that focuses less on the narrow but important question that has interested me (i.e., Why do institutions take the forms they do?) than on how institutions are maintained.

I recognize that by adding a range of institutional variables, I could achieve tighter specification of my dependent variables. It is clear that culture operates in conjunction with institutional and other variables, for culturally constrained institutional formation imperatives are indeterminate on various outcome details. But in three of my four societal examples explanatory power would have been sacrificed for relatively insignificant gains. Culture performed reasonably well in these instances. But culture was inadequate in the Japanese instance. Culture enables us to predict in the abstract that Japanese hierarchists, like hierarchists elsewhere, will be more predisposed to employ central-state institutions to cope with what they perceive as social problems than individualists are inclined to do. But culture alone does not afford a basis for explaining the division of Japanese hierarchists into two factions or the character of the resulting factions.

Validity with Respect to Purposes and Outcomes

Finally, I turn to the validity of my conclusions. With respect to what I have called the purposive process (i.e., the transformation of rival, culturally constrained beliefs and values into preferences for distinctive institutional designs), the logical relations are sufficiently tight so that I believe persons prefer certain institutions for the reasons that I suggest.[5] I do not claim that persons act from principles such as equality, liberty, or order rather than from self-interest. Rather, as I explained in Chapter 4, all persons are self-interested in some sense. But the distinctive interests that rival cultures legitimate for their adherents draw disproportionately on these various values among other elements. Further, the empirical support for my purposive hypothesis is sufficiently strong so that I feel confident about generalizing. I do not claim that there are no nonconfirming instances. In the Japanese instance culturally constrained beliefs and values predict general societal ideals, but these beliefs and values do not predict the social policy preferences of traditional Japanese hierarchists. Neither do I claim that culturally based institutional preferences are exhaustive down to the last detail; indeed they usually focus on major institutional characteristics and are indeterminate with respect to numerous specifics. But I think that three culturally constrained rationalities often predict and explain the range and essential character of rival arguments in societal controversies over social policy.

As to the causal process (i.e., how the relative influence of rival cultures among a society's relevant political elite shapes decision outcomes), I acknowledge that the small number of instances that I have examined in Part Two of this study may well be unrepresentative of political action in other contexts. I have focused on the actions of political elites rather than ordinary citizens, major—and for the most part highly developed—societies rather than smaller or developing states, societal "pressured decision points" (Cook 1993, 6) rather than overwhelming societal crises or everyday decisions, social policy decisions to the exclusion of other issues, and—within the realm of social policy—on decisions involving benefits delivered directly by the state (i.e., pensions or consumer price subsidies) rather than publicly supported social services such as national health insurance. All of these distinctions—and possibly others as well—may place limits on the degree to which my conclusions may be generalized.

I have two particular concerns in this regard. First, as I indicated both in Chapter 1 and the introduction to Part Two, the influence that I have been

5. We can rarely, if at all, be certain whether persons have acted from the motives that we attribute to them. Multiple incentives for persons making misleading statements about their motives routinely exist, and persons may not have clear conceptions of their own purposes, if only because their motives are mixed. But by the standards of contemporary social science, process tracing is an approach that is fairly well designed for dealing with the meaning of human action. We can, for instance, examine whether the institutions persons strive to construct actually do embody their expressed beliefs and values more thoroughly than alternative institutions favored by others who hold different beliefs and values.

able to isolate for culture is not as obvious outside the range of instances that Cook (1993, 6) characterizes as "pressured decision points." In less significant decisions the institutional maintenance imperatives associated with varying versions of institutional analysis are likely to become more influential (Steinmo, Thelen, and Longstreth 1992; March and Olsen 1989). And in urgent societal crises, various cultures may either be overwhelmed by the force of historical contingencies (Skocpol 1979) or be forced into adopting the same, previously constructed options as the German SPD famously (or infamously) was at the outset of the First World War.

Second, predicting and explaining the outcomes of the societal decisions hinges, not only on the institutional design preferences of rival cultures, but on other variables as well: the unpredictable character of specific historical contingencies, the frequent necessity for compromise between cultures, multiple effects of varying institutionalization patterns, and interaction among these categories of variables. Given all this, it is remarkable that the rival rationalities associated with grid-group theory's three socially interactive cultures have performed as well as they have in this study, particularly in explaining a finding, counterintuitive from an economic-man perspective, concerning why the most hard-pressed societies chose to rely more heavily on revenue increases than benefit reductions in dealing with the financial problems their social programs for the elderly encountered. Further, it is not clear to me that an analysis which carefully included all of these factors would have been better able to predict my major nonconfirming instance, the failure of Japanese hierarchists to create an adequate revenue stream for the pensions that remained after their 1985 consolidation. The relative influence of the cultures which I have employed offer a proximate first-cut at predicting other significant aspects of these cases and contribute importantly to explaining, not only what happens in important societal decisions such as those examined in this study, but—by tracing various patterns of human purposes—why.

PROTECTING THE ELDERLY: VIRTUES AND DRAWBACKS OF RIVAL CULTURES

Now let us turn to examining what a grid-group theory analysis of these four instances tells us about promise and pitfalls of using public social policy to protect the elderly. The basic lesson is that each of the three socially interactive cultures has distinctive strengths and weaknesses in this area.

While these societies vary on a host of factors that I do not consider, they also exhibit important similarities. First, all four societies were confronting more difficult economic circumstances than they had experienced a decade or so previously. With the exception of the Soviet Union, economic decline was not precipitous, but material resource allocation issues were becoming more pressing in all four societies. Second, all four societies had recognized that there were limitations on the capacities of public policy (and, with the possible exception of the Soviet Union, social policy) to improve the quality of persons' lives. And third, with the exception of the Soviet Union once again, each society was saddled with a growing proportion of elderly in its population, and in all four societies significant elderly populations were accustomed to receiving substantial public social provision benefits.

In terms of the relative difficulty of their circumstances, I rank these societies in the following order of declining severity. Although the exceptions noted for the Soviet Union above might appear to give it relative advantages over the other three, I argue that the severity of the economic problems it faced created the direst circumstances among the four. Indeed, the Soviet Union collapsed roughly six months after Gorbachev's April 1991 decision to retain reduced consumer price subsidies. While the Soviet Union had the highest worker/beneficiary ratio and likely the highest proportion of elderly actively involved in the labor force, these statistics were better indices of the stinginess of Soviet social consumption benefits and the poverty of Soviet society generally than of Soviet relative advantage. Life expectancy in the Soviet Union was considerably lower than among the advanced industrial societies, thus leaving fewer elderly, and Soviet public programs were so limited that most elderly persons had to continue to work after they became eligible for retirement benefits. Overall, the Soviet Union was on the verge of political and economic collapse in 1991.

Japan and the Federal Republic are difficult to distinguish in overall difficulty, although they differ in their particulars. Japan arguably faced more general economic difficulties in 1985 than did the Federal Republic in 1989. Yet on the particular issue of social programs for the elderly, the Federal Republic already had a distressing worker/beneficiary ratio. Its immediate situation in this regard was much worse than Japan's. The decline in Japan's worker/beneficiary ratio would arrive with alarming speed, however, falling beneath the Federal Republic's for a time in the early twenty-first century. But from the perspective of the mid-1980s, Japan's ratio was expected to rise again, whereas the Federal Republic's ratio was anticipated to remain extremely low into the distant future. Japan's net liabilities with respect to its pensions for the elderly were greater (as a percentage of GDP) than the Federal Republic's; however, the Federal Republic faced a difficult problem of trying to reverse an established practice of granting retirement benefits to ever younger workers. I put the Federal Republic's situation next to the Soviet Union's in terms of severity of circumstances, but it is a close call. Ranking the American situation in 1983 is easier. In terms of general economic circumstances, worker/beneficiary ratio, and net pension liabilities, the United States clearly faced the least severe situation (Davis 1995; Murdo 1993 and 1990; Simanis 1990, 16; WuDunn 1997).

This rough ranking of situation severity creates an intriguing mismatch with the character of these societal decisions. For instance, in terms of their relative reliance on benefit reductions as opposed to revenue increases in resolving public social provision problems, the two societies with the more difficult situations relied more heavily on revenue increases; while the two less severe cases employed benefit reductions more heavily. If the dominant elite factions of these societies had held the same interests (i.e., been adherents of the same culture), they would not have behaved in this way. Rather, this mismatch indicates that across the four societies the relative influence of rival cultures varies, and the character of decision outcomes varies with this influence. This mismatch between circumstance and cultural preferences alerts us as well to the countervailing strengths and blind spots of rival cultures as far as protecting the elderly is concerned. Which culture—hierarchy, individualism, egalitarianism, or some combination—offers the most reliable protection for the elderly? Fittingly, since grid-group theory contends that all three cultures provide society with crucial benefits that the others cannot duplicate, the answer is that it depends on the circumstances. Each culture has relative strengths and weaknesses, and each will do better in circumstances that cater to its strengths.

While hierarchists seek differentiated benefits and egalitarians strive for greater solidarity, particularly by upgrading the most modest benefits, both of these high-group cultures are more supportive of social program development than is individualism. So in generally peaceful and prosperous material circumstances, such as those existing among advanced industrial societies in the 1960s, they can be counted on to provide the elderly with more in the way of material goods and services. For hierarchists this is typically a deeply held responsibility, and their blind spot lies in persisting in providing extensive benefits even when their societies can no longer afford such generosity. The individualistic German FDP was much more realistic about the adequacy of the 1989 German decision than hierarchists in the CDU.

Egalitarians, who rarely govern on their own, differentiate even less well among disparate societal circumstances than hierarchists. In 1985, for instance, Japanese egalitarians pressed hard for more extensive benefits for large numbers of private-sector workers. Both the German SPD and the Greens were less unrealistic in this regard, but the Greens and a minority faction of the SPD were both intrigued with the prospect of using grassroots citizen groups to administer social policy. It seems unlikely that such schemes would work effectively for any length of time in such a populous society. Egalitarians are likely at their best in protecting the elderly when they enjoy prosperous times and work in close conjunction with hierarchists—as in Sweden. Across Scandinavia in the 1960s and early 1970s this cultural coalition was renown for virtuoso performances in this regard.

On social policy issues individualists are the "nattering nabobs of negativism." They may grudgingly accept social programs in the midst of historical contingencies as disruptive as the Great Depression, but these programs are at odds with their deepest beliefs and values. Individualists are correct that some persons would end up better off by exercising their ingenuity to the fullest in the market. But they likely overestimate the capacities and the inclinations of many persons to plan effectively for their retirement on their own. In prosperous times placing individualists in charge of social programs will almost surely translate into the provision of fewer goods and services to the elderly. But individualists have their own distinctive virtue with respect to social policy. They can be useful in warning the high-group cultures about the discouraging social policy implications of deteriorating societal circumstances. As the stridency of individualistic complaints about social programs grows, the high-group cultures would do well to listen and consider carefully what retrenchment steps might be appropriate. But these warnings need considerable luck to achieve this goal. In part, this is because individualists are virtually always warning society about the evils of social programs, so listeners have to be perceptive about the social circumstances in which the warnings are uttered. Yet as we just discussed, neither hierarchists nor egalitarians are particularly prone to such perceptiveness. Some German employer organizations warned themselves hoarse in 1989 to little avail.

In fact, the best example of such perceptiveness that appears among the societies examined in this study involves the bifocal (traditional/conventional) group of Japanese hierarchists associated with the Pension Bureau. When we last focused attention on them, I was contending that they had failed to confront the necessity of increasing program revenues in 1985. I close on a more positive note, giving them credit where it is clearly due. The same peculiar late-developer background that left them uneasy about taking steps to fund those benefits remaining after the 1985 decision also predisposed Pension Bureau executives to pick up warning signs about the current policy trajectory. They had acquiesced in, even abetted, program expansion during the prosperous 1960s and early 1970s, but they were also alert to the signs of trouble that appeared in the mid-1970s. Unfortunately, juxtaposing this faction's alertness on this matter with its unwillingness to act to fund Japanese pensions in a timely fashion only reinforces my claim that the strengths of various cultures with respect to protecting the elderly are narrowly focused and offset by characteristic weaknesses.

REFERENCES

Abbott, Phillip. 1991. *Political Thought in America: Conversations and Debates.* Itasca, Ill.: Peacock.

Abelshauser, Werner. 1984. "The First Post-Liberal Nation: Stages in the Development of Modern Corporatism in Germany." *European History Quarterly* 14:285–318.

Aberbach, Joel D., Robert D. Putnam, and Bert A. Rockman. 1981. *Bureaucrats and Politicians in Western Democracies.* Cambridge: Harvard University Press.

Aganbegyan, Abel. 1988. *The Economic Challenge of Perestroika.* Edited by Michael Burrett Brown. Translated by Pauline M. Tiffen. Bloomington: Indiana University Press.

Aldrich, Jonathan. 1982. "The Earnings Replacement Rate of Old-Age Benefits in 12 Countries, 1969–1980." *Social Security Bulletin* 45 (November): 3–11.

Allison, Graham T. 1971. *Essence of Decision: Explaining the Cuban Missile Crisis.* Boston: Little, Brown.

Almond, Gabriel, A. 1956. "Comparative Political Systems." *Journal of Politics* 18:391–409.

———. 1991. "Rational Choice Theory and the Social Sciences." In Kristen Renwick Monroe, ed., *The Economic Approach to Politics: A Critical Reassessment of the Theory of Rational Action,* 32–52. New York: HarperCollins.

Almond, Gabriel A., and James S. Coleman. 1960. *The Politics of Developing Areas.* Princeton: Princeton University Press.

Almond, Gabriel A., and G. Bingham Powell, Jr. 1966. *Comparative Politics: A Developmental Approach.* Boston: Little, Brown.

Almond, Gabriel A., and Sidney Verba. 1963. *The Civic Culture: Political Attitudes and Democracy in Five Nations.* Princeton: Princeton University Press.

———, eds. 1980. *The Civic Culture Revisited.* Boston: Little, Brown.

Altmeyer, Arthur. 1968. *The Formative Years of Social Security.* Madison: University of Wisconsin Press.

Andrews, Edmund L. 1996. "German Industry Loses Its Zest for Sick-Pay Battles." *New York Times*, December 10, pp. C1, 10.

Apter, David E. 1965. *The Politics of Modernization*. Chicago: University of Chicago Press.

Arrow, Kenneth J. 1951. *Social Choice and Individual Values*. New York: John Wiley and Sons.

Aslund, Anders. 1990. "How Small Is the Soviet National Income?" In Jerry S. Rowen and Charles Wolf, Jr., eds. *The Impoverished Superpower: Perestroika and the Soviet Military*, 13–61. San Francisco: Institute on Contemporary Studies.

———. 1991a. *Gorbachev's Struggle for Economic Reform*. Ithaca: Cornell University Press.

———. 1991b. "Gorbachev, Perestroyka, and Economic Crisis." *Problems of Communism* 40:18–41.

———. 1992. "Changes in Soviet Economic Policy Making in 1989 and 1990." In Anders Aslund, ed., *Market Socialism or the Restoration of Capitalism?* 92–120. Cambridge: Cambridge University Press.

Bailyn, Bernard. 1967. *The Ideological Origins of the American Revolution*. Cambridge: Belknap Press.

Baker, Kendall L., Russell J. Dalton, and Kai Hildebrandt. 1981. *Germany Transformed: Political Culture and the New Politics*. Cambridge: Harvard University Press.

Banfield, Edward C. 1958. *The Moral Basis of a Backward Society*. Glencoe, Ill.: The Free Press.

Barghoorn, Frederick. 1952. "Stalinism and the Russian Cultural Heritage." *Review of Politics* 14:178–203.

Barry, Brian, and Russell Hardin, eds. 1982. *Rational Man and Irrational Society? An Introduction and Sourcebook*. Beverly Hills, Calif.: Sage.

Bates, Robert H. 1990. "Macropolitical Economy in the Field of Development." In James E. Alt and Kenneth A. Shepsle, eds., *Perspectives on Positive Political Economy*, 31–54. New York: Cambridge University Press.

———. 1991. *Beyond the Miracle of the Market*. New York: Cambridge University Press.

———. 1997. "Area Studies and the Discipline: A Useful Controversy." *PS: Political Science and Politics* 30:166–69.

Beard, Charles A. [1913] 1965. *An Economic Interpretation of the Constitution of the United States*. New York: The Free Press.

Beard, Sam. 1996. *Restoring Hope in America: The Social Security Solution*. San Francisco, Calif.: Institute for Contemporary Studies.

Beauchamp, Edward. 1989. "Education." In Takeshi Ishida and Ellis S. Krauss, eds., *Democracy in Japan*, 225–51. Pittsburgh: University of Pittsburgh Press.

Becker, Gary S. 1976. *The Economic Approach to Human Behavior*. Chicago: University of Chicago Press.

Beer, Samuel H. 1965. *Modern British Politics*. London: Faber and Faber.

Bendix, Reinhard. 1977. *Max Weber: An Intellectual Portrait*. Berkeley and Los Angeles: University of California Press.

Benedict, Ruth. 1934. *Patterns of Culture*. Boston: Houghton Mifflin.

Bennet, James. 1995. "Buchanan, in Unfamiliar Role, Is Under Fire As a Left-Winger." *New York Times,* December 31, pp. 1, 10.

Berger, Marilyn. 1997. "Isaiah Berlin, Philosopher and Pluralist, Is Dead—at 88." *New York Times,* November 7, pp. 1, 14.

Berger, Suzanne, ed. 1981. *Organizing Interests in Western Europe.* New York: Cambridge University Press.

Berg-Schlosser, Dirk, and Ralph Rytkewski, eds. 1993. *Culture in Germany.* Houndsmill, U.K.: Macmillan.

Berlin, Isaiah. 1969. "Two Concepts of Liberty." In Isaiah Berlin, *Four Essays on Liberty,* 118–72. Oxford: Oxford University Press.

———. 1982. "The Originality of Machiavelli." In Henry Hardy, ed., *Against the Current: Essays in the History of Ideas,* 26–36. Harmondsworth, U.K.: Penguin.

———. 1998. "My Intellectual Path." *New York Review of Books,* May 14, pp. 53–60.

Berliner, Joseph S. 1983. "Planning and Management." In Abram Bergson and Herbert S. Levine, eds., *The Soviet Economy: Toward the Year 2000,* 350–90. London: Allen and Unwin.

Blyth, Mark. 1997. "Any More Bright Ideas? The Ideational Turn of Comparative Political Economy." *Comparative Politics* 29:229–50.

Börsch-Supan, Axel, and Reinhold Schnabel. 1999. "Social Security and Retirement in Germany." In Jonathan Gruber and David A. Wise, eds., *Social Security and Retirement Around the World,* 135–80. Chicago: University of Chicago Press.

Brady, Henry E., Sidney Verba, and Kay Lehman Schlozman. 1995. "Beyond SES: A Resource Model of Political Participation." *American Political Science Review* 89:271–94.

Brady, Rose. 1999. *Kapitalizm: Russia's Struggle to Free Its Economy.* New Haven: Yale University Press.

Bronfenbrenner, Martin, and Yasukichi Yasuba. 1987. "Economic Welfare." In Kozo Tamamura and Yasukichi Yasuba, eds., *The Political Economy of Japan,* vol. 1, *The Domestic Transformation,* 93–136. Stanford: Stanford University Press.

Brown, Archie. 1985. "Gorbachev: New Man in the Kremlin." *Problems of Communism* 34:1–23.

———. 1996. *The Grobachev Factor.* Oxford: Oxford University Press.

Bundesminister für Arbeit and Sozialordnung. 1988. "Rentenreform '92: Informationen über den Diskussions- und Referentenwurf." Bonn: BMA&S.

Burant, Stephen R. 1987. "The Influence of Russian Tradition on the Political Style of the Soviet Elite." *Political Science Quarterly* 102:273–93.

Calder, Kent E. 1988. *Crisis and Compensation: Public Policy and Political Stability in Japan, 1949–1986.* Princeton: Princeton University Press.

Callon, Scott. 1995. *Divided Sun: MITI and the Breakdown of Japanese High-Tech Industrial Policy, 1975–1993.* Stanford: Stanford University Press.

Campbell, John Creighton. 1992. *How Policies Change: The Japanese Government and the Aging Society.* Princeton: Princeton University Press.

Cannon, Lou. 1982. *Reagan.* New York: G. P. Putnam and Sons.

Carens, Joseph. 1981. *Equality, Moral Incentives, and the Market: An Essay in Utopian Political-Economic Theory.* Chicago: University of Chicago Press.

Cohen, Roger. 1997. "Cries of Welfare States Under the Knife." *New York Times,* September 19, pp. 1, 7.

——. 1999. "German Public Employees Protest Schroeder Austerity Plan." *New York Times,* October 20, p. 7.

Collick, Martin. 1988. "Social Policy: Pressures and Responses." In J.A.A. Stockwin, Alan Rix, Aurelia George, James Horne, Daiichi Itō, and Martin Collick, eds., *Dynamic and Immobilist Politics in Japan,* 205–36. Honolulu: University of Hawaii Press.

Collier, Irwin L., Jr. 1995. "Rebuilding the German Welfare State." In David P. Conradt, Gerald R. Kleinfeld, George K. Romoser, and Christian Soe, eds., *Germany's New Politics,* 235–52. Tempe, Ariz.: German Studies Review.

Conradt, David P. 1978. *The German Polity.* London: Longman.

——. 1980. "Changing German Political Culture." In Gabriel A. Almond and Sidney Verba, eds., *The Civic Culture Revisited,* 212–72. Boston: Little, Brown.

Cook, Linda J. 1993. *The Soviet Social Contract and Why It Failed: Welfare Policy and Workers' Politics from Brezhnev to Yeltsin.* Cambridge: Harvard University Press.

Coughlin, Richard M. 1980. *Ideology, Public Opinion, and Welfare Policy: Attitudes Toward Taxes and Spending in Industrialized Societies.* Berkeley: Institute of International Studies, University of California.

Coughlin, Richard M., and Charles Lockhart. 1998. "Grid-Group Theory and Political Ideology: A Consideration of Their Relative Strengths and Weaknesses for Explaining the Structure of Mass Belief Systems." *Journal of Theoretical Politics* 10:33–58.

Cowell, Alan. 1996. "Germany's Leader Calls for Big Cuts in Welfare State." *New York Times,* April 27, pp. 1, 4.

——. 1997a. "It's Young vs. Old in Germany As the Welfare State Fades." *New York Times,* June 4, pp. 1, 8.

——. 1997b. "Kohl's Pains: Lagging East, Inflation, The Jobless." *New York Times,* September 10, p. 13.

Coyle, Dennis J., and Richard J. Ellis, eds. 1994. *Politics, Culture, and Policy: Applying Grid-Group Analysis.* Boulder, Colo.: Westview.

Coyle, Dennis, and Aaron Wildavsky. 1987. "Requisites of Radical Reform: Income Maintenance Versus Tax Preferences." *Journal of Policy Analysis and Management* 7:1–16.

Crothers, Lane. 1996. "American Culture, Franklin Roosevelt, and the Winning of the NRA." *Journal of Contemporary Thought* 6:107–29.

Crozier, Michael, Samuel P. Huntington, and Joji Watanuke. 1975. *The Crisis of Democracy: Report to the Trilateral Commission of the Task Force on Governability of Democracies.* New York: New York University Press.

Cummings, William K. 1980. *Education and Equality in Japan.* Princeton: Princeton University Press.

Dahrendorf, Ralf. 1967. *Society and Democracy in Germany.* Garden City, N.Y.: Doubleday.

Dallek, Robert. 1984. *The Politics of Symbolism.* Cambridge: Harvard University Press.

Dalton, Russell J. 1989. "The German Voter." In Gordon Smith, William E. Paterson, and Peter H. Merkl, eds., *Developments in West German Politics,* 99–121. Durham: Duke University Press.

Davis, Christopher M. 1988. "The Organization and Performance of the Contemporary Soviet Health Service." In Gail W. Lapidus and Guy E. Swanson, eds., *State and Welfare USA/USSR: Contemporary Theory and Practice,* 95–142. Berkeley: Institute of International Studies, University of California.

Davis, Philip. 1995. *Pension Funds, Retirement-Income Security, and Capital Markets: In International Perspective.* Oxford: Clarendon Press.

Dawson, William Harbutt. [1890] 1973. *Bismarck and State Socialism: An Exposition of the Social and Economic Legislation of Germany Since 1870.* New York: Howard Fertig.

Denton, M. Elizabeth. 1981. "Soviet Consumer Trends and Prospects." In Morris Bornstein, ed., *The Soviet Economy: Continuity and Change,* 165–85. Boulder, Colo.: Westview.

Devine, Donald. 1972. *The Political Culture of the United States.* Boston: Little, Brown.

Diesing, Paul. 1971. *Patterns of Discovery in the Social Sciences.* New York: Aldine.

DiLorenzo, Thomas J. 1996. *Frightening America's Elderly: How the Age Lobby Holds Seniors Captive.* Washington, D.C.: Capital Research Center.

Dobrzynski, Judith H. 1996. "At the Top, It's Still GOP Country." *New York Times,* October 18, pp. C1, 4.

Dobson, Richard B. 1988. "Higher Education in the Soviet Union: Problems of Access, Equity, and Public Policy." In Gail W. Lapidus and Guy E. Swanson, eds., *State and Welfare USA/USSR: Contemporary Theory and Practice,* 17–59. Berkeley: Institute of International Studies, University of California.

Dore, Ronald. 1986. *Flexible Rigidities: Industrial Policy and Structural Adjustment in the Japanese Economy, 1970–80.* Stanford: Stanford University Press.

Douglas, Mary. 1978. *Cultural Bias.* London: Royal Anthropological Society.

———. 1982a. *In the Active Voice.* London: Routledge and Kegan Paul.

———. 1986. *How Institutions Think.* Syracuse: Syracuse University Press.

———. 1992. *Risk and Blame: Essays in Cultural Theory.* London: Routledge.

———, ed. 1982b. *Essays in the Sociology of Perception.* London: Routledge and Kegan Paul.

Dower, John W., ed. 1975. *Origins of the Modern Japanese State: Selected Writings of E. H. Norman.* New York: Random House.

———. 1988. *Empire and Aftermath: Yoshida Shigeru and the Japanese Experience, 1878–1954.* Cambridge: Harvard University Press.

Downey, Gary L. 1986. "Ideology and the Clamshell Identity: Organizational Dilemmas in the Anti-Nuclear Power Movement." *Social Problems* 33:357–73.

Downs, Anthony. 1967. *Inside Bureaucracy.* Boston: Little, Brown.

Dumont, Louis. 1980. *Homo Hierarchicus: The Caste System and Its Implications.* Translated by Mark Sainsbury, Louis Dumont, and Basia Gulati. Chicago: University of Chicago Press.

Durkheim, Emile. [1897] 1951. *Suicide: A Study in Sociology.* Translated by J. A. Spaulding and G. Simpson. Glencoe, Ill.: The Free Press.

Durkheim, Emile, and Marcel Mauss. [1903] 1963. *Primitive Classification.* Translated by R. Needham. Chicago: University of Chicago Press.

Dworetz, Steven M. 1990. *The Unvarnished Doctrine: Locke, Liberalism and the American Revolution.* Durham: Duke University Press.

Dyson, Kenneth. 1989. "Economic Policy." In Gordon Smith, William E. Paterson, and Peter H. Merkl, eds., *Developments in West German Politics*, 148–67. Durham: Duke University Press.

Eckstein, Harry. 1961. *A Theory of Stable Democracy*. Princeton: Center of International Studies, Princeton University.

———. 1977. "Case Study and Theory in Political Science." In Fred I. Greenstein and Nelson W. Polsby, eds., *Handbook of Political Science*, vol. 7, *Strategies of Inquiry*, 79–137. Reading, Mass.: Addison-Wesley.

———. 1988. "A Culturalist Theory of Political Change." *American Political Science Review* 82:789–804.

———. 1991. "Rationality and Frustration in Political Behavior." In Kristen Renwick Monroe, ed., *The Economic Approach to Politics: A Critical Reassessment of the Theory of Rational Action*, 74–93. New York: HarperCollins.

———. 1996. "Culture as a Foundational Concept for the Social Sciences." *Journal of Theoretical Politics* 8:471–97.

———. 1997. "Social Science as Cultural Science, Rational Choice as Metaphysics." In Richard J. Ellis and Michael Thompson, *Culture Matters: Essays in Honor of Aaron Wildavsky*, 21–44. Boulder, Colo.: Westview.

Edwards, Anne. 1987. *Early Reagan*. New York: Morrow.

Elazar, Daniel J. 1980. "Afterward: Steps in the Study of American Political Culture." *Publius* 10 (2): 127–39.

———. 1984. *American Federalism: A View from the States*. 3d ed. New York: Harper and Row.

Elkins, David J., and Richard E. B. Simeon. 1979. "A Cause in Search of Its Effect, or What Does Political Culture Explain?" *Comparative Politics* 11:127–45.

Elkins, Stanley, and Eric McKitrick. 1994. *The Age of Federalism*. New York: Oxford University Press.

Ellis, Richard J. 1993. *American Political Cultures*. New York: Oxford University Press.

Ellis, Richard J., and Fred Thompson. 1997. "Culture and the Environment in the Pacific Northwest." *American Political Science Review* 91:885–97.

Ellis, Richard J., and Aaron Wildavsky. 1989. *Dilemmas of Presidential Leadership: From Washington Through Lincoln*. New Brunswick, N.J.: Transaction.

Elster, Jon. 1989a. *The Cement of Society: A Study of Social Order*. Cambridge: Cambridge University Press.

———. 1989b. *Nuts and Bolts for the Social Sciences*. Cambridge: Cambridge University Press.

———. 1989c. *Solomonic Judgements: Studies in the Limits of Rationality*. Cambridge: Cambridge University Press.

"Ende der Stange." 1988. *Der Spiegel*. September 5, pp. 105–6.

Epstein, Leon D. 1967. *Political Parties in Western Democracies*. New York: Praeger.

Erikson, Erik H. 1956. "The Problems of Ego Identity." *Journal of the American Psychological Association* 4:56–121.

Esping-Andersen, Gøsta. 1990. *The Three Worlds of Welfare Capitalism*. Princeton: Princeton University Press.

———. 1996. "After the Golden Age? Welfare State Dilemmas in a Global Economy." In Gøsta Esping-Andersen, ed., *Welfare States in Transition: National Adaptations in Global Economies*. London: Sage.

————. 1997. "Hybrid or Unique?: The Japanese Welfare State Between Europe and America." *Journal of European Social Policy* 7:179–89.

Etzioni, Amitai. 1988. *The Moral Dimension: Toward a New Economics.* New York: The Free Press.

Evans-Pritchard, E. E. 1940. *The Nuer: A Description of the Modes of Livelihood and Political Institutions of the Nilotic People.* Oxford: Oxford University Press.

Fainsod, Merle. 1958. *Smolensk Under Soviet Rule.* Cambridge: Harvard University Press.

"Feines Ergebnis." 1988. *Der Spiegel.* November 21, pp. 22–23.

Feldman, Stanley, and John Zaller. 1992. "The Political Culture of Ambivalence: Ideological Responses to the Welfare State." *American Journal of Political Science* 36:268–307.

Ferejohn, John. 1991. "Rationality and Interpretation: Parliamentary Elections in Early Stuart England." In Kristen Renwick Monroe, ed., *The Economic Approach to Politics: A Critical Reassessment of the Theory of Rational Action,* 279–305. New York: HarperCollins.

Figes, Orlando. 1997. *A People's Tragedy: A History of the Russian Revolution.* New York: Viking.

Fisher, Paul. 1973. "Major Social Security Issues: Japan, 1972." *Social Security Bulletin* 36 (March): 26–38.

Fishkin, James S. 1983. *Justice, Equal Opportunity, and the Family.* New Haven: Yale University Press.

Fiske, Alan P. 1993. *Structures of Social Life: The Four Elementary Forms of Human Relations.* New York: The Free Press.

Flanagan, Scott C. 1979. "Value Change and Partisan Change in Japan: The Silent Revolution Revisited." *Comparative Politics* 11:253–78.

————. 1987. "Value Change in Industrial Societies." *American Political Science Review* 81:1303–19.

Flanagan, Scott C., and Russell J. Dalton. 1984. "Parties Under Stress: Realignment and Dealignment in Advanced Industrial Societies." *Western European Politics* 7:7–23.

Free, Lloyd A., and Hadley Cantril. 1967. *The Political Beliefs of Americans: A Study of Public Opinion.* New Brunswick: Rutgers University Press.

Freeman, Gary P. 1983. "Social Security in One Country? Foreign Economic Policies and Domestic Social Programs." Paper presented at the annual meeting of the American Political Science Association, September 1–4, Chicago.

Frerich, Johannes, and Martin Frey. 1993. *Handbuch der Geschichte der Sozialpolitik in Deutschland: Sozialpolitik in der Bundesrepublik Deutschland bis zur Herstellung der Deutschen Einheit,* vol. 3. Munich: R. Oldenbourg Verlag.

Friedman, Milton. 1962. *Capitalism and Freedom.* Chicago: University of Chicago Press.

————. 1999. "Social Security Chimeras." *New York Times,* January 11, pp. A21.

Fukushima, Glen S. 1989. "Corporate Power." In Takeshi Ishida and Ellis S. Krauss, eds., *Democracy in Japan,* 255–79. Pittsburgh: University of Pittsburgh Press.

Furniss, Norman, and Timothy Tilton. 1977. *The Case for the Welfare State: From Social Security to Social Equality.* Bloomington: Indiana University Press.

Fusfeld, Daniel Roland. 1956. *The Economic Thought of F.D.R. and the Origins of the New Deal*. New York: Columbia University Press.

Gaffney, John, and Eva Kolinsky, eds. 1991. *Political Culture in France and Germany*. London: Routledge.

Geertz, Clifford. 1972. "Deep Play: Notes on the Balinese Cockfight." *Daedalus* 101:1–37.

———. 1973. *An Interpretation of Cultures*. New York: Basic Books.

Gell-Mann, Murray. 1994. *The Quark and the Jaguar: Adventures in the Simple and the Complex*. New York: W. H. Freeman.

George, Alexander L., and Timothy J. McKeown. 1985. "Case Studies and Theories of Organizational Decision Making." *Advances in Information Processing in Organizations* 2:21–58.

George, Alexander L., and Richard Smoke. 1974. *Deterrence in American Foreign Policy: Theory and Practice*. New York: Columbia University Press.

German Information Center. 1996. *This Week in Germany*. October issues.

———. 1997. *This Week in Germany*. December 12.

Gewirth, Alan. 1978. *Reason and Morality*. Chicago: University of Chicago Press.

Giles-Sims, Jean, and Charles Lockhart. 2000. "Grid-Group Theory and Corporal Punishment." Unpublished.

Gitelman, Zvi. 1977. "Soviet Political Culture: Insights from Jewish Emigres." *Soviet Studies* 29:543–64.

Glazer, Nathan. 1988. *The Limits of Social Policy*. Cambridge: Harvard University Press.

Glendon, Mary Ann. 1987. *Abortion and Divorce in Western Law: American Failures, European Challenges*. Cambridge: Harvard University Press.

Golden, Miriam. 1990. *A Rational Choice Analysis of Union Militancy with Application to the Cases of British Coal and Fiat*. Ithaca: Cornell University Press.

Gorbachev, Mikhail. 1995. *Memoirs*. New York: Doubleday.

Gould, Stephen Jay. 1995. "Age-Old Fallacies of Thinking and Stinking." *Natural History* 104 (June): 6–13.

Gourevitch, Peter. 1986. *Politics in Hard Times: Comparative Responses to International Economic Crises*. Ithaca: Cornell University Press.

Gray, John. 1996. *Isaiah Berlin*. Princeton: Princeton University Press.

Greenstein, Fred I. 1992. "Can Personality and Politics Be Studied Systematically?" *Political Psychology* 13:105–28.

Greenstone, J. David. 1982. "The Transient and the Permanent in American Politics: Standards, Interests, and the Concept of Public." In J. David Greenstone, ed., *Public Values and Private Power in American Politics*, 3–33. Chicago: University of Chicago Press.

———. 1986. "Political Culture and American Political Development: Liberty, Union, and the Liberal Bipolarity." *Studies in American Political Development* 1:1–49.

Greer, Thomas H. 1958. *What Roosevelt Thought: The Social and Political Ideas of Franklin Delano Roosevelt*. Ann Arbor: University of Michigan Press.

Grendstad, Gunnar. 1999. "A Political Cultural Map of Europe: A Survey Approach." *GeoJournal* 47: 463–75.

Grief, Avner. 1994. "Cultural Beliefs and the Organization of Society: A Historical and Theoretical Reflection on Collectivist and Individualist Societies." *Journal of Political Economy* 102:912–50.

Gruber, Jonathan, and David A. Wise. 1999. "Introduction and Summary." In Jonathan Gruber and David A. Wise, eds., *Social Security and Retirement Around the World*, 1–35. Chicago: University of Chicago Press.

Haanes-Olsen, Leif. 1989. "Worldwide Trends and Developments in Social Security, 1985–87." *Social Security Bulletin* 52 (February): 14–26.

Hahn, Jeffrey W. 1991. "Continuity and Change in Russian Political Culture." *British Journal of Political Science* 21:393–421.

Hahn, Steven. 1991. "Response to Sklar." *Studies in American Political Development* 5:214–20.

Haight, David. 1976. "Collectivists, Particularists, and Individualists: An Emerging Typology of Political Life." Paper presented at the annual meeting of the Midwest Political Science Association, Chicago, Ill.

Hall, Peter A. 1986. *Governing the Economy: The Politics of State Intervention in Britain and France*. New York: Oxford University Press.

Halperin, Morton H. 1972. "The Decision to Deploy the ABM: Bureaucratic and Domestic Politics in the Johnson Administration." *World Politics* 25:62–95.

Harrington, Michael. 1958. *The Other America: Poverty in the United States*. New York: Macmillan.

Hartz, Louis. 1955. *The Liberal Tradition in America: An Interpretation of American Political Thought Since the Revolution*. New York: Harcourt, Brace.

Hashimoto, Akiko. 1996. *The Gift of Generations: Japanese and American Perspectives on Aging and the Social Contract*. New York: Cambridge University Press.

Hayek, Friedrich A. 1976. *The Mirage of Social Justice*. Vol. 2 of *Law, Legislation, and Liberty*. Chicago: University of Chicago Press.

Hazard, John H. 1982. "Legal Trends." In Archie Brown and Michael Kaser, eds., *Soviet Policy for the 1980s*, 98–117. Bloomington: Indiana University Press.

Heclo, Hugh. 1974. *Modern Social Politics in Britain and Sweden*. New Haven: Yale University Press.

———. 1977. *A Government of Strangers: Executive Politics in Washington*. Washington, D.C.: Brookings Institution.

———. 1981. "Toward a New Welfare State." In Peter Flora and Arnold J. Heidenheimer, eds., *The Development of Welfare States in Europe and America*, 383–406. New Brunswick, N.J.: Transaction.

———. 1994. "Naturalistic Inquiry in Washington and Whitehall." *Public Budgeting and Finance* 14:58–65.

———. 1998. "Community, Contract, and the Death of Social Citizenship." New York: Carnegie Council on Ethics and International Affairs.

Heidenheimer, Arnold J., Hugh Heclo, and Carolyn Teich Adams. 1990. *Comparative Public Policy: The Politics of Social Choice in America, Europe, and Japan*. 3d ed. New York: St. Martin's.

Heine, Wolfgang. 1989. "Rentenreformgesetz 1992: Kontinuitäten, Kompromisse, Konsequenzen." *Arbeit und Sozialpolitik* 43:146–56 and 196–204.

Henscheid, Eckhard. 1985. *Helmut Kohl: Biographie einer Jugend*. Zurich: Haffmans Verlag.

Hill, Ronald J. 1985. "The Cultural Dimension of Soviet Political Development." *Journal of Communist Studies* 1:34–53.

Hirschman, Albert O. 1982. *Shifting Involvements: Private Interest and Public Action.* Princeton: Princeton University Press.

Hochschild, Jennifer L. 1981. *What's Fair? American Beliefs About Distributive Justice.* Cambridge: Harvard University Press.

Hofmann, Klaus. 1985. *Helmut Kohl: Eine Biographie.* Melle: Verlag Ernst Knoth.

———. 1991. *Helmut Kohl: Eine politische Biographie.* Bonn: Aktuell.

Hoffman-Lange, Ursula, ed. 1991. *Social and Political Structures in West Germany: From Authoritarianism to Post-Industrial Democracy.* Boulder, Colo.: Westview.

Hofstadter, Richard. 1958. "Andrew Jackson and the Rise of Liberal Capitalism." In Richard Hofstadter, *The American Political Tradition.* New York: Vintage.

Howe, Daniel Walker. 1974. *The Political Culture of the American Whigs.* Chicago: University of Chicago Press.

Hume, David. [1777] 1951. "Of Parties in General." In Frederick Watkins, ed., *Hume: Theory of Politics,* 168–76. London: Nelson.

Huntington, Samuel P. 1968. *Political Order in Changing Societies.* New Haven: Yale University Press.

———. 1981. *American Politics: The Promise of Disharmony.* Cambridge: Harvard University Press.

Inglehart, Ronald. 1977. *The Silent Revolution: Changing Values and Political Styles.* Princeton: Princeton University Press.

———. 1988. "The Renaissance of Political Culture." *American Political Science Review* 82:1203–30.

———. 1997. *Modernization and Postmodernization: Cultural, Economic and Political Change in 43 Societies.* Princeton: Princeton University Press.

Inkeles, Alex. 1988. "Rethinking Social Welfare: The United States and the USSR in Comparative Perspective." In Gail W. Lapidus and Guy E. Swanson, eds., *State and Welfare USA/USSR: Contemporary Theory and Practice,* 383–457. Berkeley: Institute of International Studies, University of California.

Inkeles, Alex, and Raymond Bauer. 1968. *The Soviet Citizen: Daily Life in a Totalitarian Society.* New York: Atheneum.

Ishida, Takeshi. 1983. *Japanese Political Culture: Change and Continuity.* New Brunswick, N.J.: Transaction.

Jencks, Christopher. 1990. "Varieties of Altruism." In Jane J. Mansbridge, ed., *Beyond Self-Interest,* 53–67. Chicago: University of Chicago Press.

Jervis, Robert. 1997. *System Effects: Complexities in Political and Social Life.* Princeton: Princeton University Press.

Jillson, Calvin. 1993. "Patterns and Periodicity in American National Politics." In Lawrence Dodd and Calvin Jillson, eds., *Dynamics in American Politics,* 24–58. Boulder, Colo.: Westview.

Johnson, Chalmers. 1982. *MITI and the Japanese Miracle.* Stanford: Stanford University Press.

———. 1990. "The Japanese Economy: A Different Kind of Capitalism." In S. N. Eisenstadt and Eyal Ben-Ari, eds., *Japanese Models of Conflict Resolution,* 39–59. London: Kegan Paul.

Johnston, David. 1991. "Human Agency and Rational Action." In Kristen Renwick Monroe, ed., *The Economic Approach to Politics: A Critical Reassessment of the Theory of Rational Action,* 94–112. New York: HarperCollins.

Kagan, Jerome. 1984. *The Nature of the Child*. New York: Basic Books.

Kalberg, Stephen. 1992. "Culture and the Locus of Worth in Contemporary Western Germany: A Weberian Configurational Analysis." In Richard Muench and Neil J. Smelser, eds., *Theory of Culture*, 324–65. Berkeley and Los Angeles: University of California Press.

Kaplan, Abraham. 1964. *The Conduct of Inquiry: Methodology for Behavioral Science*. San Francisco, Calif.: Chandler.

Kaser, Michael. 1982. "Economic Policy." In Archie Brown and Michael Kaser, eds., *Soviet Policy for the 1980s*, 186–219. Bloomington: Indiana University Press.

Kato, Junko. 1991. "Public Pension Reforms in the United States and Japan: A Study in Comparative Public Policy." *Comparative Political Studies* 24:100–126.

Katzenstein, Peter J. 1977. "Conclusion: Domestic Structures and Strategies of Foreign Economic Policy." *International Organization* 31:879–920.

———. 1984. *Corporatism and Change: Austria, Switzerland, and the Politics of Industry*. Ithaca: Cornell University Press.

———. 1985. *Small States in World Markets*. Ithaca: Cornell University Press.

———. 1987. *Policy and Politics in West Germany: The Growth of a Semisovereign State*. Philadelphia: Temple University Press.

Kii, Toshi. 1991. "Retirement in Japan." In John Myles and Jill Quadagno, eds., *States, Labor Markets, and the Future of Old-Age Policy*, 268–89. Philadelphia: Temple University Press.

King, Gary, Robert O. Keohane, and Sidney Verba. 1994. *Designing Social Inquiry: Scientific Inference in Qualitative Research*. Princeton: Princeton University Press.

Kingson, Eric R., and James H. Schulz. 1996. *Social Security in the Twenty-First Century*. New York: Oxford University Press.

Kirchheimer, Otto. 1966. "The Transformation of the Western European Party Systems." In Joseph LaPalombara and Myron Weiner, eds., *Political Parties and Political Development*, 177–200. Princeton: Princeton University Press.

Krauss, Ellis S. 1989. "Politics and the Policymaking Process." In Takeshi Ishida and Ellis S. Krauss, eds., *Democracy in Japan*, 39–64. Pittsburgh: University of Pittsburgh Press.

Krauss, Ellis S., and Takeshi Ishida. 1989. "Conclusion." In Takeshi Ishida and Ellis S. Krauss, eds., *Democracy in Japan*, 327–39. Pittsburgh: University of Pittsburgh Press.

Kreps, David M. 1990. "Corporate Culture and Economic Theory." In James E. Alt and Kenneth A. Shepsle, eds., *Perspectives on Positive Political Economy*, 90–143. New York: Cambridge University Press.

Kristof, Nicholas D. 1996. "Aging World, New Wrinkles." *New York Times*, September 22, pp. E1, 5.

———. 1997. "Where Children Rule." *New York Times Magazine*, August 17, pp. 40–44.

Laitin, David D. 1986. *Hegemony and Culture: Politics and Religious Change Among the Yoruba*. Chicago: University of Chicago Press.

———. 1995. "Disciplining Political Science." *American Political Science Review* 89:454–56.

Lane, Ruth. 1992. "Political Culture: Residual Category or General Theory." *Comparative Political Studies* 25:362–87.

LaPalombara, Joseph. 1964. *Interest Groups in Italian Politics*. Princeton: Princeton University Press.

Lapidus, Gail Warshofsky. 1983. "Social Trends." In Robert F. Byrnes, ed., *After Brezhnev: Sources of Soviet Conduct in the 1980s*, 186–249. Bloomington: Indiana University Press.

Lee, Jean B. 1994. *The Price of Nationhood: The American Revolution in Charles County*. New York: Norton.

Legro, Jeffrey W. 1996. "Culture and Preferences in the International Cooperation Two-Step." *American Political Science Review* 90:118–37.

Leichter, Howard M. 1979. *A Comparative Approach to Policy Analysis: Health Care Policy in Four Nations*. New York: Cambridge University Press.

Levi, Margaret. 1988. *Of Rule and Revenue*. Berkeley and Los Angeles: University of California Press.

Levy, Michael B., ed. 1992. *Political Thought in America: An Anthology*. Prospect Heights, Ill.: Waveland.

Lichbach, Mark Irving. 1995. *The Rebel's Dilemma*. Ann Arbor: University of Michigan Press.

Lichbach, Mark Irving, and Alan S. Zuckerman, eds. 1997. *Comparative Politics: Rationality, Culture, and Structure*. New York: Cambridge University Press.

Liebfried, Stephan. 1978. "Public Assistance in the United States and the Federal Republic of Germany: Does Social Democracy Make a Difference?" *Comparative Politics* 11:59–76.

Lieske, Joel. 1993. "Regional Subcultures of the United States." *Journal of Politics* 55:888–913.

Light, Paul. 1995. *Still Artful Work: The Continuing Politics of Social Security Reform*. 2d ed. New York: McGraw-Hill.

Lijphart, Arend. 1984. *Democracies: Patterns of Majoritarian and Consensus Government in Twenty-One Countries*. New Haven: Yale University Press.

Limerick, Patricia Nelson. 1997. "The Startling Ability of Culture to Bring Critical Inquiry to a Halt." *Chronicle of Higher Education*. October 24, p. A76.

Lindblom, Charles E. 1977. *Politics and Markets: The World's Political-Economic Systems*. New York: Basic Books.

Lipset, Seymour Martin. 1990. *Continental Divide: Values and Institutions of the United States and Canada*. New York: Routledge.

———. 1991. "American Exceptionalism Reaffirmed." In Byron E. Shafer, ed., *Is America Different? A New Look at American Exceptionalism*, 1–45. Oxford: Oxford University Press.

———. 1996. *American Exceptionalism: A Double-Edged Sword*. New York: Norton.

Liu, Lillian. 1987. "Social Security Reforms in Japan." *Social Security Bulletin* 50 (August): 29–37.

Lockhart, Charles. 1991. "American Exceptionalism and Social Security: Demonstrating Complementary Cultural and Structural Contributions to Social Program Development." *Review of Politics* 53:510–29.

———. 1997. "Political Culture and Political Change." In Richard J. Ellis and Michael Thompson, eds., *Culture Matters: Essays in Honor of Aaron Wildavsky*, 91–104. Boulder, Colo.: Westview.

———. 1999. "Cultural Contributions to Explaining Institutional Form, Political Change, and Rational Decisions." *Comparative Political Studies* 32: 802–93.

Lockhart, Charles, and Richard M. Coughlin. 1992. "Building Better Comparative Social Theory Through Alternative Conceptions of Rationality." *Western Political Quarterly* 45:793–809.

Lockhart, Charles, and Richard M. Coughlin. 1998. "Foreword." In Aaron Wildavsky, *Culture and Social Theory*, ed. Sun-Ki Chai and Brendon Swedlow, ix–xxiii. New Brunswick, N.J.: Transaction.

Lockhart, Charles, and Gregg Franzwa. 1994. "Cultural Theory and the Problem of Moral Relativism." In Dennis J. Coyle and Richard J. Ellis, eds., *Politics, Policy, and Culture*, 175–89. Boulder, Colo.: Westview.

Lockhart, Charles, and Aaron Wildavsky. 1998. "The Social Construction of Cooperation: Egalitarian, Hierarchical, and Individualistic Faces of Altruism." In Aaron Wildavsky, *Culture and Social Theory*, ed. Sun-Ki Chai and Brendon Swedlow, 113–31. New Brunswick, N.J.: Transaction.

Lovejoy, Arthur O. 1961. *Reflections on Human Nature.* Baltimore: Johns Hopkins University Press.

Lowi, Theodore J. 1984. "Why Is There No Socialism in the United States?" In Robert T. Golembiewski and Aaron Wildavsky, eds., *The Costs of Federalism*, 37–54. New Brunswick, N.J.: Transaction.

Lukes, Steven. 1973. *Individualism.* New York: Harper and Row.

Lustig, Jeffrey R. 1982. *Corporate Liberalism: The Origins of American Political Theory, 1890–1920.* Berkeley and Los Angeles: University of California Press.

Lutz, Donald S. 1980. *Popular Consent and Popular Control: Whig Political Theory in the Early State Constitutions.* Baton Rouge: Louisiana State University Press.

Macaulay, Thomas Babington. 1852. "Mill's Essay on Government" [1829]. In T. B. Macaulay, *Critical and Miscellaneous Essays*, 5:268–303. Philadelphia: Hart, Carey, and Hart.

Maddox, William S., and Stuart A. Lilie. 1984. *Beyond Liberal and Conservative: Reassessing the Political Spectrum.* Washington, D.C.: Cato Institute.

Madison, Bernice Q. 1968. *Social Welfare in the Soviet Union.* Stanford: Stanford University Press.

Main, Jackson Turner. 1964. *The Antifederalists: Critics of the Constitution, 1781–1788.* Chicago, Ill.: Quadrangle Books.

Malia, Martin. 1994. *The Soviet Tragedy: A History of Socialism in Russia, 1917–1991.* New York: The Free Press.

Mangen, Steen. 1989. "The Politics of Welfare." In Gordon Smith, William E. Paterson, and Peter H. Merkl, eds., *Developments in West German Politics*, 168–89. Durham: Duke University Press.

Mansbridge, Jane J. 1990a. "The Rise and Fall of Self-Interest in the Explanation of Political Life." In Jane J. Mansbridge, ed., *Beyond Self-Interest*, 3–22. Chicago: University of Chicago Press.

———. 1990b. "On the Relation of Altruism and Self-Interest." In Jane J. Mansbridge, eds., *Beyond Self-Interest*, 133–43. Chicago: University of Chicago Press.

March, James G., and Johan P. Olsen. 1989. *Rediscovering Institutions: The Organizational Basis of Politics*. New York: The Free Press.

Marcus, George E., John L. Sullivan, Elizabeth Theiss-Morse, and Sandra L. Wood. 1995. *With Malice Toward Some: How People Make Civil Liberties Judgments*. New York: Cambridge University Press.

Marer, Paul. 1985. *Dollar GNPs of the U.S.S.R. and Eastern Europe*. Baltimore: Johns Hopkins University Press.

Margolis, Howard. 1982. *Selfishness, Altruism and Rationality*. Cambridge: Cambridge University Press.

Marshall, John Douglas. 1993. *Reconciliation Road: A Family Odyssey of War and Honor*. Syracuse: Syracuse University Press.

Marshall, S.L.A. 1947. *Men Against Fire*. New York: William Morrow.

Marshall, T. H. [1949] 1963. "Citizenship and Social Class." In T. H. Marshall, *Sociology at the Crossroads and Other Essays*. London: Heinemann.

Maruyama, Magoroh. 1980. "Mindscapes and Science Theories." *Current Anthropology* 21:589–600.

Maser, Werner. 1990. *Helmut Kohl: Der Deutsche Kanzler*. Berlin: Verlag Ullstein.

Masters, Roger D. 1978. "Of Marmots and Men: Human Altruism and Animal Behavior." In Laren Wispe, ed., *Altruism, Sympathy, and Helping: Psychological and Sociological Principles*, 59–77. New York: Academic Press.

Matthews, Mervyn. 1986. *Poverty in the Soviet Union: The Life Styles of the Underprivileged in Recent Years*. Cambridge: Cambridge University Press.

———. 1989. *Patterns of Deprivation in the Soviet Union Under Brezhnev and Gorbachev*. Stanford, Calif.: Hoover Institution Press.

McAdam, Doug. 1994. "Culture and Social Movements." In Enrique Larana, Hank Johnson, and Joseph R. Gusfield, eds., *New Social Movements: From Ideology to Identity*, 36–57. Philadelphia: Temple University Press.

McAuley, Alastair. 1979. *Economic Welfare in the Soviet Union: Poverty, Living Standards, and Inequality*. Madison: University of Wisconsin Press.

———. 1982. "Social Policy." In Archie Brown and Michael Kaser, eds., *Soviet Policy for the 1980s*, 146–69. Bloomington: Indiana University Press.

McClosky, Herbert, and John Zaller. 1984. *The American Ethos: Public Attitudes Toward Capitalism and Democracy*. Cambridge: Harvard University Press.

McKean, Margaret A. 1989. "Equality." In Takeshi Ishida and Ellis S. Krause, eds., *Democracy in Japan*, 201–24. Pittsburgh: University of Pittsburgh Press.

Mead, Lawrence M. 1986. *Beyond Entitlement: The Social Obligations of Citizenship*. New York: The Free Press.

Medvedev, Zhores A. 1987. *Gorbachev*. New York: Norton.

Monroe, Kristen Renwick. 1991a. "The Theory of Rational Action: Origins and Usefulness for Political Science." In Kristen Renwick Monroe, ed., *The Economic Approach to Politics: A Critical Reassessment of the Theory of Rational Action*, 1–31. New York: HarperCollins.

———. 1995. "Psychology and Rational Actor Theory." *Political Psychology* 16:1–22.

———, ed. 1991b. *The Economic Approach to Politics: A Critical Reassessment of the Theory of Rational Action*. New York: HarperCollins.

Montesquieu, Baron de. [1748] 1900. *The Spirit of the Laws*. Translated by Thomas Nugent. New York: Collier.

Moynihan, Daniel Patrick. 1973. *The Politics of a Guaranteed Income: The Nixon Administration and the Family Assistance Plan.* New York: Random House.

Münch, Richard. 1992. "The Production and Reproduction of Inequality: A Theoretical Cultural Analysis." In Richard Münch and Neil J. Smelser, eds., *Theory of Culture,* 243–64. Berkeley and Los Angeles: University of California Press.

Murarka, Dev. 1988. *Gorbachev: The Limits of Power.* London: Hutchinson.

Murdo, Pat. 1990. "Japan's Social Security and Pension Systems Face Need for New Reforms." Japan Economic Institute Report, no. 21A. May 25.

———. 1993. "Japan's Social Security Reforms Target Equity, Solvency Issues." Japan Economic Institute Report, no. 32A. August 27.

Namenwirth, Zvi. 1973. "Wheels of Time and the Interdependence of Value Change in America." *Journal of Interdisciplinary History* 3:649–83.

National Commission on Social Security Reform. 1983. *Report of the National Commission on Social Security Reform* (January 20). Washington, D.C.: GPO.

Noguchi, Yukio. 1986. "Overcommitment in Pensions: The Japanese Experience." In Richard Rose and Rei Shiratori, eds., *The Welfare State East and West,* 173–92. New York: Oxford University Press, 1986.

———. 1987. "Public Finance." In Kozo Yamamura and Yasukichi Yasuba, eds., *The Political Economy of Japan,* vol. 1, *The Domestic Transformation,* 186–222. Stanford: Stanford University Press.

Noll, Roger G., and Barry R. Weingast. 1991. "Rational Actor Theory, Social Norms, and Policy Implementation: Applications to Administrative Processes and Bureaucratic Culture." In Kristen Renwick Monroe, ed., *The Economic Approach to Politics: A Critical Reassessment of the Theory of Rational Action,* 237–58. New York: HarperCollins.

North, Douglass C. 1990. *Institutions, Institutional Change and Economic Performance.* New York: Cambridge University Press.

Nove, Alec. 1986. *The Soviet Economic System.* 3d ed. Boston: Allen and Unwin.

Nozick, Robert. 1974. *Anarchy, State, and Utopia.* New York: Basic Books.

Ofer, Gur, and Aaron Vinokur. 1988. "The Distributive Effects of the Social Consumption Fund in the Soviet Union." In Gail W. Lapidus and Guy E. Swanson, eds., *State and Welfare USA/USSR: Contemporary Theory and Practice,* 251–77. Berkeley: Institute of International Studies, University of California.

Olson, Mancur. 1993. "Dictatorship, Democracy, and Development." *American Political Science Review* 87:567–76.

Organisation for Economic Co-operation and Development. 1985. *Social Expenditure, 1960–1990: Problems of Growth and Control.* Paris: Organisation for Economic Co-operation and Development.

———. 1992. *OECD Economic Surveys, 1991–1992: United States.* Paris: Organisation for Economic Co-operation and Development.

———. 1993. *OECD Economic Surveys, 1992–1993: Japan.* Paris: Organisation for Economic Co-operation and Development.

———. 1994a. *OECD in Figures: Statistics on the Member Countries.* Paris: Organisation for Economic Co-operation and Development.

———. 1994b. *OECD Economic Surveys, 1993–1994: Sweden.* Paris: Organisation for Economic Co-operation and Development.

———. 1995. *National Accounts: Volume II, Detailed Tables.* Paris: Organisation for Economic Co-operation and Development.

————. 1996. *OECD Economic Surveys, 1995–1996: Germany.* Paris: Organisation for Economic Co-operation and Development.

Ostrom, Douglas. 1997. "Aging and Pensions in Japan: Economic Issues." *Japan Economic Institute Report*, no. 12A. March 28.

Padgett, Stephen. 1989. "The Party System." In Gordon Smith, William E. Paterson, and Peter H. Merkl, eds., *Developments in West German Politics*, 122–46. Durham: Duke University Press.

Parsons, Talcott, and Edward Shils, eds. 1951. *Toward a General Theory of Action.* Cambridge: Harvard University Press.

Passell, Peter. 1996. "Can Retirees' Safety Net Be Saved?" *New York Times*, February 18, pp. F1, 4.

Pear, Robert. 1997. "Panel on Social Security Urges Investing in Stocks But Is Split Over Method." *New York Times*, January 7, pp. 1, 8.

Pempel, T. J. 1982. *Policy and Politics in Japan: Creative Conservatism.* Philadelphia: Temple University Press.

————. 1989. "Prerequisites for Democracy: Political and Social Institutions." In Takeshi Ishida and Ellis S. Krauss, eds., *Democracy in Japan*, 17–37. Pittsburgh: University of Pittsburgh.

Pempel, T. J., and Keiichi Tsunekawa. 1979. "Corporatism Without Labor? The Japanese Anomaly." In Philippe C. Schmitter and Gerhard Lehmbruch, eds., *Trends Toward Corporatist Intermediation*, 231–70. Beverly Hills, Calif.: Sage.

Peters, B. Guy. 1996. *The Future of Governing: Four Emerging Models.* Lawrence: University Press of Kansas.

Peterson, Peter G. 1996. *Will America Grow Up Before It Grows Old? How the Coming Social Security Crisis Threatens You, Your Family and Your Country.* New York: Random House.

Petracca, Mark K. 1991. "The Rational Actor Approach to Politics: Science, Self-Interest and Normative Democratic Theory." In Kristen Renwick Monroe, ed., *The Economic Approach to Politics: A Critical Reassessment of the Theory of Rational Action*, 171–203. New York: HarperCollins.

Pierson, Paul. 1994. *Dismantling the Welfare State? Reagan, Thatcher, and the Politics of Retrenchment.* New York: Cambridge University Press.

Pipes, Richard. 1994. *Russia Under the Bolshevik Regime.* New York: Knopf.

Popkin, Samuel. 1979. *The Rational Peasant: The Political Economy of Rural Society in Vietnam.* Berkeley and Los Angeles: University of California Press.

Powell, Margaret, and Masahira Anesaki. 1990. *Health Care in Japan.* London: Routledge.

Puidak, Peter. 1987. "Developments in the Equalization of Treatment of Men and Women Under Social Security in the Federal Republic of Germany." *Social Security Bulletin* 52 (February): 49–52.

Pulzer, Peter. 1989. "Political Ideology." In Gordon Smith, William E. Paterson, and Peter H. Merkl, eds., *Developments in West German Politics*, 78–98. Durham: Duke University Press.

Putnam, Robert D., with Robert Leonardi and Raffaella Y. Nanetti. 1988. "Institutional Performance and Political Culture: Some Puzzles About the Power of the Past." *Governance: An International Journal of Policy and Administration* 1:221–42.

———. 1993. *Making Democracy Work: Civic Traditions in Modern Italy.* Princeton: Princeton University Press.

Pye, Lucian W. 1962. *Politics, Personality and Nation Building: Burma's Search for Identity.* New Haven: Yale University Press.

———. 1988. *The Mandarin and the Cadre: China's Political Culture.* Ann Arbor: University of Michigan, Center for Chinese Studies.

Pye, Lucian W., and Sidney Verba, eds. 1965. *Political Culture and Political Development.* Princeton: Princeton University Press.

Rae, Douglas W. 1967. *The Political Consequences of Electoral Laws.* New Haven: Yale University Press.

Rae, Douglas W., and Michael Taylor. 1970. *The Analysis of Political Cleavages.* New Haven: Yale University Press.

Ragin, Charles C. 1992. "Casing and the Process of Social Inquiry." In Charles C. Ragin and Howard S. Becker, eds., *What Is a Case? Exploring the Foundations of Social Inquiry,* 217–26. Cambridge: Harvard University Press.

Reagan, Ronald, with Richard G. Hubler. 1965. *Where's the Rest of Me?* New York: Duell, Sloan, and Pearce.

Reagan, Ronald, with Robert Lindsey. 1990. *An American Life.* New York: Simon and Schuster.

Rein, Martin. 1982. "The Social Policy of the Firm." *Policy Sciences* 14:117–35.

Renshon, Stanley. 1989. "Psychological Perspectives on Theories of Adult Development and the Political Socialization of Leaders." In Roberta S. Sigel, ed., *Political Learning in Adulthood: A Sourcebook of Theory and Research,* 203–64. Chicago: University of Chicago Press.

Resnick, David, and Norman C. Thomas. 1990. "Cycling Through American Politics." *Polity* 23:1–21.

Richardson, Bradley M. 1974. *The Political Culture of Japan.* Berkeley and Los Angeles: University of California Press.

Rimlinger, Gaston V. 1971. *Welfare Policy and Industrialization in Europe, America, and Russia.* New York: John Wiley and Sons.

Roberts, Geoffrey K. 1984. " 'Normal' or 'Critical?' Progress Reports on the Condition of West Germany's Political Culture." *European Journal of Political Research* 12:423–31.

Rogers, Carl. 1961. *On Becoming a Person.* Boston: Houghton Mifflin.

Rogowski, Ronald. 1974. *Rational Legitimacy: A Theory of Political Support.* Princeton: Princeton University Press.

———. 1978. "Rationalist Theories of Politics: A Midterm Report." *World Politics* 30:296–323.

———. 1989. *Commerce and Coalitions: How Trade Affects Domestic Political Alignments.* Princeton: Princeton University Press.

Rohrschneider, Robert. 1994. "Report from the Laboratory: The Influence of Institutions on Political Elites' Democratic Values in Germany." *American Political Science Review* 88:927–41.

Rokeach, Milton. 1973. *The Nature of Human Values.* New York: The Free Press.

Rose, Richard, and Rei Shiratori. 1986. "Welfare in Society: Three Worlds or One?" In Rose and Shiratori, *The Welfare State East and West,* 3–12. New York: Oxford University Press.

Rosenberg, Shawn. 1988. "The Structure of Political Thinking." *American Journal of Political Science* 32:539–66.

———. 1991. "Rationality, Markets, and Political Analysis: A Social Psychological Critique of Neoclassical Political Economy." In Kristen Renwick Monroe, ed., *The Economic Approach to Politics: A Critical Reassessment of the Theory of Rational Action*, 386–404. New York: HarperCollins.

Ross, Marc Howard. 1997. "Culture and Identity in Comparative Political Analysis." In Mark Irving Lichbach and Alan S. Zuckerman, eds., *Comparative Politics: Rationality, Culture, and Structure*, 42–80. New York: Cambridge University Press.

Rossiter, Clinton. 1949. "The Political Philosophy of Franklin Delano Roosevelt." *Review of Politics* 11:87–95.

Rowen, Jerry S., and Charles Wolf, Jr., eds. 1990. *The Impoverished Superpower: Perestroika and the Soviet Military Burden.* San Francisco: Institute on Contemporary Studies.

Safran, William. 1967. *Veto-Group Politics: The Case of Health Insurance Reform in West Germany.* San Francisco, Calif.: Chandler.

Sakwa, Richard. 1990. *Gorbachev and His Reforms.* New York: Prentice-Hall.

Sanger, David E. 1997. "The Last Liberal (Almost) Leaves Town." *New York Times,* January 9, p. 9.

Schlesinger, Arthur M. 1945. *The Age of Jackson.* Boston: Little, Brown.

Schlesinger, Arthur, M., Jr. 1957. *The Crisis of the Old Order.* Vol. 1 of *The Age of Roosevelt.* Boston: Houghton Mifflin.

———. 1959a. *The Coming of the New Deal.* Vol. 2 of *The Age of Roosevelt.* Boston: Houghton Mifflin.

———. 1959b. *The Politics of Upheaval.* Vol. 3 of *The Age of Roosevelt.* Boston: Houghton Mifflin.

———. 1986. "The Cycles of American Politics." In Arthur M. Schlesinger, Jr., *The Cycles of American History,* 23–48. Boston: Houghton Mifflin.

Schmidt-Häuer, Christian. 1986. *Gorbachev: The Path to Power.* Translated by Ewald Osers and Chris Romberg. Topsfield, Mass.: Salem House.

Schumacher, E. F. 1973. *Small Is Beautiful: Economics as if People Mattered.* New York: Harper and Row.

Schumpeter, Joseph. 1950. *Capitalism, Socialism and Democracy.* 3d ed. New York: Harper and Row.

Schwarz, John E. 1988. *America's Hidden Success: A Reassessment of Public Policy from Kennedy to Reagan.* New York: Norton.

Schwarz, Michiel, and Michael Thompson. 1990. *Divided We Stand: Redefining Politics, Technology, and Social Choice.* Philadelphia: University of Pennsylvania Press.

Seager, Henry Rogers. 1910. *Social Insurance: A Program of Social Reform.* New York: Macmillan.

Searle, John R. 1995. *The Construction of Social Reality.* New York: The Free Press.

Sen, Amartya. 1977. "Rational Fools: A Critique of the Behavioral Foundations of Economic Theory." *Philosophy and Public Affairs* 6:317–44.

Shafer, Byron E. 1993. "Political Eras in Political History: A Review Essay." *Journal of Policy History* 5:461–74.

Shalev, Michael. 1990. "Class Conflict, Corporatism and Comparison: A Japanese

Enigma." In S. N. Eisenstadt and Eyal Ben-Ari, eds., *Japanese Models of Conflict Resolution*, 60–93. London: Kegan Paul.

Sharkansky, Ira. 1969. "The Utility of Elazar's Political Culture: A Research Note." *Polity* 2:66–83.

Shinkawa, Toshimitsu, and T. J. Pempel. 1996. "Occupational Welfare and the Japanese Experience." In Michael Shalev, ed., *The Privatization of Social Policy? Occupational Welfare and the Welfare State in America, Scandinavia and Japan*, 280–326. London: Macmillan.

Shoup, Paul S. 1981. *The East European and Soviet Data Handbook: Political, Social and Developmental Indicators, 1945–1975*. New York: Columbia University Press.

Shweder, Richard A. 1991. *Thinking Through Cultures: Expeditions in Cultural Psychology*. Cambridge: Harvard University Press.

Sigel, Roberta S., ed. 1989. *Political Learning in Adulthood: A Sourcebook of Theory and Research*. Chicago: University of Chicago Press.

———. 1995. "New Directions for Political Socialization Research: Thoughts and Suggestions." *Perspectives on Political Science* 24 (Winter): 17–22.

Silbey, Joel H. 1991. *The American Political Nation, 1838–1893*. Stanford: Stanford University Press.

Silk, Leonard. 1972. *Nixonomics: How the Dismal Science of Free Enterprise Became the Black Art of Controls*. New York: Praeger.

Simanis, Joseph G. 1990. "National Expenditures on Social Security and Health in Selected Countries." *Social Security Bulletin* 53 (January): 12–16.

Simon, Herbert A. 1955. "A Behavioral Model of Rational Choice." *Quarterly Journal of Economics* 69:99–118.

———. 1983. *Reason in Human Affairs*. Stanford: Stanford University Press.

Sklar, Martin J. 1991. "Periodization and Historiography: Studying American Political Development in the Progressive Era, 1890s–1916." *Studies in American Political Development* 5:173–213.

Skocpol, Theda. 1979. *States and Social Revolutions: A Comparative Analysis of France, Russia and China*. New York: Cambridge University Press.

———. 1987. "America's Incomplete Welfare State." In Martin Rein, Gøsta Esping-Anderson, and Lee Rainwater, eds., *Stagnation and Renewal in Social Policy*. Armonk, N.Y.: M. E. Sharpe.

———. 1992. *Protecting Soldiers and Mothers: The Political Origins of Social Policy in the United States*. Cambridge: Harvard University Press.

Skowronek, Steven. 1982. *Building a New American State: The Expansion of National Administrative Capacities, 1877–1920*. New York: Cambridge University Press.

———. 1993. *The Politics Presidents Make: Leadership from John Adams to George Bush*. Cambridge: Harvard University Press.

Smeeding, Timothy, Barbara Boyd Torrey, and Martin Rein. 1988. "Patterns of Income and Poverty: The Economic Status of Children and the Elderly in Eight Countries." In John L. Palmer, Timothy Smeeding, and Barbara Boyd Torrey, eds., *The Vulnerable*, 89–119. Washington, D.C.: Urban Institute Press.

Smith, Hedrick. 1990. *The New Russians*. New York: Random House.

Smith, Patrick. 1997. *Japan: A Reinterpretation*. New York: Pantheon.

Smith, Rogers M. 1993. "Beyond Tocqueville, Myrdal, and Hartz: The Multiple Traditions in America." *American Political Science Review* 87:549–66.

Smoler, Frederick. 1989. "The Secret of the Soldiers Who Didn't Shoot." *American Heritage* 40 (March): 36–45.

Sniderman, Paul M., Richard A. Brody, and Philip E. Tetlock, with Henry E. Brady, et al. 1991. *Reasoning and Choice: Explorations in Political Psychology.* New York: Cambridge University Press.

Snyder, Louis L. 1967. *The Blood and Iron Chancellor: A Documentary Biography of Otto von Bismarck.* New York: Van Nostrand.

Starr, Paul. 1982. *The Social Transformation of American Medicine: The Rise of a Sovereign Profession and the Making of a Vast Industry.* New York: Basic Books.

Steinmo, Sven H. 1994. "American Exceptionalism Reconsidered: Culture or Institutions?" In Lawrence Dodd and Calvin Jillson, eds., *Dynamics in American Politics*, 106–31. Boulder, Colo.: Westview.

———. 1995. "Why Is Government so Small in America?" *Governance: An International Journal of Policy and Administration* 8:303–34.

Steinmo, Sven, Kathleen Thelen, and Frank Longstreth, eds. 1992. *Structuring Politics: Historical Institutionalism in Comparative Analysis.* New York: Cambridge University Press.

Steven, Rob. 1983. *Classes in Contemporary Japan.* New York: Cambridge University Press.

Stevenson, Richard W. 1999. "Lawmakers in Both Parties Are Weighing Compromise Plans to Revamp Social Security." *New York Times*, January 14, p. A16.

Strathern, Andrew. 1971. *The Rope of Moka: Big-Men and Ceremonial Exchange in Mount Hagen, New Guinea.* Cambridge: Cambridge University Press.

Swidler, Ann. 1995. "Cultural Power and Social Movements." In Hank Johnson and Bert Klandermans, eds., *Social Movements and Culture*, 25–40. Vol. 4 of Bert Klandermans, ed., *Social Movements, Protest, and Contention.* Minneapolis: University of Minnesota Press.

Tate, Dale. 1982. "Budget Battle Erupts on Hill as Compromise Talks Fizzle." *Congressional Quarterly Weekly Reports* 40 (May 1): 967–69.

Tawney, R. N. 1926. *Religion and the Rise of Capitalism: A Historical Study.* New York: Harcourt, Brace.

Taylor, A.J.P. 1955. *Bismarck: The Man and the Statesman.* New York: Knopf.

Teske, Nathan. 1997. *Political Activists in America: The Identity Construction Model of Political Participation.* New York: Cambridge University Press.

Thompson, Michael. 1982. "The Problem of the Center: An Autonomous Cosmology." In Mary Douglas, ed., *Essays in the Sociology of Perception*, 302–27. London: Routledge and Kegan Paul.

Thompson, Michael, Richard Ellis, and Aaron Wildavsky. 1990. *Cultural Theory.* Boulder, Colo.: Westview.

Thurow, Lester. 1992. *Head to Head: The Coming Economic Battle Among Japan, Europe, and America.* New York: Morrow.

Titmuss, Richard M. 1971. *The Gift Relationship: From Human Blood to Social Policy.* New York: Random House.

Toulmin, Steven. 1961. *Foresight and Understanding: An Enquiry into the Aims of Science.* Bloomington: Indiana University Press.

Triandis, Harry C. 1995. *Individualism and Collectivism*. Boulder, Colo.. Westview.

Tsurumi, Kazuko. 1970. *Social Change and the Individual: Japan Before and After Defeat in World War II*. Princeton: Princeton University Press.

Tucker, Robert C. 1987. *Political Culture and Leadership in Soviet Russia: From Lenin to Gorbachev*. New York: Norton.

Tugwell, Rexford G. 1992. "A Constitution for the New States of America." In Steven R. Boyd, ed., *Alternative Constitutions for the United States: A Documentary History*. Westport, Conn.: Greenwood.

Turnbull, Colin. 1972. *The Mountain People*. New York: Simon and Schuster.

Turner, Christena. 1989. "Democratic Consciousness in Japanese Unions." In Takeshi Ishida and Ellis S. Krauss, eds., *Democracy in Japan*, 299–323. Pittsburgh: University of Pittsburgh.

Turner, Frederick Jackson. 1962. *The Frontier in American History*. New York: Holt, Rinehart and Winston.

Uchendu, Victor C. 1965. *The Igbo of Southeast Nigeria*. New York: Holt, Rinehart, and Winston.

Uchitelle, Louis. 1997. "A Shift to Self-Reliance." *New York Times*, January 13, pp. 1, 11.

United Nations. 1992. *National Accounts, Statistics: Main Aggregates and Detailed Tables, 1990, Part II*. New York: United Nations.

———. 1993. *Yearbook of National Accounts Statistics, 1981*. Vol. 2, *International Tables*. New York: United Nations.

United States Department of Commerce. 1994. *Statistical Abstract of the United States*. Washington, D.C.: GPO.

Van Wolferen, Karel. 1990. *The Enigma of Japanese Power: People and Politics in a Stateless Nation*. New York: Random House.

Verba, Sidney, Steven Kelman, Gary R. Orren, Ichiro Miyake, Joji Watanuki, Ikuo Kabashima, and G. Donald Ferree, Jr. 1987. *Elites and the Idea of Equality: A Comparison of Japan, Sweden, and the United States*. Cambridge: Harvard University Press.

Verba, Sidney, Norman H. Nie, and Jae-on Kim. 1978. *Participation and Political Equality: A Seven Nation Comparison*. New York: Cambridge University Press.

Volkogonov, Dmitri. 1994. *Lenin: A New Biography*. Edited and translated by Harold Shukman. New York: The Free Press.

———. 1998. *Autopsy for an Empire: The Seven Leaders Who Built the Soviet Union*. Edited and translated by Harold Shukman. New York: The Free Press.

Walzer, Michael. 1983. *Spheres of Justice: A Defense of Pluralism and Equality*. New York: Basic Books.

———. 1995. "Are There Limits to Liberalism?" *New York Review of Books*, October 19, pp. 28–31.

Weiner, Myron. 1967. *Party Building in a New Nation: The Indian National Congress*. Chicago: University of Chicago Press

Weinstein, Michael M. 1998. "Uttering the P-Word With Social Security." *New York Times*, June 28, pp. 3–1, 3–12.

Weir, Margaret, Ann Shola Orloff, and Theda Skocpol, eds. 1988. *The Politics of Social Policy in the United States*. Princeton: Princeton University Press.

White, Stephen. 1979. *Political Culture and Soviet Politics*. London: Macmillan.

Whiting, Beatrice Blyth. 1983. "The Genesis of Prosocial Behavior." In Diane L.

Bridgeman, ed., *The Nature of Prosocial Development*, 221–42. New York: Academic Press.

Wildavsky, Aaron. 1985. "Change in Political Culture." *Journal of the Australian Political Science Association* 20:95–102.

——. 1987. "Choosing Preferences by Constructing Institutions: A Cultural Theory of Preference Formation." *American Political Science Review* 81:3–21.

——. 1991. "Can Norms Rescue Self-Interest or Macro Explanation Be Joined to Micro Explanation?" *Critical Review* 5:301–23.

——. 1994. "Why Self-Interest Means Less Outside of a Social Context: Cultural Contributions to a Theory of Rational Choices." *Journal of Theoretical Politics* 6:131–59.

Wilensky, Harold L. 1975. *The Welfare State and Equality: The Structural and Ideological Roots of Public Expenditures*. Berkeley and Los Angeles: University of California Press.

——. 1976. *The "New Corporatism," Centralization, and the Welfare State*. Beverly Hills, Calif.: Sage.

Will, George F. 1985. "Fresh Start." *Washington Post*, October 31.

Wills, Gary. 1978. *Inventing America: Jefferson's Declaration of Independence*. Garden City, N.Y.: Doubleday.

——. 1987. *Reagan's America: Innocents at Home*. Garden City, N.Y.: Doubleday.

Wilson, James Q. 1973. *Political Organizations*. New York: Basic Books.

——. 1993. *The Moral Sense*. New York: The Free Press.

Wilson, William Julius. 1987. *The Truly Disadvantaged: The Inner City, the Underclass, and Public Policy*. Chicago: University of Chicago Press.

Wirt, Frederick. 1980. "Does Control Follow the Dollar: Value Analysis, School Policy, and State-Local Linkages." *Publius* 10 (2): 69–88.

Wolfe, Alan. 1993. *The Human Difference*. Berkeley and Los Angeles: University of California Press.

Wood, Gordon S. 1969. *The Creation of the American Republic, 1776–1787*. Chapel Hill: University of North Carolina Press.

WuDunn, Sheryl. 1997. "The Face of the Future in Japan." *New York Times*, September 2, pp. C1, 14.

Yavlinsky, Grigory, Boris Fedorov, Stanislav Shatalin, et al. 1991. *500 Days: Transition to the Market*. Translated by David Kushner. New York: St. Martin's.

Young, Michael. 1959. *The Rise of Meritocracy*. Harmondsworth, U.K.: Penguin.

Young, Peyton H. 1996. "The Economics of Conventions." *Journal of Economic Perspectives* 10:105–22.

Zapf, Wolfgang. 1986. "Development, Structure, and Prospects of the German Social State." In Richard Rose and Rei Shiratori, eds., *The Welfare State East and West*, 126–55. New York: Oxford University Press.

Zeitzer, Ilene R. 1983. "Social Security Trends and Developments in Industrialized Countries." *Social Security Bulletin* 46 (March): 52–61.

Zisk, Betty. 1992. *The Politics of Transformation: Local Activism in the Peace and Environmental Movements*. New York: Praeger.

INDEX

Abalkin, Leonid, 151, 159–61
Abbott, Phillip, 98, 122
Abelshauser, Werner, 82, 175
Adams, Carolyn Teich, 74
Adams, Henry Carter, 99
Adenauer, Konrad, 48, 50, 107–8, 172–75, 181
adequacy principle, social security revisions and, 129
adolescence, spheres of socialization during, 30–31
adult development, spheres of socialization and, 29–33
affiliation, strength of, grid group theory and, 6–8
AFL/CIO, social security revisions and, 133
Aganbegyan, Abel, 151, 161, 165 n. 16
Aldrich, Jonathan, 200
Allison, Graham T., 89
Almond, Gabriel A., 23
Altmeyer, Arthur, 99, 109
American Association of Retired Persons (AARP), 133
Anasaki, Masahira, 195
Andrews, Edmund I., 177
Andropov, Yuri, 45–47, 152, 158
Archer, William, 129
Aristotle, 68, 70
Armstrong, William, 129
Arrow, Kenneth J., 23
Articles of Confederation: American cultural

coalitions and, 95–96, 123; institutional formation imperatives and, 32; Soviet economic reforms compared with, 160
Aslund, Anders, 147, 151–52, 157–58, 160, 163–66

Bailyn, Bernard, 94
Baker, James, 138
Baker, Kendall L., 107, 173, 175
Ball, Robert, 131, 138
Banfield, Edward C., 33, 175
Barghoorn, Frederick, 143
Barry, Brian, 23
Basic Law of 1949 (Germany), 172–73
Basic Pension (Japan), 208–9
Bates, Robert H., 23
Bauer, Raymond, 144
Beard, Charles A., 32, 95
Beauchamp, Edward, 197
Beck, Robert, 129
Becker, Gary, 12, 27, 92, 112
beliefs: culturally constrained value clusters and, 12–16; grid-group theory and, 8–10, 55–57, 227–29; Japanese cultural coalitions and, 193–202; pension program policies and, 118–20; revision of social security and role of, 129 n. 7; Soviet consumer price subsidies and role of, 164–67
Bendix, Reinhard, 31
benefits reductions: comparison of U.S.-German reforms, 191–92; German pension reforms and, 177, 187–89; Japanese pension

Pulzer, Peter, 173, 175
purposive process: decision outcomes and,
232–34; pension program case studies and,
117–20
Pye, Lucian W., 33

rational action theory: cross-societal institutional differences and, 62–73; rival ontologies and, 62–64, 220–21; value clusters
and, 64–68
rational choice theory: comparative politics
and, 5, x–xi; instrumental rationality and,
10–12; political change and, 111–12; political culture theory and, 92–93; social relations preferences and, 27–59; Soviet
consumer price subsidies and, 150–61
rationality: comparative politics and, 19–21;
culturally constrained value clusters and,
13–16; instrumental rationality, 10–12;
political change and, 110–12; "thick" rationalities, 15
rational-legal authority, spheres of socialization and, 31
Reagan, Nancy, 41
Reagan, Ronald, 4, 152, 175; individualism
of, 55–56; social relations preferences of,
36–42, 56–57; social security revisions
and, 128–29, 134–40
"Realos" movement, German partisan politics and, 180
Rein, Martin, 74
relevance, boundaries of, spheres of socialization and, 31–32
Renner, Hannelore. See Kohl, Hannelore
Renshon, Stanley, 28
Republic, The, 8
Republican Party: conservatism within, 84;
cultural coalitions in, 179, 229–31;
Reagan's membership in, 39–40; social security revisions and role of, 129, 136–37
retirement age increases: German pension reforms and, 188–90; Japanese pension reform and, 205–12; U.S. social security
revisions and, 138–39
revenue increases: German pension reforms
and, 187–90; Japanese pension reforms
and, 209–12, 226; pension reforms and, international comparisons, 236–328; Soviet
economic reforms and, 160–63; U.S. social
security revisions and, 128, 132, 134, 141

Revolutionary War: cultural coalitions and,
122–24, 180 n. 10; institutional formation
imperatives and, 32
Richardson, Bradley M., 193
Rimlinger, Gaston V., 101, 103
rival ontologies: German partisan politics
and, 175–87; institutional preferences and,
217–23; pension program case studies and,
116–20; rational action theory and, 62–64;
Soviet consumer price subsidies and,
151–61; stratification and, 69–71; U.S. so-
cial security reform and, 128–36; value
clusters constrained by, 219–21, 236–38
Roberts, Geoffrey K., 172
Rogers, Carl, 30
Rogowski, Ronald, 92, 105–7
Rohrschneider, Robert, 62, 108, 173, 194,
231
Roosevelt, Franklin Delano, 39–40, 91, 98–
101, 111–12
Rosenberg, Shawn, 23
Ross, Marc Howard, 23
Rossiter, Clinton, 98
Rostenkowski, Dan, 132
Rousseau, Jean-Jacques, 8, 71
Rowen, Jerry S., 147
Russian Jewish emigrés, hierarchist beliefs of,
143–44
Russo-Japanese War, 195
Rytkewski, Ralph, 172
Ryzhkov, Nikolai, 153–54, 156, 158–61,
164, 166–67, 195 n. 2, 202, 231

Safran, William, 181
Sakwa, Richard, 45
Sanger, David E., 133
Scandinavia, egalitarianism's prevalence in,
76 n. 6, 237
Schlesinger, Arthur, 98
Schlozman, Kay Lehman, 29
Schmidt, Helmut, 181–82, 183 n. 13
Schmidt-Häuer, Christian, 42, 44–45
Schmoller, Gustav, 182 n. 2
Schnabel, Reinhold, 188, 190
Schumacher, E. F., 13, 180
Schumacher, Kurt, 48
Schumpeter, Joseph, 64, 72
Screen Actors Guild (SAG), Reagan's mem-
bership in, 38–42
Searle, John R., 62

tions surrounding, 109–10; German pension reforms compared with, 185, 190–92; long-term financial costs of, 140; reform and revision of, 121–42; worker/beneficiary ratios in, 4–5, 118–20, 127–28, 139 n. 13, 141–42

Soviet Union: consumer price subsidies in, 79–82, 143–67; dissolution of, 187 n. 14, 235; grid-group theory coalitions in, 24–25, 223–26; hierarchist culture of, 143–67, 195 n. 2, 231; pension reforms in, 117–20, 184, 235–38; value cluster constraints in, 221

spheres of socialization: agents of, 30–31; boundaries of relevance and, 31–32; culture and personality and, 32–33; early stages of, 29–30; grid-group theory and, 33–35, 55–57; political change and, 92–93; social relations preferences and, 28–33

Stalin, Joseph, 42–44, 47, 144, 146, 152–53

Stamp Act, 122

State Commission on Economic Reform, 159

state-industry collaborations, Japanese interventionism and, 86–87

Steinmo, Sven, 27, 87, 142, 234

Steven, Rob, 194

Stevenson, Richard W., 140, 190

Stockman, David, 135–36, 138

stratification: American cultural coalitions and, 94–101; in Japanese society, 194–202; rival ontologies regarding, 69–71

Strauss, Franz Josef, 50

structured-focused comparison: American political structure, 124–27; grid-group theory and, 21

Suslov, Mikhail, 45

Sweden: egalitarianism in, 104 n. 6, 237; Japanese elite attitudes compared with, 86, 226–27

Takeuchi Tsuna, 51

Tanaka Kakuei, 229

Tate, Dale, 138

Tawney, R. N., 103

tax revenues: American social security revisions and, 128, 132, 134, 141; German pension reforms and, 187–89; Japanese pension reforms, 209–12; Soviet economic reforms and, 160–63

Taylor, A. J. P., 101

Teske, Nathan, 11, 23

Thatcher, Margaret, 4, 175

Thelen, Kathleen, 27, 87, 234

Thompson, Michael, 23, 27, 33, 63, 91, 96 n. 3, 227

"three-legged stool" model of pension programs: German pension programs and, 181; Japanese pension reforms, 210–11; U.S. social security reforms and, 129, 181 n. 11

Thurow, Lester, 55

Titmuss, Richard M., 72

Titorenko, Raisa. See Gorbachev, Raisa

Torrey, Barbara Boyd, 74

Trotsky, Leon, 80 n. 7

Trowbridge, Alexander, 129

Tsunekawa, Keiichi, 202, 204

Tsurumi, Kazuko, 193–94

Tucker, Robert C., Soviet consumer price subsidies and, 79–80, 145

Tugwell, Rexford, 99

Turner, Christena, 194, 198

Turner, Frederick Jackson, 121

Uchitelle, Louis, 229

unemployment: in Federal Republic of Germany, 177–79; German insurance programs, increases in, 178; impact on U.S. social security program, 127–28; Japanese assistance programs and, 200; Soviet consumer price subsidies and, 82 n. 9, 148–50

United States: German pension reforms and, 212–13; grid-group theory coalitions in, 24–25, 223–26; historical contingency and cultural shifts in, 229–31; institutional formation imperatives, 222; Japanese public expenditure compared with, 82–83, 212–13; "neoliberal" wage erosion in, 75; pension programs in, 117–20; public sector expenditures in, 78–79; rival cultural coalitions in, 94–101; social security reform in, 121–42, 236–38

value clusters: core clusters, 65; cultural constraints on, 12–16; institutional preferences and, 68; rational action theory and, 64–68

value-priority pluralism, 15

values: coalitions and sharing of, 100–101;